Beyond Sixty-Five

The Dilemma of Old Age in America's Past

Beyond Sixty-Five

The Dilemma of Old Age in America's Past

CAROLE HABER

CAMBRIDGE UNIVERSITY PRESS

Cambridge

London   New York   New Rochelle

Melbourne   Sydney

Published by the Press Syndicate of the University of Cambridge
The Pitt Building, Trumpington Street, Cambridge CB2 1RP
32 East 57th Street, New York, NY 10022, USA
296 Beaconsfield Parade, Middle Park, Melbourne 3206, Australia

© Cambridge University Press 1983

First published 1983

Printed in the United States of America

Library of Congress Cataloging in Publication Data
Haber, Carole, 1951–
Beyond sixty-five.
Bibliography: p.
Includes index
1. Aging – United States – History – 19th
century. 2. Aged – Services for – United States –
History – 19th century. I. Title.
HQ1064.U5H18 1982   305.2'6'0973   82-12786
ISBN 0 521 25096 X

To Peter

Contents

Tables

Acknowledgments

Most scholarly monographs, supposedly the work of a single author, are actually filled with the insights and ideas of many. Certainly, this is true of my work. Throughout the course of my research and writing, a number of individuals have made significant contributions. I would especially like to thank Drew Gilpin Faust, John Modell, Peter Stearns, Maris Vinovskis, and Robert Zemsky for reading and commenting on parts or all of the manuscript, Walter Licht for unselfishly sharing his knowledge of unions and railroads with me, and Saul Jarcho for saving me from making numerous medical errors. My fellow graduate students in the Department of American Civilization at the University of Pennsylvania and my colleagues at the University of North Carolina at Charlotte (UNCC) have listened patiently to me as I formulated my ideas and added their own expertise and knowledge. Department secretaries Mary Bottomly and Sandy Bergo typed the manuscript with more understanding and accuracy than I had thought possible. Frank Smith, editor at Cambridge University Press, and Helen Greenberg, copy editor, made suggestions that greatly improved the manuscript. Personal thanks are due both to my parents and to my husband, Peter Rothstein, who always offered me great encouragement and never questioned when, or whether, I would ever be finished. Material support came in part from NIH Grant LM02904 from the National Library of Medicine and from a summer grant from UNCC. The editors of the *Journal of Social History* and the *Pennsylvania Magazine of History and Biography* kindly granted me permission to reprint materials that first appeared in their journals.

My greatest debt – one far too large to acknowledge in a single paragraph – is to Charles E. Rosenberg. Since I began my graduate studies, he has served as my chief instructor, critic, and editor, as well as my model of a good historian. Without his assistance and moral support, this work would not only never have been completed, it probably would not even have been begun.

Classifying Society's Superannuated

Old age, in mid-twentieth-century America, is a stage of life both clearly and categorically defined. The man and woman who reach sixty-five seemingly undergo a dramatic change. Once beyond this year, they pass into the final stage of existence; they have become bureaucratically defined as geriatrics and senior citizens. Age, more than any other criterion, sets the elderly apart from society. Business policies, government regulations, and community standards uniformly dictate retirement. The active, as well as the sedentary, the healthy and the disabled are all perceived as superannuated.

The belief that disease and dependence often accompany old age is certainly not new. Few societies, in fact, have failed to recognize the infirmities of the elderly. Even in those cultures in which only a minority outlived adolescence, the presence of individuals of advanced age is a well-noted phenomenon. Since biblical times, the aged patriarch, stooped, bearded, and toothless, has served as a physical representation of the nature of senescence.

Every culture has also recognized that at some point elderly individuals may be forced to withdraw from society; the onset of physical or mental infirmities will hinder their activities. Regardless of past accomplishments or former skills, they might then find themselves judged incompetent. So stereotyped, the elderly will fall into a new category, that of the "overaged" or superannuated. According to anthropologist Leo W. Simmons, this is a classification that exists even in small, preindustrial cultures. "Among all people," Simmons contends:

> a point is reached in aging at which any further usefulness appears to be over and the incumbent regarded as a living liability. "Senility" may be a suitable label for this. Other terms among primitive people are the "overaged," the "useless stage," the "sleeping period," and the "already dead." Then, without actual death, the prospects are gloomy. There is no question about the generalized social decision. All societies

1

differentiate between old age and this final pathetic plight. Some do something positive about it. Others wait for nature to do it or perhaps assist nature in doing it.[1]

As Simmons points out, each culture recognizes this distinctive categorization and assigns specific persons to its ranks. The criteria by which it makes this classification, however, are hardly universal. Every society, through standards shared by its members, must define the nature of health and disease. Illness itself is a subjective classification; symptoms defined by one group as pathological may be accepted by another as normal and easily tolerable part of everyday life. The Omaha Indians, for example, continued to defer to their elders well beyond the onset of physical weakness. Bodily infirmities did not deter such aged leaders from playing an active role in society; their status was based on their knowledge and experience.[2] In contrast, the Shilluk usually labeled their king overaged at an early stage of his existence. Unable to meet the sexual demands of his many wives, he was considered to have outlived his usefulness and was put to death by the tribal chieftains.[3] Other groups equated disease with individuals' inability to provide for their own basic necessities. Once the aged became a burden to others, they lost their value to society. Like the sickly Hottentots left in a deserted hut, or the decrepit Lapps bludgeoned to death, these aged individuals were literally eliminated from playing any part in their societies.[4]

In America as well, certain types of persons have always been characterized as overaged and outdated. Even in colonial times, those elderly individuals who lacked family, wealth, or occupation composed a powerless group. They passed from town to town, were boarded out with neighbors, or spent their final years as almshouse residents. Weakness and poverty defined the distinctiveness of their final years. Retaining few ties integrating them into society, they were inevitably seen as superannuated.[5]

Such an evaluation did not pertain only to the most poverty-stricken and debilitated persons. In some cases, even pillars of colonial society experienced feelings of uselessness as their final days approached. Cotton Mather, for example, repeatedly noted the discontent of his elderly father and searched for the proper activity to occupy his aging mind. No longer consulted on matters of great importance, Increase Mather felt himself segregated by reason of his age and infirmities. In the more than two decades he spent preparing for death, the elder Mather expressed numerous complaints about his assumed decrepit condition. As an old man, he believed he was shown little respect or veneration.[6]

Mather was not alone in his feelings. Throughout American history, old people have voiced similar complaints; in contrast to their status in middle age, senescence seemed a time of uselessness. Despite the deferential admonitions of ministers and moralists, they discovered that respect, in actuality, did not always accompany senescence. In 1805, for example, Joseph Lathrop repeated an often-heard old man's lament:

> Once we were men; now we feel ourselves to be but babes. Once we possessed active powers; now we have become impotent. Once we sustained our children and ministered to them with pleasure; now we are sustained by them, and we are sure, our once experienced pleasure is not reciprocated. Once we were of some importance in society; now we are sunk into insignificance. Once our advice was sought and regarded; now we are passed by with neglect and younger men take our place.[7]

In 1950, in response to a sociologist's inquiry about modern-day old age, one elderly man characterized his plight in similar terms. "I have no family," he explained. "I have no money, and all my close friends are dead. No one cares what happens to me. My fling is over and I would just as soon die as not. My life is perfectly meaningless."[8] Although living more than a century after Lathrop, he would have understood the nineteenth-century man's condition. Both individuals found themselves severed from former responsibilities; they were left few roles through which to exert authority. As such, each became classified as superfluous; each had become part of society's overaged.[9]

This characterization has always existed in America. It is easy to identify persons who portray themselves or are depicted as superannuated. The qualities ascribed to this stage, however, have not always remained the same. Persons deemed worthy of honor in one century may have little to offer future generations. The attributes that had earned them respect might later help define them as outdated. In colonial America, as we shall see, in contrast to Increase Mather, there were elderly individuals who held great power until the end of their lives. Through the structure of society, its laws, traditions, and demographic patterns, they retained an active role in the culture. To a large degree, their merits were judged individually and according to function. No experts forced them as a group into retirement; no set of regulations demanded their departure from positions of authority. To these aged persons, at least, threescore and ten implied a long life. It did not, however, preclude all interaction with the community.

In the nineteenth century, however, both the labile nature of society and significant intellectual trends affected attitudes toward senescence. By the end of the century, the category of the overaged had become far more rigid. A person's advanced years began to represent the primary criterion for classifying him as unproductive and useless. Regardless of past achievements or assets, age marked the onset of his superannuated state.

These structural changes and evolving beliefs are not unrelated. The demographic, social, and economic transformation altered the position of the old as it shaped the culture's perception of the final stage of existence. With urbanization and industrialization, those old people who had once held power discovered that their authority was eroding. The often tight-knit family over which they ruled or the landholdings that granted them control no longer served to integrate them into society. In growing numbers, they were thought to possess little deemed worthy of honor.

Such individuals – and, consequently, their life stage as a whole – became the subject for countless tracts focusing upon the problems of the old. In the nineteenth century, for the first time, writers produced a growing body of literature devoted strictly to the ills of senescence. Doctors, statisticians, welfare advocates, and business planners all formulated theories on the nature and needs of the elderly. Relying on their rising status as professionals and scientists, they felt themselves well qualified to comment on all aspects of the aging process. The fact that these experts approached senescence from different fields did little to alter their vision or prescriptions; the conception of old age uniformly emphasized its infirmities and limits. The old, they believed, by reason of their altered physiological, anatomical, and psychological state, were no longer able to play an active or necessary role in society.

The policies that these writers endorsed clearly reflected this belief. Without exception, their recommendations rested on the notion that senescence was a distinctive and debilitated state of existence. The elderly were best served, they argued, through measures that limited their interaction and competition with younger persons. Mandatory retirement, pension plans, geriatric medicine, and old-age homes were not designed to reintegrate the elderly into the culture, nor did they attempt to confer new power and prestige on those who had reached senescence. Rather, these programs and institutions ensured

4

the separation of the old from work, wealth, and family. In their rules and regulations, they emphasized that the elderly profited by severing all ties with the community. Old-age homes sheltered the elderly in a consciously segregated environment; geriatric medicine tended to divide the life cycle into distinct and irreversible stages; and pension plans removed the elderly from the labor market, forcing them into retirement. In turn, each of these measures served to segregate the old according to their advanced age.

These new policies, however, must not be interpreted as an indication of a suddenly developed social distaste for the elderly. Clearly, there was never a golden age of senescence in which the old were treated with veneration. For many individuals, even in colonial America, gray hair and wrinkles seemed reason for contempt instead of honor; their age alone was not deemed worthy of respect. Nor did attitudes toward the old ever veer sharply from adoration to contempt. The aged were not loved as a group at one moment, only to be hated collectively the next.[10]

Instead, as we shall see, the nineteenth-century measures that defined and limited the roles of the old were based on a transformation in the way society attempted to eliminate disease and dependence. Incorporating the findings of science, technology, statistics, and medicine, these programs were created to meet the needs of the superannuated. Such policies, in fact, did help scores of the elderly. Without these measures, and lacking family, wealth, or the ability to work, many aged individuals spent their final days in poverty and isolation. To them, the pension plan or even the old-age home was a preferable alternative to unrelenting indigence. But these programs were not addressed to the poverty-stricken alone. By the early twentieth century, their scope had broadened to include nearly all senescent persons. In an increasingly complex culture, they reflected a bureaucratic approach to the problems of senescence, classifying their recipients primarily according to age.

Not all elderly individuals, of course, were immediately influenced by such sweeping bureaucratic changes. At first, these newly established policies and institutions directly affected only a few. During the nineteenth century, nearly three-fourths of all aged men remained in the labor force.[11] With only forty-nine pension programs in existence by 1910, retirement was never a real option for the great majority of workers.[12] Nor did many aged people resort to the final shelter of an old-age home or hospital. Until recent decades, only about 2 percent of the old made their homes in such residences; there simply

5

were not enough of these institutions to accommodate those who petitioned for entrance.[13] Throughout the nineteenth century, the overwhelming majority of elderly persons continued to follow traditional patterns of employment and residence.

This does not mean that the ideas of the early gerontological specialists were of little importance. Although their policies and programs initially affected only a limited number, they were based on well-structured models of the nature of old age. Nursing homes, geriatric medicine, and pension plans all incorporated contemporary beliefs about the aging process. In their rules and regulations, they dictated how the experts believed the old thought, acted, and behaved. The programs of these specialists, then, serve as a useful perspective by which to evaluate attitudes toward senescence. In their development, acceptance, and implementation, such measures reflect changing beliefs about old age in nineteenth-century America.

For the twentieth century, the ideas of these early reformers have importance as well. The questions these individuals asked, the categories they constructed, and the solutions they proposed continue to the present day to structure our attitudes toward the old. A great majority of the elderly now retire from the work force when they reach sixty-five; many spend their final days in a hospital or old-age home.[14] Without question, their lives have been permanently altered by programs developed over a century ago. These early policies, therefore, have an immediate relevance to the modern study of gerontology. In their innovations and beliefs, the reformers and writers helped form many of the intellectual assumptions and institutional continuities on which our contemporary programs are based.

This study is intended to examine the ideas of these early specialists and the classification of superannuation that they developed. It will focus upon the beliefs of those groups that assumed control over the elderly – the doctors, sociologists, and welfare advocates, as well as the business and government planners who conveyed and acted upon a clear conception of what it meant to be old in America. Through these newly emerging professions and the solutions they proposed, the broad, age-based categorization of superannuation was formulated, justified, and finally implemented.

This study begins, however, not with the nineteenth century but with an examination of the treatment of the old in the colonial era. This perspective is essential if we hope to gain a broader understanding of the direction and shape of attitudes. Even in this early period, a classification of the elderly existed; clear and important criteria distinguished useful old age from superannuation. Those persons able to retain their authority in society were likely to be treated with respect, if not great love. But for the elderly who had lost status and power, the future was bleak. Gray hair, wrinkles, and increasing infirmities did indeed become signs of ridicule. Despite biblical prescriptions that called for respect of the old, one did not gladly pass into this stage of existence.

Such a categorization, then, became the basis for attitudes in the early nineteenth century. And in time, this classification was broadened and transformed, in terms of both the social conditions that created it and the individuals who claimed expertise in its formation. This evolution of belief represented neither a sharp break with the past nor a radical reinterpretation. Instead, the early experts simply attempted to solve traditional, age-old problems of the elderly, problems that, in the course of urban and industrial growth, seemed to be greatly expanding. As we shall see, however, the solutions they formulated tended to increase the distance and distinctiveness between active adulthood and superannuation. Through policy innovations and reforms, they created a conception of senescence that emphasized its need for isolation and medical intervention. Hospitals, old-age homes, and mandatory retirement plans segregated the old primarily according to chronological age and attempted to minister to their specific age-related problems. These programs reflected assumptions that pervaded the culture; by the beginning of the twentieth century, nearly all elderly individuals began to be perceived as superannuated.

This study, though, does not propose to examine the beliefs about old age that existed throughout America's history. It will not attempt to delineate these conceptions as portrayed in art, literature, and philosophy.[15] Nor, for the most part, will it focus upon the differences in perceptions according to class and ethnic groups. Rather, it is intended to examine the creation of formal "scientific" classifications of aging and the effect these categorizations had upon the care of the elderly. These models – whether sociological, medical, or institutional – were formulated by a small elite group of professionals. In a society, though, that was becoming increasingly dependent upon this class for its expertise, these notions had significance far beyond this limited circle; their assumptions and recommendations were presented with the power and authority of science. In the works of these early specialists, therefore, lies an influential portrayal of old age in America's past.

CHAPTER ONE

Aging in Colonial America

In the eighteenth century, an individual who approached his sixth decade was almost certain to think of himself as growing old. Those "who have attained to threescore," asserted an aged Increase Mather,"are everywhere accounted as old men."[1] In early America, such longevity seemed great indeed. The median age was not far from sixteen; most people died before forty. Only about 5 percent of the population lived beyond sixty.[2] Thus, persons who survived to this extreme age often assumed a peculiar and highly visible status. In colonial New England, religious and civil leaders lectured on the glories inherent in old age. Through speeches and sermons, they expatiated on the nature of senescence and its rightful place in society. For Puritans, at least, old age seemed more than merely the last segment of the life cycle; it became a tangible expression of God's benevolent order. "There is," declared Reverend Samuel Willard:

> that Relation and Order that arises from the Condition of Man, whose God's Providence disposeth to dwell in such Societies . . . There are in all Places, some that are *Aged*, and others that are *Younger*, and both of these in Plenty are promised to a People whom God has blessed.[3]

In this divinely appointed universe, each individual had age-related roles and responsibilities. Children, servants, and parents were joined in a well-established hierarchy of law and tradition. The old were to assume the highest rank, their longevity a sign from Providence of chosen status. "If a man is favored with long life," Increase Mather explained, "it is God that has lengthened his days."[4] In the biblically based communities of early America, such longevity demanded universal respect. "Honor thy father and thy mother," admonished the fifth commandment, and this prescription applied not just to one's immediate family but to all elderly individuals. As long as they were physically able, the old were to rule over society and dispense the wisdom of past generations. In return, the young were to follow them with unquestioned deference and veneration.

Such, at least, was the scriptural ideal. And in part, colonial society was organized in accordance with these principles. Some elderly persons did, in fact, enjoy great power and prestige. A good many ministers and magistrates were men of advanced years; only death caused such leaders to retire. In times of crisis, the young even rallied behind certain of these "grey champions."[5] But these men did not assume their exalted rank merely because they were old; other colonists, equally aged, were treated in quite a different manner. Far from being respected and esteemed, these elderly men and women found themselves characterized as too ancient to participate in society and too outdated to adapt to the changing times. In early America, the stereotypes used to describe the final stage of life ranged from a favorable portrayal of the knowledge and experience of the elderly to a pejorative caricature of their weaknesses and infirmities. If the old were called saintly and wise, they were also pictured as decrepit and decayed; many found that they became targets of increasing contempt as they grew older.[6]

The status of old persons, as we shall see, rested not on an unwavering adherence to pious prescriptions but on a variety of social, economic, and demographic factors. These realities shaped the nature of senescence as they defined its legitimate (and varied) responsibilities. Elderly persons who were able, or required, to participate in society were likely to be treated with respect; the authority they exerted over valued assets guaranteed their continued importance. But for others, feeble in health or bereft of property, senescence assumed a strikingly different form. These aged individuals were characterized in terms of their declining physical abilities and labeled as superannuated. In early America, then, the relationship between age and honor was neither direct nor simple. For some, great age contributed to their high status; for others, it led only to ridicule and neglect.

*   *   *   *

To understand the manner in which colonial society classified its elderly, we must first suspend modern conceptions of old age. In the mid-twentieth century, the final stage is marked by sharp boundaries: Work has ended; children have grown, married, and departed. These turning points, according to one sociologist, are "role exits"; they signify the separation of the old from past positions and functions.[7] In modern society, such role exits divide the final phases of the life cycle into distinct sections. Without children to raise or a job to fulfill, the individual is assumed to have passed beyond active adulthood. He may then be designated a grandparent or retiree; at sixty-five or seventy, he is classified as superannuated.

In the eighteenth century, however, old age was often a more am-

9

biguous stage of existence. The boundary separating it from maturity was less explicit and segmented. A person might retain both his family and his occupation until death. But this was not the result of a well-established "colonial gerontocracy," nor even of widespread respect for age as such.[8] Instead, numerous factors combined to keep the old active members of society.

In contrast to their twentieth-century counterparts, the elderly of colonial America rarely experienced role exits marking the decline of their influence in the family. High fertility and mortality rates, along with a late age of marriage, combined to guarantee their parental position well into their final years. The demographic pattern of their lives thus ensured their continued authority. The couple that married in the bride's early twenties (as the majority did) was likely to bear children over the next two decades.[9] As a result, a woman – if she lived to an advanced age – would be likely to spend almost half her married life pregnant or nursing. On the average, her last child would not leave home until she reached her sixty-third birthday.[10] The final decades of her adult life, then, much like the first, would be devoted to the responsibilities of childrearing. Her role as the mother of growing children blurred the distinctiveness of her final years.

Large families and widely spaced offspring also added ambiguity to old age by shading the lines between generations. The aging colonial couple might be both parents of infants and grandparents at the same time. Rarely was there a period when they were simply the third generation of an extended family network. It was not unusual, in fact, for the birth of both their children and grandchildren to occur simultaneously. Consenquently, for many, old age differed little from their middle years; the lines separating the stages of life remained imprecise.

Such, for example, was the life experience of one large eighteenth-century family. Thomas Willing, a Philadelphia merchant and politician, was born in 1731, the oldest of eleven children. His youngest sister, Margaret, was born in 1753, twenty-two years and an entire generation later. Had Willing's parents lived until all their children were grown, they would have spent over forty years raising a family – well into the period of advanced old age. This was true for Willing as well. From 1764 (a year after his marriage) to 1781 (the year of his wife's death), Willing and his wife had thirteen children. One result of this large family was that the couple's parental status remained secure. The marriage of their oldest daughter hardly characterized Willing as overaged; the older generation did not pass into the role

Table 1.1. *Demographic Life Cycle in America, 1650–1950*

	1650	1700	1750	1800	1850	1890	1950
Men							
Mean age at:							
First marriage	24	25	26	25	26	26	23
Last birth	42	42	43	42	37	37	29
Last child comes of age	63	63	64	63	58	57	50
Last child marries	65	64	66	67	61	59	50
Death	52	52	c.52	c.56	62	66	77
Women							
Menarche	n.a.	n.a.	n.a.	15.2	14.6	14.2	12.8
First marriage	20	21	23	22	24	23	20
Last birth	38	38	39	39	35	32	26
Last child comes of age	59	59	60	60	56	53	47
Last child marries	60	61	63	64	59	56	48
Death	c.50	c.50	c.50	c.56	61	71	81

Source: From *Growing Old In America* by David Hackett Fischer. Copyright ©
1978 by David Hackett Fischer. Reprinted by permission of Oxford University
Press, Inc.

of superannuated grandparents, divorced from their own nuclear
family. Instead, in 1781, the year their daughter Anne married William Bingham, Thomas Willing and his wife had their final child.
Thus, Willing approached his seventh decade before his last surviving
son matured beyond his teens. In the next generation, the pattern of
broad age distribution of children and vague generational lines had
a similar effect upon the shape of an individual's old age. In 1799,
Anne and William Bingham became grandparents for the first time;
a year later, their own son was born. Again, almost two decades
separated the birth of their first and last child. Well into advanced
age, they retained their parental roles and responsibilities.[11]

This demographic pattern is illustrated in Table 1.1. In contrast to
the old of the twentieth century, the elderly of colonial America rarely
lived apart from their children. Few would undergo the common
modern-day experience of the "empty nest" syndrome. Rather, for
the great majority, old age would be spent within a nuclear family.

The life cycle of the family, then, greatly influenced the concerns
of the elderly. For most aged persons, there was little question of the
proper and legitimate roles. Until their children were grown, parents
– whatever their age – had few alternatives but to remain integral

family members. Despite their increasing physical weakness, fathers were still responsible for meeting the needs of their kin. According to law, parents had to provide materially for their children and see that they were well educated, trained for a career, and settled into a proper marriage.[12] Until these obligations were met, aged individuals could not – even if they desired – separate themselves from the community.

As this role gave the elderly man continued responsibilities, it also provided him with numerous rights. In colonial America, the head of the family exerted considerable power over his children. In studies of both Maryland and Massachusetts, historians have found that eighteenth-century fathers strongly influenced the choice of their children's spouses as well as the order and timing of their marriages.[13] But this was not the result of great age, nor did it extend beyond the nuclear family. Only as long as the individual maintained control of the family property was he assured the rights and duties of the patriarch.[14]

Many fathers, then, chose to retain their parental roles well beyond the maturity of their sons. In the rural communities of the eighteenth century, age alone was not enough to signify a child's adulthood or a parent's old age. Social and economic constraints combined to blur further the distinctiveness of the life cycle. Before a son could be truly independent of his father, he had to own a sufficient portion of the family's estate or accumulate wealth of his own. Fathers who held on to their homes and property, therefore, also retained the obedience of their offspring.[15] Patriarchy rested not only on biblical admonitions but on the promise of land. The son who failed to honor his father and mother might face grave repercussions.

James White was one individual who learned this lesson, if perhaps a bit too late. Raised in Maryland as a Catholic, White disobeyed his father by joining the Anglican Church. In return, the elderly White left him out of his will; he refused to let his son inherit the estate that he had farmed for thirty years. Contesting the will in 1768, White called his deceased, ninety-year-old father an "ignorant Illerate man wholly biggetted to all the Follies and Superstitions of the Roman Church." In death, as well as in life, White's father received neither the respect nor the honor supposedly the right of the aged patriarch. The bonds tying father to son had dissolved, along with the assurance of property.[16]

For most elderly fathers, however, their dominant economic position guaranteed their continued authority. Usually, sons dared not

12

question the moral or intellectual abilities of their parents. Whatever the fathers' physical capabilities, they could rarely be labeled as useless and outdated. As James White learned, parents possessed assets that were of value to both their families and their communities. In the colonial period, the old, although not as rich as persons in their fifties, did in fact control a sizable proportion of the town's wealth. Although their estates decreased as their children married and departed, their economic standing rarely underwent a radical change. On the average, they retained enough property to assure the importance of their old age.[17] And if they chose – as many did – to give their land to their children only upon death, their last decades were even more secure.[18] Rarely did the son elected to inherit the home move away and begin his own family, nor did three complete generations reside in the same house.[19] Instead, until they gained ownership of the land, many sons remained dependent on their fathers' good will and family affection.

Such, for example, was the life course of Joseph Abbot of Andover, Massachusetts. Joseph, one of six sons, was chosen to inherit the family residence upon his father's death. Until the senior Abbot died in 1731, at seventy-three, the son remained a bachelor, living in his parents' home. A year after his father's death and his inheritance of the house, Joseph finally married – at forty-five. His continued residence with his parents not only defined his status as a dependent but guaranteed the role of household head to his aging father.[20]

In the eighteenth century, the strength of this patriarchal system varied from place to place. In the Chesapeake colonies, fathers' power seems to have grown through the decades. Increasing life spans and longer marriages produced generations of elderly parents able to dominate their offspring through the promise of valuable inheritances. By the time of the American Revolution, according to Allan Kulikoff, half of all male householders under the age of fifty had fathers who were still living. The economic standing of the elders was clearly superior to that of the sons; the younger generation had to wait for their fathers' demise to assume the social status of their elders.[21]

In contrast, in the older villages of Massachusetts, the patriarchal power of the old appeared to weaken as the century progressed. The growth of western towns, the decreasing size of family estates, and the practice of giving the land away by deed, rather than will, all tended to result in a greater degree of independence for the children.[22] But even in these areas, old age did not immediately assume

Table 1.2. *Age and Wealth in Colonial America*

Age	Five New England towns,[a] 17th century	Guilford, Conn.,[b] 18th century	Maryland,[c] 18th century
20–29	£112	n.d.[d]	£90
30–39	134	£58.71	244
40–49	431	79.10	352
50–59	555	87.61	658
60–69	434	65.58	410
70–79	308	40.87	n.d.[d]
80–89	286	n.d.[d]	n.d.[d]

[a] The towns are Hampton, N.H., Springfield, Mass., Northampton, Mass., Wetherfield, Conn., and Easthampton, L.I.
[b] Age divisions are for cohort, 1732–77, for the following ages: 37, 45, 52, 65, 72 (the figure is a mean of wealth for the group).
[c] Age divisions are for groups: –25; 26–45; 46–60; 61+.
[d] No data are available for these age categories.
Source: John Demos, "Old Age in Early New England," in *The American Family in Social-Historical Perspective*, 2d ed., ed., Michael Gordon (New York: St. Martin's Press, 1978), p. 236; From John J. Waters, "Patrimony, Succession, and Social Stability: Guilford, Connecticut in the Eighteenth Century," *PAH*, 10 (1976), p. 157, published by the CWC. for Studies in American History, Harvard University; Allan Kulikoff, "Tobacco and Slaves: Population, Economy, and Society in Eighteenth-Century Prince George's County, Maryland" (Unpublished Ph.D. diss., Brandeis University, 1976), p. 512.

a new shape. Fathers rarely ceded their parental control as soon as their sons approached maturity. The older generation usually transferred their property only after their heirs had aged considerably. In a study of Andover, Massachusetts, Philip Greven found that by the mid-eighteenth century, a majority of landholders had deeded their property to their children prior to death. The sons, however, were hardly striplings; the average age of fifty-one individuals who received land was thirty-one.[23] Given the late date of many last pregnancies, the parents, in turn, were also generally beyond middle age.

Many were well advanced in years before giving up the means of ensuring power and respect. Thus, even in these cases, the social position of the old remained tied to control over both children and land.

Not all aged individuals, of course, were guaranteed enough family or wealth to ensure the comfort and continuity of their final years. But even those without these assets sometimes escaped being categorized as outdated. In colonial society, the expectation that the old might continue to work until physically disabled kept them active participants in the community. This was, however, not always a matter of choice. Lacking land or material goods, their only alternatives to work were dependence and destitution. Thus, ancient individuals often sought employment, if only to provide for their own basic necessities. In the early eighteenth century, for example, Francis Righton petitioned the selectmen of Boston for an innkeeper's license. Due to their advancing years, he explained, he and his wife had to leave their trade:

> & solisiting some honest way of Support do thearfore pray your favor in granting them the liberty of Retailing Liqors in wich they hope to behave themselves with all vertious Regard to the Publick & to the laws in that Case provided & your petitioners shal ever pray.[24]

Many other old persons followed a similar course, although they did not always "behave themselves with all vertious Regard to the Publick & to the Laws."[25] In Philadelphia in 1741, Alexander McKensie and his wife were charged with operating a public house without a license. According to the Common Council records, McKensie explained that as he was "old and infirm and his wife a Cripple," there was little else he could do to support himself.[26] McKensie was not alone in his crime or original in his defense; other aged Philadelphians pleaded guilty to the same offense. And in almost every case, the council, noting the age and condition of the criminals, allowed them to remain in business.[27] Age brought with it a few prerogatives, if not always veneration and respect.

For many people in eighteenth-century America, then, senescence was necessarily a time of activity. Their roles as parents and providers dictated their continued participation in society. The value of the individual and the positive characteristics ascribed to his age were determined by his particular circumstance. If he owned a great deal of land or personal property, he was likely to be treated with considerable deference. William Byrd, for example, an eighteenth-century Virginia gentleman, retained his plantation – and social position –

Table 1.3. *Age of Elected Officials*

Age	Hampton, N.H., 1645–1720		Hingham, Mass., 1650–1750			
			First election		Last election	
	No.	%	No.	%	No.	%
20–29	2	1	10	8	1	1
30–39	31	19	44	34	12	9
40–49	45	27	44	34	35	25
50–59	52	32	27	21	60	43
60–69	30	18	3	2	23	17
70 +	5	3	0	0	8	6

Source: John Demos, "Old Age in Early New England," in *The American Family in Social-Historical Perspective*, 2d ed., ed., Michael Jordan (New York: St. Martin's Press, 1978), p. 242; Daniel Scott Smith, "Old Age and the 'Great Transformation': A New England Case Study," in *Aging and the Elderly*, eds. Stuart F. Spicker, Kathleen M. Woodward, and David D. Van Tassel (Atlantic Highlands, N.J.: Humanities Press, 1978), p. 293. Reprinted by permission of Humanities Press Inc., Atlantic Highlands, N.J. 07716.

until his death; no one questioned his right to preside with authority over his estate. At the advanced age of seventy, in fact, he became president of the Virginia Council.[28] Like Byrd, such highly respected men might be elected to government posts, sit at the front of meetinghouse, or be consulted in times of crisis.

Not every old man, however, held such an exalted position; age itself guaranteed little power and recognition. The elderly did not automatically assume their place in the front of the meetinghouse or sit on all lawmaking councils. As both John Demos and Daniel Scott Smith have shown, these symbols of status were not reserved for the old; at times, they were dominated by far younger men.[29] The majority of political leaders, in fact, seem to have been middle-aged. As a rule, the elderly were reelected only to seats that they had won in their younger days. In eighteenth-century Hingham, Massachusetts, for example, only 1 selectman out of 101 attained his initial post after his sixtieth birthday; not a single individual assumed his first office after he reached seventy.[30] It was not age, then, but accomplishments, wealth, and influence that determined the election of colonial officials.

16

Similarly, not all elderly persons sat in the places of honor in the town's meetinghouse. Here, too, other factors determined their prescribed positions. Property, influence, and family background could cause younger men to sit in front of the old, whereas aged persons of middling wealth would find seats in a middle row. And if the old were very poor, they would be likely to take their places in the rear. Their position, like their political power, rested not on their many years but on their attainments and economic status.[31]

Such was the case even for those who addressed the meetinghouse. In the eighteenth century, aging ministers were hardly assured of veneration. As they approached senescence, some religious leaders were forced off the pulpit, to be replaced by the young; others spent their last days pleading for their congregations' support. Without a comfortable estate, they often discovered that respect for the old was more alive in the ideals of their sermons than in the reality of their own existence.[32]

In colonial society, then, the experience of the elderly clearly varied from individual to individual. For persons such as William Byrd, their accumulated wealth and influence assured them the respect of the community. Such men did, in fact, attain political office and front-row meetinghouse seats; few would question their significance in society. For other elderly persons, such as the Rightons and the McKensies, their last years were a time of activity – though not adoration; their activity can hardly be viewed as a symbol of honor. Despite advancing age and increasing infirmities, they had little choice but to remain employed. Their only protection against poverty and destitution was their own daily labor.

But this is hardly the total picture of old age in eighteenth-century America. Not every person lived like the McKensies, much less like William Byrd. Many men and women lacked strong ties to family, property, and occupation. And if, as I have suggested, such factors were of great importance in shaping the nature of old age, these persons would have seen their last years from a very different perspective. Because they no longer possessed means of integrating themselves into society, their old age would have been characterized by deprivation and disdain.

This, in fact, was the experience of scores of elderly persons. The retired, the childless, the widowed, and the poor often found themselves segregated from society in their last years. Few bonds existed to define their roles or solidify their status. Without these links, the prestige and power of the aged disappeared. For such elderly individuals, old age was a distinctive stage of life that brought neither comfort nor respect.

This was true not only for the decrepit pauper but for the once respected and influential as well. Increase Mather, for example, viewed his final years with bitter discontent. In extreme old age, Mather no longer occupied the status of adored and venerated elder. Instead, he discovered that he had been categorized as useless and outdated. "My aged father," wrote Cotton Mather, "too much laies to Heart; the withdrawal of a vain, proud, foolish people from him in his Age."[33]

At the time, Mather was eighty-two, certainly well advanced in years. But more important to understanding his position, I believe, was the fact that he was retired. Beginning in his late sixties, Mather started to complain of a loss of esteem. Once he left the pulpit, the young no longer sought Mather's advice, and the founding of a new church proceeded without his active intervention.[34] Shorn of his identity as a minister, he had, he discovered, also sacrificed a great deal of prestige. Despite his continued good health, he had little to occupy his time.[35] In his advice to the old, therefore, Mather lamented, "it is a very undesirable thing for a man to outlive his work."[36] His own authority, he found, had been based on the roles he had fulfilled, not merely his advanced years. Thus, without an occupation, his age was deprived of its dignity and esteem. Instead, according to Mather, senescence divorced from daily, meaningful work became a divine test of man's power of resignation. "If God will have it so," he wrote, "His holy will must be humbly and patiently submitted to."[37]

Retirement, in fact, was not unknown in the eighteenth century; individuals did leave the work force. In Hampton, New Hampshire, for instance, selectmen lived an average of eleven years between the time they left office and their death.[38] But just when each person experienced this crucial role exit is not easy to determine. In colonial society, few legal restrictions dictated an individual's withdrawal from work.[39] Certainly, as we have seen, many persons did manage to stay employed throughout their entire lives. Personal circumstance, need, and ability combined to keep them active. Yet even these persons, if they lived long enough and became physically disabled, would be expected one day to retire. The aged man was certainly aware that his declining physical strength might hamper his effectiveness as he entered his sixth decade.[40] Samuel Sewall, for example, repeatedly examined his own failing health and advanced age, anxious to determine the point at which he had to resign. Finally, at seventy-five, he decided that he had grown too old and feeble to continue as Supreme Court justice.[41]

Such admissions were not easy to make. In essence, they were an acknowledgment that a radical change had occurred in one's social status. Old age, without activity or a source of income, appeared a distinctive and less honored stage of existence. In most cases, those who were judged to be in this phase received little of the biblically prescribed adoration. As we have seen, even the elite of colonial society suffered an extreme decline in prestige when they retired. Understandably then, those who voluntarily made this transition were to be praised – if no longer venerated. Sewall, in fact, congratulated a fellow judge who was able to admit his own age-related weaknesses and step down from the bench. The justice, Sewall wrote, "has given us further Instance of his Integrity, by resigning his place because of apprehending himself incapable of sustaining it by reason of the infirmities of Age (hardness of hearing)."[42] The advanced years of the individual, rather than bringing him respect and esteem, had suddenly become a physical hindrance. Other elderly persons, therefore, seemed far less willing to resign from positions of importance. Sewall noted, for example, that many of the deacons of his church were very old and infirm, yet would not retire.[43] This, it seems, was not an uncommon predicament. In 1726, Cotton Mather publicly berated the elderly for their refusal to withdrawal voluntarily from significant positions. Simple pride, he believed, inhibited them from duly stepping aside for the younger generation. "Old folks," he wrote:

> often can't endure to be judged less able than ever they were for *public appearances*, or to be put out of offices. But good, sir, be so wise as to *disappear* of your own accord, as soon and as far as you lawfully may. Be glad of a *dismission* from any *post*, that would have called for your activities.[44]

Despite Mather's advice, it is hardly surprising that aged Puritans did not view retirement with a great deal of pleasure. In the religiously oriented towns of New England, a person's identity was strongly linked to his "calling"; he served both God and the community by his daily labor. Leisure, even leisure due to age-based difficulties, was not valued. The old, therefore, were expected always to keep busy, if only with "good works and deeds."[45] But such activity did not give them great prestige. By retiring from their principal calling, they were acknowledging an end to their primary role in society. As a result, they were drawing a sharp line between the final stage and the rest of the life cycle.

19

Retirement, however, was only one means of marking the start of superannuation. Other events symbolized an individual's passage into this stage as well. For an elderly woman, in particular, the death of her husband might represent a crucial, if involuntary, role exit. As an aged widow, she often entered a new set of relationships with both her family and her community. Her past status had been based on her position as wife of the household head; her security, in turn, had rested on her husband's accumulated wealth and influence. Without these assets, the comfort of her final years was no longer assured. There was little guarantee that she would now be perceived as a valuable member of society.

To some degree, the laws of early America attempted to ease the precariousness of the widow's condition. According to legal statute and tradition, the woman was to receive one-third of her husband's property. In addition, an eighteenth-century landholder usually prepared a will that clearly described his wife's portion of the estate. Document after document listed the room that she would inhabit, the clothes she would receive, and the land reserved for her income and benefit.[46] The woman, for example, might be promised "the bedstead we lie on, the bedding thereto belonging . . . and the best green rug . . . the best low chair and a cushion" or "two cows, by name of Reddy and Cherry, and one yearling heifer."[47] These precisely drawn wills were not limited to established towns and cities; they followed the frontier as it moved west. Adam Deemus of Allegheny County, Pennsylvania, for instance, made a will in 1789 in which he reserved for his wife "the privilege to live in the house we now live in until another one is built and a room prepared for herself if she chuses, the bed and beding she now lays on, saddel bridle with the horse called Tom: likewise ten milch cows, three sheep . . ."[48]

Provisions such as these guaranteed that the aging widow would never become completely dependent. Many wills went even further, granting the woman additional control over her offspring. According to the terms of such documents, children would continue to receive their inheritance only if they showed their mother lasting respect and obedience. Their fate, in effect, was tied to how well they treated their aging parent. In 1715, for example, Timothy Richardson of Woburn, Massachusetts, was not to be granted his father's estate until he agreed to "give, sign, and pass unto his mother, the widow of the deceased, good and sufficient security . . . during her widowhood.[49] As long as she lived, Susanna Richardson was assured that her son would be both supportive and attentive. Such wills, then, gave widows considerable assets – in the form of property, wealth, or the threat of repossession – and, consequently, endowed them with a degree of authority in society.[50]

At the same time, these documents symbolized a significant change in the status of the elderly woman. Although she may have retained some of her possessions, or limited power over the young, she nevertheless experienced a radical alteration in both rights and duties. With the loss of property, the aged widow left the secure ranks of the active landholder. Her place in the house was now limited to a single room; the provisions allotted to her satisfied only her basic necessities. She was no longer married to the master of her own home or the spouse of the principal provider for her children. Once the estate changed hands, the younger generation assumed these duties and, with them, the dominant role in the family. The conditions established by such wills, therefore, both underscored the new, precarious position of old age and defined the obligations of a transformed relationship. In listing the room, food, and apparel reserved for the elderly, such bequests broadly paralleled the obligations parents had once owed to their children. Now, however, it was the children who had become accountable by law for the care and feeding of their parents. By the transfer of land, the established hierarchy was reversed; the aged, rather than being respected without question, had assumed the subservient role in the relationship.

Not surprisingly, then, the aged widow was often characterized as superannuated. In the older coastal towns of colonial America, there appear to have been large numbers of such overaged women. In 1756, widows made up 11 percent of the population of Guilford, Connecticut; the Boston census estimated that in 1743, there were about 1,200 of these women out of a population of 16,382. The great majority of those individuals, the survey reported, were both aged and poor. There was little chance that such persons would remarry or possess assets that might assure them continued respect and status.[51] Accordingly, in 1728, Cotton Mather admonished his townsmen to have pity on these persons. "A State of Widowhood," he wrote, "is a state of Affliction; and very singularly so, if the widow is bereaved of the Main Support that after the Death of her Husband Sorrows Embittered by New Anxieties and Encumbrances coming upon her; Debts to be Paid and Mouths to be fed."[52]

The provisions of wills, of course, often eased the woman's condition. If her husband provided for her security, she would at least escape complete dependence. As long as she lived, she would be assured residence in her own home and care by her relatives. But for those aged persons forced to seek shelter in the houses of their grown children, there was little question of the nature of their last years. Their old age lost its unchallenged authority; it was neither a venerated nor an esteemed state, but one based on economic dependence.

This was true not only for elderly women but for elderly men as well. In times of extreme need, they too had to resort to the care of their adult offspring. In eighteenth-century Hingham, Massachusetts, for example, about 20 percent of the old resided in households in which they were not listed as the head.[53] Similarly, in Bedford, New York, at the very end of the seventeenth century, two of the town's six elderly persons lived in their children's home. One was a seventy-five-year-old man who resided with his son; the other was a sixty-year-old widow living with her married son.[54] For these individuals, there was little question of their altered status. As their children became the head of the family, their own power and prestige diminished. The young adults, rather than the elderly, now made the decisions for the group. With the transformation of the traditional hierarchy, they assumed control of the household. In terms of child-rearing, for example, parents, not grandparents, were thought to be the best and final authority. John Wesley made this point quite clear. "Your mother or your husband's mother may live with you," he advised:

> and you will do well to show her all possible respect. But let her on no account have the least share in the management of your children. She will undo all that you have done; she will give them their own will in all things. She would humour them to the destruction of their souls if not their bodies to.[55]

As Wesley realized, the presence of the old within the household might lead to familial conflict. The elderly, once able to control their children, now found themselves dependent and subservient. The result, at times, was a public confrontation between generations. In the late seventeenth century, for instance, John Barbor appeared in Boston complaining of the harsh treatment he received from his son James. In response, the selectmen petitioned James:

> to acquaint you that your father John Barbor is come to Boston, and being by the select men of Boston; Demanded to give a Reson; there of; he Saith you have not been kind to him but macketh him worcke; Two or three miles: aborde which is burdensum to him and more than he can do in his old age; the Select of Boston; do Requir you; as you; will keep your Covinant; which you maid with them; 27 octob. 90. To

come and take Caer of your father, or Ealse you may expect wee shall; prosecute the Law upon you.[56]

The young Barbor had been criticized more than once for the treatment of his father. He was not alone in his seeming negligence; other children as well appeared less then eager to accept their familial responsibilities.[57] The many speeches and sermons extolling the value of age may well be seen as one way of dealing with the problem. Often they defended, not glorified, the old; they called for greater understanding of the weaknesses and dependence of the elderly. In 1723, for example, Thomas Foxcroft asked his readers not to condemn the aged for their failing abilities. "It is not expected of the Ancient," he wrote:

> nor is it commonly needful, that they attend their secular Affairs with that Industry and Application, which is both lawful and commendable in younger People. Persons in years may be allowed more Relaxation, and may, in some cases, exchange a difficult or inferior calling, for a more easy and honorable Employment.[58]

According to ministers and magistrates, the old were to be respected not for their valuable possessions but for the selfless qualities that appeared (or, at least, should appear) in old age. The elderly were to be sober, temperate, grave, and patient.[59] Without such characteristics, however, their old age would hardly be noble or honorable. Cotton Mather, for instance, sharply criticized the elderly who did not possess these virtues. Those who were not sober and temperate had certainly sunk to a disgraceful condition. "For them that stagger with age," he exclaimed, "at the same time to stagger with drink; to see an old man reeling, spewing, stinking, with the excess of the tavern, 'tis too loathsome a thing to be mentioned without a very zealous detestation."[60] The old, therefore, were to be warned: If they wished to be loved and adored – or invited to reside with their children – they should adhere strictly to the qualities Mather enumerated.

Many sons and daughters, nonetheless, chose to place the old in the homes of others. In 1715, for example, Mrs. Mary Thomas advised the selectmen of Boston that she would board her widowed mother in Dorchester.[61] This decision, I believe, reflected more than a desire for space. In colonial America, after all, privacy was not even a possibility for most persons. The average household was filled with children, servants, and even distant relatives.[62] Instead, this course of action may well have allowed both parents and children to avoid confronting the radical change in generational position and, at the same time, gave both the aging parent and the young adult greater independence. As a boarder, the elderly person could be treated according to the terms of the contract; as a resident grandparent, he or she would have to live with the transformed status.[63]

Neither ministers nor magistrates objected to the boarding out of parents. As long as the children fulfilled their financial responsibilities to their kin, they met the minimum obligation. When the young did default on these duties, however, religious leaders rose to denounce their actions. From his pulpit, Samuel Willard criticized such ungrateful offspring. "Children," he declared, "that have been the Charge of their Parents, to bring them up to be capable of doing something, should not presently, in hope of doing better for themselves, desert their helpless Parents, as thinking it now time to look to themselves, and left them shift as they can."[64]

Those old persons left to "shift as they can" were among the most helpless individuals in eighteenth-century society. Lacking any ties to family, wealth, or occupation, they were perceived to be of little worth. They certainly did not possess the high status associated by prescription with great age. Instead, these elderly persons were seen as a drain on the resources of the community. By law and tradition, such old people were prohibited from remaining in any area in which they were not official residents. In 1792, for example, the province of Pennsylvania passed an act requiring a bond from any person importing an aged individual into the region. If the old man or woman became a "charge to the City, Town, or Community," the money would be used to transport this person to his or her original county of residence.[65] This was not simply a threat; age awarded paupers little special treatment. Instead, their many years and helpless condition seemed even more reason to hasten their departure. In 1707, for instance, Nicholas Warner was repeatedly warned to leave the city of Boston. Although Warner protested that he was over eighty and infirm, the selectment held sternly to their judgment.[66]

For poor persons who were official inhabitants of the community, alternate plans had to be created. The authorities, of course, could not bar all the established, poverty-stricken elderly from residence. The solutions they devised generally reflected the physical condition (rather than simply the age) of the needy recipients. The elderly who could still work were expected to do so. As long as their health and capabilities prevailed, they were to provide for their own necessities. Those too weak to find steady employment, though able to care for themselves, were usually given the necessary financial support. As

24

outdoor pensioners, they might receive money to pay the rent or a cord of wood to heat their dwellings. Ministers, as well, participated in the care of the needy aged, contributing both economic assistance and religious admonitions. Cotton Mather, for example, repeatedly recorded cases of forsaken elderly persons in the community who were to benefit from his support and his comforting sermons. In one instance, in 1713, he noted: "There is an Aged Woman in my Neighborhood, poor, and lame, and sick, and in miserable Circumstances. I must not only releeve her myself but also summon together her several Relatives, that they agree to have her well-provided for."[67]

Whenever possible, civil and religious leaders such as Mather turned to the family to care for the poor. The individual household, they believed, was the ideal setting for moral and financial support. In colonial America, it served as the center for charity and relief. Obviously, the old persons left "to shift as they can" lacked the relatives essential to the efficient operation of this plan. As a substitute, surrogate families were provided by the community through the boarding out of the needy. The aged widow, alone in the world, might take in lodgers to complete her household and add to her income.[68] Or, if she was too weak, she would assume her place in the homes of others. Again, the physical condition of the aged poor – as with all poverty-stricken individuals – determined their fate. Rarely, however, did they reside alone. According to colonial regulations, they were expected to enter the households, and the lives, of their neighbors.

Even in the eighteenth century, however, the family system of support could not meet the needs of all the poverty-stricken. Especially in large cities, aged paupers were placed in public almshouses, often composing one-quarter to one-half of the institutionalized inmates.[69] Generally, these were the most broken and ancient of the senescent; their all too apparent infirmities served as a clear sign of their need for charitable attention. Thus, unlike the able bodied or the vagrant, such elderly persons were not made the target of the public's contempt. Their decrepit state left little doubt that they were worthy recipients of the community's care.[70] Yet their broken physical condition also granted them few privileges. Like the "infants, maimed, and lunaticks" with whom they were placed, these individuals were distinguished by their seemingly worthless and unproductive nature. For the incarcerated old, the isolation of the asylum stood as a tangible symbol of their superannuated state.

*   *   *   *

In colonial America, therefore, attitudes toward old age were hardly uniform or unvaried. Despite the admonitions of ministers and the prescriptions of the Scriptures, age alone was not the ultimate source of respect. Power was embodied primarily in younger men; honor was awarded to those of wealth and influence. The status of the elderly, then, was generally based on the assets they possessed. Their control of property, occupation, and kin determined how they would be treated. The aging patriarch, of course, was certain to receive respect – but only as long as he retained his authority within his own family. In large part, of course, his parental position was assured. The great majority of the old never experienced a time when they were not responsible for the upbringing of a child. Moreover, in the agricultural society of eighteenth-century America, they could depend on their landholdings to preserve their strength even if they were robbed of all physical powers. Thus, economic, social, and demographic factors combined to guarantee that they would experience few role exits placing them among the ancient and broken.

But for those without these assets, the life cycle took a very different form. Even in the eighteenth century, attitudes toward the old were hardly static. As the availability of land lessened and the size of estates decreased, many elderly persons lost their assurance of power.[71] Those without valued possessions were rarely treated with great honor. For them, in fact, great age could become an overwhelming handicap. Having failed to accumulate enough to guarantee the comfort of their final years, they appeared of little use to the community. As John Demos has pointed out, language, as well as actions, separated such persons from the elderly of high status. Whereas the wealthy of advanced years were listed in township records by both their first and last names, the aged poor were simply called by the latter – along with the derogatory prefix "old."[72] It was clear that "Old Moore" and "Old Hammond" were the recipients of little esteem. They had passed beyond the years of activity; they were simply characterized as overaged.

The unhappy plight of such persons was especially apparent in the growing cities of America. Urbanization per se did not create superannuation; scores of aged, powerless persons resided in rural areas as well. But in the city, the proportion of such elderly individuals rapidly expanded. There was, after all, little in urban America that could have guaranteed their continued esteem or veneration. The newcomer in a large city lacked the family to offer a home and the kinship network to serve as a source of employment and support.

26

And as they aged, elderly men and women were separated from the important links that had traditionally guaranteed their status. In leaving the farm, migrants also left behind the power and prestige inherent in the ownership of land and goods. They could no longer ensure their own senescent comforts or depend on others to meet their needs. Furthermore, in highly populated urban areas, authorities were far less able to demand a family's continued support of an aged pauper or threaten deportation to the original county of residence. The most common official response was to confine the needy elderly man or woman to an almshouse. Here, in old age, paupers were no longer an integral part of society; they spent their final years surrounded by the signs of their weakness and dependence.

In the nineteenth century, this would become the fate of a growing number of elderly persons. The Philadelphia Almshouse, for example, which before 1750 had never admitted more than 50 paupers a year, enrolled nearly 500 indigent persons annually by the end of the century.[73] By 1815, this number has risen to 2,250.[74] About one-third of this group cited old age as the cause of their destitution.[75] In order to meet the demands of the poverty-stricken, city officials had to raise the poor tax from 4 to 80 cents per $100 of assessed property.[76] The individuals supported by the 1815 tax had not suddenly become the target of society's contempt and neglect. They had merely fallen into the long-standing category of old persons unable to care for themselves. In the years to come, as we shall see, an increasing proportion of the elderly would be classified in this manner. In the nineteenth century, social, economic, and demographic realities would have a significant effect upon society's perception of its aged population.

CHAPTER TWO

Social Realities and Perceptions of Old Age in the Nineteenth Century

In the early republic, the presence of large numbers of the poverty-stricken could easily be explained. Their existence was part of God's plan; the Bible had stated it clearly: The poor will always be with you. The American experience offered ample evidence of this scriptural wisdom. Even in a land of vast opportunities, some individuals would never prosper. The sick, the crippled, the insane, and the aged formed a seemingly permanent class, destined by misfortune and disease to depend on the benevolence of others. To the almshouse manager or the supervisor of outdoor relief, there seemed little reason to question the legitimacy of the elderly's need or to institute a policy that might isolate them from other destitute persons. According to the philosophy of charity popular in the early nineteenth century, such victims of circumstance, age, and misfortune were all simply part of the worthy poor, valid recipients of compassion and relief.

As the century progressed, however, this perception of the elderly would be altered significantly. In time, the old would be distinguished from other groups, separated by their advanced age and seemingly helpless condition. By virtue of their sheer number and destitution, the aged poor came to be categorized as a serious and growing welfare problem. This widespread belief, as we shall see, sprang from two not unrelated phenomena. In large part, it was based on changing social and economic conditions faced by a sizable proportion of the elderly. Especially in the nation's largest cities, the old found their traditional means of retaining prestige eroding. For a significant percentage of the aged, urban and industrial growth led to diminished control over family, wealth, and possessions. Without such traditional props, these old individuals lost their independence and power. At the same time, the elderly poor found themselves under the care and scrutiny of newly professionalized charity workers and social scientists whose perception of old age was undergoing a marked transition. These experts came to reject the notion that the

28

elderly were similar to other needy groups. Instead, they would characterize senescence as a unique and particularly perilous stage of existence.

*   *   *   *

This new conception of the aged did not develop overnight. In the nineteenth century, no single event or innovation triggered an instant aversion to senescence. The country did not experience a rapid "graying of America"; the proportion of persons over sixty rose gradually from 4 percent in 1830 to only 6.4 percent by 1900.[1] Yet, if the country was not suddenly overwhelmed by the aged, the urban and industrial transformation of the nation did not seem to affect their rights and duties adversely.

Basic to the elderly's diminishing control was a changing relationship with their children. In the colonial era, as we have seen, the old rarely faced a time when they were separated from parental responsibilities. Due to their large families and the mother's extended period of childbirth, most couples lived out their days as the parents of growing children. In the nineteenth century, however, important alterations in the structure of the family began to limit the influence many Americans exerted over their offspring. As the average number of children per marriage declined from 7.04 in 1800 to 3.56 by 1900, and the average period of childbirth decreased from seventeen to nine years, it became increasingly likely that a significant proportion of the old would survive to see all their children grown and married.[2] In 1890, only slightly more than half (55.9 percent) of all women aged sixty lived with both husband and children. For women of this age who were still married, more than one out of five had already witnessed the departure of all their children from home. By 1910, this empty nest syndrome had become the familiar condition of nearly one in four.[3]

For those who experienced it, the empty nest could have decisive effects. Losing their identities as the parents of dependent children, they also ceded a great deal of security. Such aged adults had no guarantee that they would retain the care and support of their offspring. Moreover, changes in family structure influenced perceptions of the elderly's precise place in the life cycle. As women limited the size and planned the timing of their families, the birth of their youngest child and oldest grandchild no longer routinely coincided. As a result, the line separating the generations became increasingly distinct. Now, there seemed little doubt of when the old stopped being

29

Table 2.1. *Percentage of Native-Born,
Ever-Married Persons Aged 40–69
Living Without Children, Providence,
Rhode Island, 1865–1900*

Age	Men	Women
40–44	22.7	16.8
45–49	19.2	17.5
50–54	22.3	24.1
55–59	27.1	23.0
60–64	36.2	35.0
65–69	38.1	40.0

Source: Howard P. Chudacoff and Tamara K. Hareven, "Family Dissolution: Life Course Transition into Old
Age," *The Journal of Family History*, 4,
no. 1 (Spring, 1979), p. 72.

responsible for their children. At least in terms of their family relationships, these elderly persons often appeared both overaged and
unnecessary.

For aged urban dwellers, the empty nest was an especially common
occurrence. Throughout the nineteenth century, white city residents
tended to have smaller families than their rural counterparts. In contrast to farm areas, which in 1840 had a ratio of 1.138 children under
five to 1,000 women aged twenty to forty-four, cities with a population
between 250,000 and 500,000 had a ratio of 663. By 1910, these proportions had dropped to 794 and 427, respectively.[4] And understandably, the fewer children the couple had, the more likely they were
to experience old age without parental responsibilities.[5]

By the second half of the nineteenth century, a significant proportion of the urban elderly had come to live apart from their offspring.
In Providence, Rhode Island, for example, between 1865 and 1900,
38.1 percent of ever-married men and 40.0 percent of ever-married
women aged sixty-five to sixty-nine lived without children in their
homes.[6] For these individuals, the absence of their sons and daughters meant the loss of one of the primary means of retaining respect
and authority. If they wished to exert power, they had to rely increasingly upon other valued assets.

Urbanization, however, while limiting family size, simultaneously
tended to diminish the wealth and possessions of the elderly. In the
large city, it was often difficult for the old to rely upon the constant

Table 2.2. *Ratio of Children Under Age Five to Women of Ages Twenty to Forty-Four, by Size of Community, 1840–1910*

		Whites	
Size of community	1840	1890	1910
Rural	1,138	731	782
2,500–25,000	739		507
25,000–100,000	663	487	460
100,000–250,000	778	529	409
250,000–500,000	665	500	427
500,000+		513	474

Source: Warren S. Thompson and P. K. Whelpton, *Population Trends in the United States* (New York: Gordon & Breach, Science Publishers, 1969), p. 279.

control of land or other material goods for their continued high status. Unlike their white rural contemporaries or the elderly of the colonial era, these old persons who lived in the city were rarely able to threaten their negligent children with loss of the family property.[7] Only a small proportion of these aged individuals possessed real estate. By 1890, in fact, only 35.82 percent of the elderly who lived in the nation's eleven largest cities were homeowners; the rest were tenants. In rural areas, though, 83.42 percent of all persons over sixty still owned their own farms. For women, the contrast between rural and urban homeowners was even more striking. Whereas over 90 percent of all aged females heading farm households were owners, the proportion of elderly city women who retained their homes was only 34.20 percent.[8] In the countryside, the aged widow or spinster often inherited the family estate and the status inherent in it. In the rapidly expanding city, she was more likely to be found among the helpless and needy.

But it was not land or houses alone that the aged lacked. In the second half of the nineteenth century, there seemed little likelihood that the average old man or woman would remain in control of great wealth of any kind. In Wisconsin, for example, Lee Soltow discovered that by 1870, in contrast to earlier times, "there was an absence of wealthy native born and foreign born in the state over sixty."[9] Predictably, the most poverty-stricken of all the state's elderly were the immigrants living in the city of Milwaukee. Their average wealth dropped precipitously upon reaching old age.[10] This pattern of dim-

31

Table 2.3. *Home/Farm Ownership of Persons Over Age Sixty, 1890*

	Owners	Tenants
Farms	83.42	16.58
Males	82.38	17.62
Females	91.10	8.90
Homes	57.93	42.07
Males	55.96	44.04
Females	61.78	38.22
Homes, 58 largest cities, pop. 50,000+	40.47	59.53
Males	41.10	58.90
Females	39.16	60.84
Homes, 47 largest cities, pop. 50,000–250,000	47.13	52.87
Males	47.55	52.45
Females	46.27	53.73
Homes, 11 largest cities, pop. 250,000+	35.82	64.18
Males	36.61	63.39
Females	34.20	65.80

Source: Eleventh Census of the United States (1890): Housing, "Report on Farms and Homes: Proprietorship and Indebtedness" (Washington, D.C.: Government Printing Office, 1895), pp. 216–25.

inished wealth in old age was true for the urban areas of Canada as well as the United States. In Hamilton, Canada West, for instance, Michael Katz found that in the period 1851–61, the old experienced the most frequent decline in economic rank of any age group. Over a quarter (27.6 percent) of all men beyond sixty lost at least a portion of their property and wealth.[11]

Moreover, as these individuals were unable to exert authority through their estates, they found it increasingly difficult to earn respect by their employment and knowledge. With urban and industrial growth, the elderly tended to face the problem of occupational segregation. In the course of the nineteenth century, they came to be vastly underrepresented in the fields that would dominate modern America. By 1890, although men over sixty-five made up 4.6 percent of the work force, they filled only 3.5 percent of the manufacturing and mechanical jobs and 3 percent of trade and transportation.[12] Even within these fields, the old were likely to occupy traditional crafts and positions. In transportation, they were merchants (38.5 percent) or agents (10.7 percent) rather than engineers (0.5 percent); in manufacturing, they were carpenters (22.7 percent) rather than steelworkers (1.5 percent) or printers (0.7 percent).[13] In contrast, the great

Table 2.4. *Occupational Rank, by Age,*
Hamilton, Canada, 1851–61

Age, 1851	Stable	Up	Down
–30	70.6	117.1	12.4
30–39	75.3	16.0	8.6
40–49	76.3	16.3	7.4
50–59	71.6	16.2	12.2
60+	60.0	16.7	23.3

Source: Michael B. Katz, *The People of Hamilton, Canada West* (Cambridge, Mass.: Harvard University Press, 1975), p. 161. Reprinted by permission.

majority of the elderly filled professions and trades rapidly declining in wealth and prestige. Most aged men (60 percent) continued to follow the traditional careers of farming, fishing, and mining, whereas only 47.8 percent of men between forty-five and sixty-four and 41.7 percent of men under forty-five were employed in these fields.[14] Other professions of declining status also employed a large proportion of the old. Men over sixty-five, for example, comprised an overwhelming 25 percent of the nation's ministers.[15] And perhaps most suggestive of the growing powerlessness of the old was the fact that they were extremely overrepresented in the least profitable field of all: Twelve percent of unskilled laborers were men of advanced years.[16]

Again, it was in the city that the elderly faced the greatest decline in occupational rank. For individuals entering old age in America's urban areas, job opportunities seemed to diminish rapidly. The aging farmer was likely to be employed far longer than the urban laborer; his ability to do some type of farm work provided status and security that the city resident lacked.[17] This situation occurred in Canada as well. Many of the elderly of mid-nineteenth-century Hamilton, for example, "could not retain their jobs, and those who had been unable to save or acquire independent means were forced into unskilled work or sometimes poverty."[18] As a group, Hamilton's old people were the most likely of any age category to experience a decline in occupational position. Such individuals had few modern vocational skills. They could no longer guarantee their status through professional knowledge or technical expertise.[19]

Not surprisingly, then, the rapid industrialization of the late nineteenth century did affect the labor force participation of the old. As agriculture and self-employment declined in importance, so too did the proportion of employed elderly men. Whereas labor force participation rates for the old remained relatively stable through the nineteenth century, at the close of the century they suddenly began to decline. In 1890, 73.8 percent of all old men were gainfully employed; in 1900 the figure was 68.4 percent, and in 1910 approximately 63 percent; by 1920, the number had dropped to 59.9 percent.[20] For the first time in American history, it became apparent that large numbers of old persons no longer held jobs.

This growing rate of unemployment among elderly workers had an impact upon their status even within their own homes. In the nineteenth century, the old married man who remained employed was almost always guaranteed that he would also continue as household head. If he lost his job, however, he was often forced to enter the homes of his children or board with strangers. By 1900, 35 percent of all married unemployed men over the age of fifty-four no longer retained the dominant role in their households.[21] Moreover, the elderly often experienced greater dependence if they became widowed. For men, the death of a spouse increased the likelihood that they would no longer be considered the head of their home. In 1900, only a minority of widowers over the age of fifty-four retained control of their households. The majority (52 percent) faced a decline in power as they sought shelter outside their traditional economic and familial positions.[22] For many, widowhood and retirement were important role exits that marked the beginning of superannuation.

By the end of the nineteenth century, then, a significant percentage of America's elderly had been adversely affected by the nation's economic transformation. Not every old person, of course, had become destitute or left abandoned. A majority, in fact, remained secure in their families, their employment, and the ownership of their homes. The prosperous among the aged, however, rarely attracted notice. Rather, it was the old who crowded into overflowing almshouses and placed great demands on the relief rolls that drew public attention. To contemporaries, it seemed that dependence among the aged was rapidly expanding. With continued industrial and urban growth, they predicted a time when most aged persons would require charitable assistance.

This perception, however, rested on more than simple economic trends. In a sense, the poverty of the aged needed to be discovered;

34

their declining power had to be publicized and made a national concern. And in the course of the nineteenth century, such a recognition clearly occurred. As urbanization and industrialization progressed, so too did a parallel realization of their negative effects on individuals of advanced age. In the late nineteenth century, it was widely believed that the average elderly man was a likely candidate for pauperism. In developing this notion, charity experts, statisticians, and sociologists played a critical role. In their writing, they presented a persuasive view of senescence that emphasized its weaknesses and problems. The fact that these new professional groups were influential in shaping this perception is hardly surprising. They were, after all, the first to be directly confronted with the harsh realities of growing old in an urban, industrial environment. As a result, their characterization of needy old age, although exaggerated, reflected their daily experience with the elderly.[23] Moreover, as we shall see, the methodology and philosophy of their studies led them to perceive senescent dependence as inherently different from all others and hardly conducive to reform. According to their studies, old age was clearly a time of dependence and struggle.

*   *   *   *

The early welfare worker and charity expert did not set out to depict the old in such negative terms. In the first decades of the nineteenth century, in fact, they took little, if any, special notice of their aged clientele. The impoverished orphan, the crippled, and the insane – as well as the aged – all merged into a homogeneous group characterized primarily by their unquestionable need for public benevolence.

The welfare expert's failure to recognize the aged poor as a special indigent class was vividly reflected in the nation's early relief measures. Rarely did these regulations prescribe one type of treatment for the orphan, another for the insane or senescent.[24] Most smaller towns, in fact, chose to apply the same poor laws to all their worthy poverty-stricken citizens. The community that placed its needy in their neighbors' homes boarded the young and the old, the lunatic and the incapacitated.[25] Similarly, areas with public, tax-supported asylums frequently demanded the institutionalization of all their paupers. Within poorhouse walls, they mixed the dependent of every age, sex, and degree of incapacity.[26] Even larger cities followed similar policies, differing only in scale. Apparent physical capabilities always outweighed the individual's particular life stage. Apart from small children, for example, the able-bodied were usually expected to work. Even aged paupers were not made an exception to this regulation as long as they remained in good health. The old as well as the young could be confined to a workhouse, given a strenuous labor test, or supplied with enough food, fuel, or employment to ensure their continued survival.[27] In contrast, the cities' most ancient and broken, critically ill, and raving insane of all ages were likely to spend their final years isolated (though often laboring) behind the walls of a public institution.[28]

In the first decades of the nineteenth century, then, there was clearly no single, accepted method of dealing with indigent old age, nor did the charity experts define the problems of the elderly as more intractable than those of other groups. The aged poor certainly existed in large numbers, but they were simply grouped with other needy persons. Along with the rest of the worthy poor, they might receive aid not only within the walls of the poorhouse but as outdoor pensioners, as neighborhood boarders, as piecework employees, or, in some cases, as the welcomed tenants of privately endowed hospitals and asylums. To welfare experts, such persons seemed little in need of reformation or uplifting; they were just vivid proof of the enduring nature of poverty. Disease, desertion, and misfortune – rather than self-indulgence – had been the sources of their destitute state.

Beginning in the 1830s, however, the notion of homogeneous, stable class of worthy indigents was challenged – with results that would be critical to perceptions of the aged poor. In time, the sources of the elderly's poverty, as well as the acceptable measures for their relief, would be distinguished from all others. The effects of urban and industrial growth on the old would be discovered and labeled hopeless. The motivating force behind this discovery was the Second Great Awakening. With the religious revivals, evangelically inspired Americans set out to rid the city of the ever-present poor. Members of organizations such as the Philadelphia Temperance Society and the New York Protestant Episcopal City Mission Society hoped to uplift the poor through the distribution of religious pamphlets and moral exhortations.[29] With their energy and enthusiasm, the vast number of friendly visitors were sure that they could save even the greatest of sinners.

But life in the slums did not often correspond to this optimistic picture. Many of the volunteers discovered that poverty was far more enduring than they had originally believed. Venturing into the basements and back alleys of the city, they came upon a lower class seemingly impervious to both moral reform and their own middle-class respectability. Although few of these charity workers ever really questioned the link between weak character and dire poverty, many did come to realize that particular social factors also played a part in shaping the existence of the lower class.[30] Especially in the large port cities, the mass of unskilled workers often greatly outnumbered the available jobs. During every period of economic stagnation, this situation grew worse. In the years 1837–44 and 1857–8, the number of unemployed dramatically swelled. Even the hardworking artisan became unable to support himself.[31] Opportunities, it appeared, were not always unlimited, nor were jobs available for all. The lesson of urban life was that some persons would continue to be poor.[32] Moreover, the environment of the slum seemed to breed an irreversible tendency toward destitution; all who lived in it showed the permanent scars of despair. Given such conditions, moral reform seemed almost useless, even among the youngest inhabitants of the tenements. The downtrodden could hardly succeed while caught up in an inescapable cycle of poverty, illness, and unemployment.

The solution, according to many midcentury reform groups, such as the New York Association for Improving the Condition of the Poor (NYAICP) and, later, the many Charity Organization Societies, was to concentrate primarily on persons who showed the greatest promise of improvement. These individuals were to be selected through a system of rigorous investigation. By classifying the indigent in terms of their background, character, and ability, the concerned volunteer would be able to separate the redeemable poor from the unworthy mass. Past reform societies, according to a spokesman for the NYAICP, had been far too lax in allocating charity. By distributing aid to all who asked for it, they had only guaranteed that most of the poor would continue to lead a life of useless pauperism.[33] Instead, the association gave a radical new meaning to the concept of the worthy poor. It declared that it would assist only five groups of needy persons: industrious laborers; indigent widows and deserted wives with children; educated single females; the sick and the bereaved, who would improve; and mechanics who suffered a temporary loss of employment. For all these individuals – and only these – financial assistance would result in respectable, productive futures.[34]

Consciously omitted from the list of worthy candidates, however, were persons who had reached old age. For the first time, they were not deemed to be worthy of private charitable assistance. The NYAICP reasoned that, as its resources were limited, its first responsibility was to the industrious poor who were young or middle-aged. Their failure to lead virtuous lives would be a loss not only to themselves but to the entire society. "It is well known," the NYAICP wrote in 1854, "that men in health usually labor until sixty or sixty-five. Every man, therefore, who dies in early life, subtracts from the wealth of the community all that he would have earned if he had lived and continued to labor."[35] The old, on the other hand, had little left to contribute. Their weakened physical state detracted from their value; they would never again retain full productive power. Thus, the association resolved "to give no aid to persons who, from infirmity, imbecility, old age, or any other cause, are likely to continue unable to earn their own support, and consequently to be permanently dependent."[36] The evangelicals' belief in progress and perfection had led them to separate the old from other needy – though significantly younger – persons. Their newly established system of classification of the poor created limits corresponding to the stages of life.

Other midcentury reform organizations, such as the Five Points Mission and the New York House of Industry agreed with this policy of age categorization.[37] Although only a minority of all private charity societies adhered to programs that excluded the old, the idea, at least, was endorsed by many. In ideology, if not always in practice, these organizations expressed little faith in the ability of the old to reform and become self-reliant. In the eyes of their founders, the future of the city, as well as the nation, rested on the reformers' ability to mold the corrupt into hardworking Americans. At least by uplifting the young, their leaders reasoned, they might prevent old-age dependency in the future. Once the impoverished individual had become thrifty and diligent, he would be able to save for his own senescence. Moreover, most concerned volunteers believed that it was far easier to transform children and adolescents into good citizens than those who had grown old. With habits and ideas deeply ingrained by time, the elderly had become resistant to all change; poverty had left a permanent mark upon their characters. With the very young, however, the welfare worker retained the hope that a complete reformation might still be achieved. "If the vicious, reckless, improvident habits of adults prove incorrigible to its efforts," the NYAICP wrote in 1860, "in the ductile character of the young there is still hope."[38] The Children's Aid Society, established in 1853, was founded on this basic belief. According to the author of one of its earliest annual reports, work with adults was next to useless; success would reward only those societies that concentrated on the young. "We have begun," the writer explained in 1856:

> where we believe begins the disease, *with the children*. No permanent
> result, we are persuaded, can be hoped for works of reform, taking a
> broad view of society, which do not bear upon the young. It is a griev-
> ous and laborious trial to strive against human evil on every side, but
> when to the effect of unfavorable circumstances and bad passions and
> selfishness is added the influence of time and habit, the labor under
> usual restraints becomes almost hopeless.[39]

The ideologically justified refusal of many midcentury charity organizations to assist the old, therefore, was based on two assumptions: first, that the characters of the old were intractable; and, second,
that the elderly had outlived their years of maximum productivity.
As such, the elderly were unlikely candidates for a popular form of
charity in the middle and late nineteenth century. For a number of
private societies, improvement of the poor was most likely to occur
if they could be removed from the corrupt atmosphere of the slum.
Many volunteers came to despair of helping the indigent while they
lived in the tenement. Salvation and escape from the toils of pauperism, therefore, lay in placing the poor in good homes and jobs in
the countryside.[40]

There was little doubt, however, that such a scheme was inappropriate for the old. In advertising for candidates for rural migration,
organizations such as the Women's Protective Emigrant Society and
the New York City Labor Bureau stressed that only able-bodied persons need apply. They wanted young men and women who could
"turn their hands to anything for which they might be competent"
and, as a result, be turned themselves into productive adults.[41] The
old and weak, in contrast, could play little part in this program. Lacking the elastic personalities of children or the strength and flexibility
of young adults, they had few of the qualities that might have ben-
efited by a sojourn in the countryside.

Even in the city, however, most mid-nineteenth-century philanthropists devoted little time or money to assisting the aged. The same
negative perception of senescence barred the old from urban welfare
programs as well. Houses of industry, piecework employment, and
training centers increasingly catered to the young.[42] In the second
half of the nineteenth century, those volunteers who had labored to
find work for even the most able-bodied had learned the lesson of
restricted employment; if opportunities were limited, they had to be
directed primarily toward the young. The negative aspects of age

39

meant that in contrast to children or adults, the elderly would be unable to learn or labor enough to make these programs profitable. Two generations after the establishment of the NYAICP, reform advocates continued to remark upon the hopelessness of senescence. "In work with the aged," charity expert Amos Warner explained in 1892, "one is conscious that, for the individuals dealt with there is no possibility of success."[43] Thus, regardless of whether the private charity organization was city-oriented or promoted rural migration, attention to the old implied only failure – for the reform society itself as well as its aged clients. If the old and weak were routinely assisted, the NYAICP argued, "the entire fund of the Association would soon be depleted in support of a permanent list; and its primary objects – the elevation of the moral and physical condition of the poor – be defeated."[44] In a society that placed great faith in progress, it was easy to rationalize the growing acceptance of a classification system that excluded the old from the use of private funds.

This philosophy marked a new and significant way of categorizing the poor. Age alone served as the criterion for distinguishing among the indigent. No longer would the young and old receive the same types of assistance. The elderly would find themselves confined to an almshouse, whereas able-bodied adults were offered rural migration and labor. By the late nineteenth century, as a growing proportion of the old applied for charitable assistance, the age-based categorization of the poor gained increasing popularity. Charity workers had discovered that the poverty of the old was indeed unique; because of their advanced age, elderly paupers could be neither reformed nor, it was believed, ultimately relieved.

The rejection of the old, though, was not the result of any sudden aversion to age as such. The welfare experts' characterization of the poverty-stricken elderly bore a striking similarity to much older notions. As we have seen, even in early America, the most broken of the aged, deprived of both family and property, were never held in high esteem. Although they may have received the community's support (provided, of course, that they were established town residents), they were not expected to attain positions of power; clearly, their place in the meetinghouse was in the rear. And in the course of the nineteenth century, this conception of needy senescence did not really change. Dependence in old age was still linked to the elderly's lack of material goods and a suitable family network. The superannuated rejected as proper candidates for private relief would certainly have been among the overaged of their community a century earlier.

Yet, by the second half of the nineteenth century, the condition of the old had evolved; poverty had begun to seem the elderly's usual state. As we have seen, economic changes were eliminating the traditional basis for the authority of the older generation. As a result, growing numbers were being categorized as helpless. Especially from the charity administrator's perspective, the average old person – rather than the exception – had lost control over family, work, and possessions.

Such a perception, of course, marked a new way of viewing old age. Instead of making a distinction between the powerful, responsible elderly and the overaged, welfare authorities endorsed a system that placed most old persons in the category of superannuated simply because of great age and apparent weakness. But this conception was not limited to those who dealt with the aged poor on a day-to-day basis. Academics who attempted to reach an understanding of the forces behind poverty came to a similar conclusion. Beginning in the mid-nineteenth century, a variety of sociological, economic, and scientific works also emphasized the seemingly obvious and unchangeable link between old age and indigence. From their statistical (and therefore seemingly objective) viewpoint, these studies concluded that poverty was indeed a common condition for the old; it grew logically and naturally out of their superannuated state. Like the welfare tracts, these academic works depicted the effects of urbanization and industrialization upon the old in harshly negative terms. They, too, viewed the elderly, poverty-stricken city resident as the typical aged person. According to their findings, men and women beyond sixty-five, or at most seventy, had little hope of exerting authority or power in the modern industrialized world.

One of the first and most important scientific studies to emphasize this fact was the groundbreaking work by the Belgian statistician L. A. Quetelet. In his *Treatise on Man and the Development of His Faculties*, written in French in 1835 and translated into English in 1842, Quetelet sought to explore human capabilities at each stage of existence.[45] According to the great Belgian statistician, other scientists had overlooked the significance of age. In the past, he wrote:

> they have not determined the age at which [man's] faculties reach their maximum or highest energy, nor the time when they commence to decline. Neither have they determined the relative value of his faculties at different epochs or periods of his life nor the mode according to which they mutually influence each other, nor the modifying causes. In like manner, the progressive development of moral and intellectual man has scarcely occupied their attention; nor have they noted how the

41

faculties of his mind are at every age influenced by those of the body nor how his faculties mutually react.[46]

Quetelet attempted to rectify these omissions by "long and laborious study, and by the comparison of a vast number of individuals."[47] Dividing his subjects according to age, he proposed to "establish correct average proportions" for each stage of the "average man's existence."[48]

Quetelet left little doubt as to the negative aspects of senescence. In old age, a person was far less likely to be productive, creative, or agile. The biographies he collected, the author explained, had definitely proven this fact.[49] Although man's "genius" remained highly original in middle age, it disappeared during the last stage of life; his intellect had suffered as well as his moral sense. This was also true for the average worker. He could no longer hope to compete physically at the rate set by a young person. In sum, the brilliant as well as the mediocre were mere shadows of what they had been during the prime of existence. Moreover, in this advanced state, an individual's death was never far distant. Most persons, of course, had already succumbed; only a small minority even survived to senescence. And after seventy, all hope of additional decades of life had to be forsaken. As Quetelet's aggregate death records revealed, the biblical count of threescore and ten closely reflected the maximum length of human existence.[50]

Quetelet's treatise was only one of many that studied individual abilities in correlation with age. In the mid-nineteenth century, the fledgling insurance industry, along with the medical profession, pioneer public health advocates, and census officers, made statistical studies of the length and limitations of the human life span. With ever-increasing sophistication in the gathering and interpretation of data, these experts worked to dispel age-old notions of the possibility that an individual's life might continue for centuries.[51] Legends of persons such as Thomas Parr or Henry Jenkins, who were believed to have lived well beyond 100, were shown to be false. According to often-quoted statisticians such as the English William J. Thoms or the American Edward Jarvis, it was only wishful thinking – and not the strength of old age – that had made certain individuals appear to live for centuries.[52] In 1873, in his, *Human Longevity*, Thoms wrote:

> the unquestioning confidence and the frequency with which the public is told of instances of persons living to be a hundred years of age and upward so familiarizes the mind to the belief that Centenarianism is a

matter of everyday occurrence, that the idea of questioning the truth of any such statement never appears to have suggested itself.[53]

Yet, once enough facts had been presented, the author doubted that many persons could believe that old age might be infinitely extended. As a stage of life, senescence was limited to a few short years.

To many mid-nineteenth-century American and English statisticians, these figures revealed more than the average life course; they scientifically depicted God's rational plan for the operation of his universe. Each life span and every decade had been divinely formulated. "The results [of his statistical study]," wrote the English physician and public health reformer Southwood Smith, "clearly indicate that certain fixed periods are marked by nature as epochs of human life."[54] High mortality in childhood and sensecence, for example, was balanced by low death rates in middle age. Similarly, an individual's productive power rose and declined according to age.[55] Even sickness could be directly correlated with life stage: The older the man, the more days he suffered from any ailment. Dr. Daniel Maclachlan, for instance, charted the ill health of the patient according to age. At fifty, the "average man" could count on nine or ten days of illness; by sixty-five the number had risen to thirty; and it more than doubled to seventy-three or seventy-four by the time he reached seventy.[56] Like infants susceptible to myriad diseases – and highly likely to die – the old were placed in a similarly precarious role. "Mortality is subject to laws," explained Smith, "the operation of which is as regular as gravity."[57] The elderly's weakness, diseases, and death, therefore, were all products of their position at the end of the life cycle.

For the social scientists of post–Civil War America, these studies served a critical function; they helped to explain a major source of the nation's poverty. In studying the increasing almshouse population, the overcrowded labor market, or the growing mass of unskilled workers, economists and sociologists repeatedly discovered that a large proportion of the destitute were quite old. This fact was reported time and time again in the journals of the newly formed social science associations. Articles such as Davis R. Dewey's "Irregularities of Employment," F. J. Kingsbury's "Pensions in a Republic," Mary Roberts Smith's "Almshouse Women," and Amos Warner's "Notes on the Statistical Determination of Poverty" left little doubt as to the direct relationship between old age and poverty.[58] According to their statistics and charts, the worker had little hope of retaining his position into his sixties and seventies. At around fifty, his abilities began to falter. And with each passing year, he became more of a liability. His strength and flexibility – as well as his salary – all declined with age. By sixty-five, he had little chance of remaining self-sufficient. Such articles agreed that old age, both as a biological and a social reality, undermined the human struggle for subsistence.

The social scientist hardly needed to convince the worker of this fact. By the last quarter of the nineteenth century, the industrial laborer appeared only too aware of the fate that might await him. In a survey distributed by the Massachusetts Bureau of Labor Statistics in 1879, the worker was asked to assess his chances for a comfortable old age. Would he, after sixty-five, be able to support himself and not depend on charity? Of the 202 individuals who replied, less then 25 percent (forty-three men) responded positively: They had, or expected to have, enough to exist. The rest of the sample viewed their final years with grave misgivings. Wrote one man, "With the present conditions of business, don't want to survive [sic]."[59]

In publishing the results of his survey, statistician Carroll Wright emphasized that the laborer was hardly responsible for his predicament. Along with other social scientists, he argued that even the most industrious and moral individual was likely to suffer in his final years.[60] The worker, after all, was only a minute part of the labor market, subject to its demands and fluctuations. As he aged, it was likely that he would be replaced by the young and vigorous. The pauperism of the old, therefore, was hardly unusual or unexpected. It was simply the outcome of the elderly's inability to keep up with the ever-quickening pace of industrialization.[61]

In the late nineteenth century, no social scientist was more influential in drawing this fact to public attention than the English writer Charles Booth. In his books, *Pauperism and the Endowment of Old Age* and *The Aged Poor in England and Wales*, both published in the 1890s, Booth focused upon the extent of old-age pauperism. In one-third of all poverty cases, he discovered that old age was the primary cause of destitution; neither disease nor alcohol was responsible for such a high percentage of the country's indigence. In the industrial world, he concluded, the old were simply regarded as unnecessary and were discarded. They then had little choice but to become the inmates of almshouses or to join the list of those receiving the public dole.[62]

In America, Booth's results were widely publicized and discussed.[63] His conclusions seemed to justify the social scientists' contention that the elderly could do little to rectify their poverty-stricken condition. By the early twentieth century, state commissions in Massachusetts and Pennsylvania had been appointed to discover the nature and extent of such destitution. With statistical care, they duplicated the focus of Booth's investigation and repeated many of his procedures. Counting the percentage of elderly persons in almshouses, benevolent homes, and on relief, they found that about one-fifth of all pauperism in their states was related to senescence. Although this was far less than the English case, the commissioners were hardly encouraged by the results. Even those elderly persons who reported themselves to be self-sufficient were not far from the level of poverty. It seemed clear to the authors of the states' reports that a large proportion of the elderly population would eventually be forced to accept some type of charitable assistance.[64]

With the publication of the commissions' findings, poverty in old age had clearly attained public recognition as a serious and growing condition. In the first two decades of the twentieth century, numerous social scientists wrote studies that focused on the special problems of the elderly. Sociologists such as Edward T. Devine, Abraham Epstein, I. M. Rubinow, and Lee Welling Squier depicted the last years as a stage in which the individual was likely to be relegated to "the industrial scrap heap."[65] All agreed on the reason for this displacement: With the economic transformation of the nation, the old had fallen victim to uncontrollable economic forces. "The socio-economic problem of the old man or woman, as we know it," wrote I. M. Rubinow, "is specifically a problem of modern society, a result of the rapid industrialization within the last century."[66]

These social scientists, like scores of charity workers, had come to support a theory of poverty that separated the elderly from other needy persons. They agreed that there was little that could be done to change the condition of the old. With welfare authorities, they shared a conception of senescence emphasizing its handicaps and deficiencies; in the modern world, great age seemed reason enough for a penniless condition. In reality, as we have seen, the poverty of the elderly had not suddenly appeared. Even before the nineteenth century, there had been numerous aged paupers who received little community respect. But the proportion of needy elderly persons had never seemed great. The overaged comprised only a small minority of the elderly population. With industrial and urban growth, however, social analysts constructed a classification system based on the assumption that all elderly individuals would lose control over valued resources and eventually outlive their usefulness. Because of the nature of society and the weaknesses of age, they would one day become

45

indigent. The social scientist and the welfare authority endorsed this conception not because they despised the elderly; they were just vividly aware of the negative effects America's economic growth seemed to have had on many elderly persons. Growing numbers of aged persons appeared to have been forced into destitution. To these professionals, then, there was little question that old age was a distinctive and less than golden stage of life. By the sixth decade, an individual was likely to have passed out of self-sufficiency into a period of poverty and need. "After the age of sixty has been reached," wrote Lee Welling Squier in his study *Old Age Dependency in the United States*:

> the transition from non-dependence to dependence is an easy stage – property gone, friends passed away or removed, relatives become few, ambition collapsed, only a few short years left to live, with death a final and welcome end to it all – such conclusions inevitably sweep the wage-earner from the class of hopeful independent citizens into that of the helpless poor.[67]

This conception of aging gained widespread and rapid recognition. In the popular press of the late nineteenth and early twentieth centuries, old age was characterized by poverty and uselessness.[68] In addition, the last years were pictured as a time of serious, body-wasting illnesses. The old were not only apt to be poor but also disease-ridden and in need of a physician's constant care. Such a perception was supported by the medical model that developed in the late nineteenth century. As we shall see, the doctor, like the charity worker and the social scientist, would come to depict the elderly as both senile and overaged.

46

CHAPTER THREE

Medical Models of Growing Old

The late-nineteenth-century physician who wrote about old age had few medical traditions on which to base his work. Prior to the nineteenth century, medical practitioners did not prescribe specifically for the old. They treated most adults alike, with little regard for chronological age. Even a century later, a specialization in the diseases of senescence could hardly be considered well established; no medical school offered courses on the aged, nor did some prestigious journals publish the latest findings in gerontological research. The term *geriatrics*, in fact, did not enter the medical lexicon until 1909.[1] Compared with such popular specializations as gynecology, pediatrics, or surgery, the study of the illnesses of the old attracted little official recognition.

This does not mean, however, that doctors had little to say about the nature of old age. Throughout the nineteenth century, physicians discussed the importance of studying senescence, in order both to understand the dynamics behind growing old and to offer the elderly sufficient therapeutic care. As we shall see, important developments in the theory and practice of medicine had a significant effect upon the physician's perception and treatment of the elderly. By the end of the century, he would view most aged persons – not only the chronically ill – as patients in need of his constant professional attention. Paradoxically, perhaps, this conception would deter him from specializing in the diseases of old age while leading him to prescribe for every aspect of the senescent's care. Through articles and texts written for the popular and medical press, he presented a consistent and influential view of the needs and abilities of the elderly.

*   *   *   *

In the nineteenth century, no ambitious physician had to "discover" old age to prove it physically or socially different from adulthood.[2] Since ancient times, medical experts had included senescence as a fundamental part of the life cycle.[3] Certain medical writers in classic antiquity, in fact, believed that they had determined the precise point at which the last stage began. According to this view of the body, the organism renewed itself in cycles that corresponded to the number seven and certain "powerful" squares. Ages seven, fourteen, twenty-one, forty-nine, sixty-three, and eighty-one were designated "climacterics," crisis years during which an individual completed one cycle and began the next. Some physicians warned that these were periods of particular danger. Weakened by its total transformation, the body became peculiarly susceptible to disability and disease. One of the most crucial of these years was sixty-three, the "grand climacteric." At this point, productive life ended and the final segment of existence began. Now, according to this classic theory, an individual entered old age.

Almost two thousand years after the Greeks, writers of medical texts still discussed the body's innate developmental cycle, although they often ridiculed the ancients' belief in magic numbers. "Such were once the trifles dignified by the name of science!" declared an exasperated Bartholomew Parr in his early-nineteenth-century dictionary.[4] The predetermined segments, he assured his readers, had little to do with the organism's constant state of alteration and repair. Yet such early-nineteenth-century experts did not disregard the stages of life, nor, as we shall later see, were they entirely willing to abandon the notion of climacterics. A physician rarely chose to portray the human life span as a straight line, unbroken by distinct and important physical developments. Instead, since at least the sixth century, writers of medical texts had come to rely upon the life cycle as a description – if not really an explanation – of the course of human existence.[5] Visible developmental changes, such as dentition, puberty, and menopause, were repeatedly cited as signs that the body evolved according to well-established and predictable patterns. Moreover, these fundamental physiological divisions represented distinct psychological states; to act in accordance with each was to follow the dictates of nature. Physicians cautioned the young against appearing too cynical and the aged against a lighthearted and callous manner. Such admonitions were aimed at both medical and moral well-being. In the seventeenth century, for example, the renowned English physician Sir Thomas Browne instructed his readers to adhere closely to the basic traits of their respective stages for the sake of health and happiness. "Confound not the distinctions of thy life with nature hath divided," he warned:

that is, youth, adolescence, manhood, and old age; nor in these divided periods, wherein thou art in manner four, conceive thyself but one. Let every distinction be happy in its proper virtues nor one vice run through all. Let each distinction have its salutary transition and critically deliver these from the imperfections of the former, so ordering the whole, that prudence and virtue may have the largest section.[6]

Browne chose to divide life into four stages; others portrayed it in as few as three or as many as eight. But regardless of its brevity or length, no scheme ever omitted old age as a separate and distinct segment of the life cycle. Although youth and adolescence were often united, or infancy and childhood represented as one, old age and maturity were never merged. Their physical and mental attributes contrasted too greatly to be included in a single category. In depicting the life cycle, most illustrators – whether writers, artists, or physicians – selected similar and stereotypical images. The young man was pictured at the height of his growth, his body and mind vividly reflecting his strength and unlimited possibilities. The old man, on the other hand, was portrayed in a far more ambiguous fashion. Even if depicted as extremely wise – and thus an apt judge or lawmaker – he could never escape the negative aspects of his years. Bent, decayed, and wrinkled, his body revealed an approaching final demise.

Yet, despite the marked contrast between the adult life stages, and the importance attributed to this difference by physicians such as Browne, in practice most medical writers ignored the basic divisions. Prior to the nineteenth century, no body of literature instructed practitioners on how to care for the particular needs of the elderly. In most books, the life cycle was limited to the introduction or included in an appendix; it bore little relation to the body of the text.[7] As we shall see, only authors who focused on longevity hygiene discussed senescence, but this was a final goal, not a reason for devising age-specific treatments. Most physicians prescribed for the old – if they prescribed at all – much as they would for younger persons. As conventionally described in materia medica texts, traditional therapeutics did not consider differences in age. Instead, treatment centered on the effects of specific drugs on the individual's system as a whole. Certain compounds stimulated, others calmed, and still others were noted for their ability to produce vomiting, sweating, or a purge.[8] Once an individual had survived childhood, however, the stage of life had little effect on the theoretical operations of the chemical. A large dose of calomel was likely to produce the desired – and highly visible – result whether the patient was twenty or seventy.

Similarly, medical texts that classified diseases, either as specific entities or as general states, rarely considered the age of the adult. There were, to be sure, diseases that were routinely associated with senescence. Physicians believed that gout and rheumatism, for example, were particularly prevalent in the elderly. Yet, neither the diagnosis nor the treatment of these illnesses altered with advancing years. Once the appropriate symptoms appeared, a well-defined treatment was sure to follow, regardless of the patient's age. Other more general disease states, such as fevers or catarrhs, were classified by their external appearance, course, and cure, or by their seat and cause. These nosologies, though, took little notice of life stages.

In addition, age played only a small part in those systems that explained disease in terms of a single factor. Since antiquity, scores of medical experts had attempted to find a single cause of all maladies. Depending on their chosen philosophy, they pinpointed the way to cure any disease. The practitioner need only relieve the pressure on the blood vessels, balance the humors, control the electric field around the body, or do whatever else might be called for in the logic of his explanatory system. Here again, life stages played but a small part. If all diseases had a single cause, there could hardly be one set of ailments for the old and another for the young.[9]

Yet, pre–nineteenth-century physicians were not oblivious to the changes that came with age, nor did they expect all patients to react in precisely the same fashion. The scarcity of medical texts containing information on the care of the elderly was due to an unquestioning acceptance of their disabilities rather than to a failure to recognize them. The weakness of the old was not considered a state amenable to cure. Instead, physicians believed that this was the essential, irremediable quality of growing old. In describing senescence, writers consistently called upon the centuries-old metaphor in which the body was conceived of as a limited fund of vitality. At birth, the organism was endowed with a supply of energy that it used for growth and activity. As that supply diminished, the body was by adulthood merely able to maintain itself. Finally, its energy spent, it slowly decayed. Here, then, were the primary and highly visible stages of life: childhood, maturity, and old age. Loss of vitality explained this basic transformation and the obvious changes that came with the passage of years.

This hypothetical model also served to explain the numerous and often incurable illnesses that afflicted the elderly. Viewing the body in holistic terms, physicians believed that a change in any part of the system would affect the entire constitution. Thus, the organism's loss of vitality quickly led to a "predisposing debility"[10] that might cause either systemic ailments or specific diseases. In this sense, it mattered little whether a physician adhered to the belief that illness was an entity that entered the body from without, an imbalance among the humors, or the result of improper stimulation. Drained of energy, the elderly individual was unable to sustain the vital balance between the body and the environment. Disease was, then, an inevitable and predictable aspect of this stage of existence.

This model of aging did not require physicians to create a distinct senile therapeutics. Although the weakened condition of the old allowed the disease to "take over" the system, the manifestations of illness did not alter with age. The lack of vital energy, though, did have a systemic effect. Not only did it lead to a variety of ailments, but it also caused the dimming sense perceptions and weakening motor skills of the aged. The physician, however, had few remedies for this condition. Usually, he simply attempted to increase the body's power temporarily through the use of appropriate foods and tonics. This was neither a revolutionary nor an age-distinctive treatment. Traditional therapeutics had long been based on the notion that the body was a product of the dynamic interactions between its own internal functions and the outside environment. By introducing stimulants into the bloodstream, medical authorities believed that they could revitalize the entire system, giving power to the senses and agility to the muscles, and thus making the body less susceptible to disease. In addition, they might hope to monitor and "adjust" the primary organs of the body in order to create a harmonious relationship among all the parts. In the early nineteenth century, for example, Anthony Carlisle recommended regular bloodletting for the aged patient with a debilitated heart.[11] Again, the prescription followed the logic of rational therapeutics: The enervated organ, unable to pump at full capacity, would be greatly relieved if less blood flowed through the system. Once a new equilibrium was established, the body would operate at a lower, though presumably more efficient, level.

Such prescriptions were not abundant, however. Few physicians devoted themselves to the development of novel treatments for the aged. The debilitated state of such patients discouraged the application of experimental procedures – both for the sake of the patient and the reputation of the physician. Because he could not hope to restore completely the vitality of the old, the doctor's active intervention might only raise public doubt about the power and efficacy of his practice. "The prudent physician," advised one such medical man:

> will not interfere, or if at all, with care and limitation, in cases where changes irresistible in their actions have occurred in any organ or function of the body. To urge medical treatment in the face of distinct proof to this effect is to sacrifice at once the good faith and usefulness of the physician.[12]

The doctor would not, in any case, have to face harsh criticism if his aged patient died without his therapeutic intervention. The same model that justified the numerous infirmities of the old also explained their demise. It was hardly the physician's fault. Each person, after all, had been allocated only a limited amount of energy and time. "The last calamity . . . in old people," concluded Richard Mead in 1762:

> is that the whole body is afflicted. The very course of the blood is interrupted; hence the wretched man is seized with difficulty of breathing, apoplexies, or lethargies. The heart also, the principle and fountain of life, sinks through want of its usual force, and "the broken chariot falls into the pit."[13]

Mead, quoting the words of Seneca, asserted, in fact, that old age was itself a disease. Yet this eminent English physician felt no need to cite specific evidence; his proof rested upon the words of King Solomon, "the wisest of kings," and common sense.[14] It did not take a medical expert to evaluate the damage to age. The years took their toll externally: The stooping posture, loss of hearing, and addition of wrinkles were all clearly apparent – as much to the philosopher or the poet as to the physician. Once nature had set a determined course, no one expected the medical man to be able to perform miracles. The age of "wonder drugs" was yet to come. Instead, the physician fulfilled his professional responsibilities and, at the same time, demonstrated his medical skill by merely warning that death was near. The old, it was often contended, faced the news with resignation and relief; as their vital energy declined, so too did their desire for continued existence.[15] The prognostic skills of the physician, the argument followed, allowed the elderly to prepare for their passing. In the end, even science had to acknowledge the presence of a far more powerful life-giving and life-denying force. For the aged, a better world was shortly to be theirs.[16]

Thus physicians easily rationalized the demise of their elderly patients. For centuries, they had attributed their deaths to "old age" or "decay" – imprecise diagnoses, perhaps, but ones that corresponded to widely accepted conceptions of development and decay.[17] Before the twentieth century, most aged persons did not go to the hospital to die; few "extra ordinary measures" existed in this institution to sustain their lives. Instead, death usually took place in the home, without the physician's active therapeutic intervention. Given such conditions, and barred from performing autopsies, doctors often recorded the cause of mortality in extremely broad terms. "Senility," "old age," and "debility" continued to be listed as the causes of death well into the late nineteenth century. The general weakness of the patients, after all, could hardly be denied. They had died natural deaths, the consequence of living long, and thus necessarily debilitating, lives.

Far more perplexing to the medical profession, however, were those ancient persons who continued to retain their strength and vigor. These individuals, of course, were not in the majority. At the beginning of the eighteenth century, only about one out of every eight persons born in America would reach seventy.[18] Yet, even this minority aroused wide scientific interest. Despite (or, in some cases perhaps, because of) the medical profession's generally accepted therapeutic techniques, most patients succumbed well before they attained sensecence. How had these atypically long-lived persons been able to preserve their precious vitality?

Prior to the nineteenth century, in fact, physicians who wrote about old age usually concentrated more on the uncommon phenomena of survival than on the diseases that often accompanied longevity. The illnesses of the elderly tended to be both too predictable and (in most cases) too incurable to benefit from extensive study. Far more interestingly, however, were those old persons whose health and longevity seemingly defied the acceptable laws of nature. In the only general American medical text written in the early eighteenth century, for example, Cotton Mather focused on the inexplicable reality of senescence. His chapter in *The Angel of Bethesda* provided no advice on curing senile ailments or alleviating disease. The individual who had outlived the biblical allotment of threescore and ten hardly required medical recommendations; he was already well "past the danger of Dying before his Time." Mortal persons could ask for no more. Instead, Mather instructed the elderly to contemplate the sheer wonder of their continued survival. "O my God," he led them to implore, "why am I not *feeble* and *Sore broken* and roaring by reason of *Disquietness* of my Heart and under those Terrible Distempers which Defy the *Physicians* and which Torture the *Patients* and under which *all the Days* of the Afflicted are *Evil Days*?" In subsequent verses, the elderly

53

could marvel at how they had been spared the inflictions of Stone, Gout, Palsy, and Broken Bones. Surely, the Puritan minister surmised, this was little less than "a Miricle."[19]

Mather's interest in the reasons for human longevity was not unique in eighteenth-century American medical literature. In 1797, for example, Benjamin Rush's chapter on old age in *Medical Inquiries and Observations* echoed many of the concerns of the Puritan minister. Reporting on the physical condition of a group of octogenerians, Rush, like Mather, focused neither on their illnesses nor possible cures but on the reasons for their continued survival. Unlike Mather, however, he concluded that the reason for such longevity lay not in the hands of God but with the subjects themselves: They were all descendants of long-lived ancestors, had been temperate in food and drink, and moderate in business, politics, and religion. Moreover, these individuals had been wise enough to emigrate to America. The postrevolutionary environment, the nationalistic physician assured his readers, was conducive to a long and happy existence.[20]

In conducting his survey, Rush placed himself within a long literary tradition. Since at least the time of Cicero, physicians and laymen alike had written on the means of attaining longevity. These authors hardly constituted an organized school of thought; they adhered to no single philosophy of medicine and adopted no unified, single view of nosology. In their writings, in fact, they often emphasized two quite different ultimate goals.[21] Some advocates of longevity accepted threescore and ten as the natural span of human existence and attempted to improve individuals' day-to-day health and vitality. Other more radical longevity spokesmen dreamed of adding unlimited years to the average life span. Biblical patriarchs, after all, had counted their ages by centuries, not decades. In their longevity tracts, many of these advocates related the popular belief that historical figures and exotic tribesmen had lived well past 100.[22] This phenomenon, they asserted, was not limited to the distant past. In 1635, for example, an Englishman, Thomas Parr, died, allegedly at 152. His claim received the support of the scientific community, for his autopsy was performed by the eminent William Harvey. Here seemed proof that people could live far beyond the scriptural allotment of threescore and ten.

The difference in the two approaches to longevity, however, should not be overemphasized.[23] The writers agreed on the basic principle on which their tracts were based: Individuals might secure a long and prosperous life if they lived according to certain strict rules. The writers' prescriptions for attaining this goal varied. Some endorsed the use of wines; others demanded abstinence; still others debated the merits of vegetables or red meat. But they all believed that in order to reach a healthy old age, a person had to follow the law of moderation in every aspect of life. The proof for this assertion, as almost every writer of longevity tracts proclaimed, was the well-known case of Liugi Cornaro. Cornaro was an Italian nobleman of the Renaissance who, at thirty-five, had been warned by the most respected authorities that his death was imminent. His indulgent style of life had prematurely dissipated his supply of vitality. Reforming his habits, Cornaro managed to outlive both the predictions and the respected authorities; he did not succumb to death until ninety-eight. In his later years, Cornaro explained the secret of his successful longevity in *Discourses on the Temperate Life*. Published in Italian, Latin, English, French, German, and Dutch, the treatise achieved an immortality that even its author had not attained. In England alone, the work went through fifty editions during the eighteenth and nineteenth centuries. The lesson it preached was simple: All one had to do was to imitate Cornaro's lifestyle, and old age was assured.[24]

In time, other authors were to follow in Cornaro's footsteps, each outlining his own plan for longevity. In accordance with popular beliefs about aging, these writers viewed senescence and natural death as the result of declining energy. In the publications of these advocates of longevity, however, this metaphoric model became the basis for literal prescription. If death resulted from an exhausted supply of energy, then the goal was to retain it at all cost. This could easily be achieved, they argued, by eating the correct foods, wearing the proper clothes, and performing (or refraining from) certain activities. Such regimens, like the model on which they were based, were straightforward indeed: The more wisely people used the energy they had been given, the more likely they would be to attain a healthy and long-lived sensecence.

On one level, then, in contrast to most medical authorities, longevity writers seemed to instruct the reader on the concerns of old age. These authors unanimously sang the praises of a decades-long existence and rhapsodized over the deeds that were yet to be performed by the mature and experienced individual. Upon closer scrutiny, however, this literature, like the literature of clinical medicine generally, had little to say about senescence as such. In stressing the joys of longevity, the writers wanted it clearly understood that there was to be a total redefinition of the last stage of life. None wanted to spend endless, unproductive years filled with infirmities and disease; this would hardly be a future for which one would strive. Their goal instead, as Christopher William Hufeland, one of the most popular of the late-eighteenth-century longevity writers, explained, was "to preserve oneself in a state of youth to an advanced period of life."[25] The age-old characterization of the elderly as bent, decayed, and wrinkled would vanish. In its place, longevity publicists created the image of an individual who, "without loss of physical power and energy," [26] would continually live in the prime of life. Death, when it came, would be spontaneous; all organs and functions were to cease in a single painless instant.[27]

For those who had actually aged, however, this optimistic view was rarely applicable. By their weakened condition, the old revealed that their energy had already been squandered and little more could be done. Cornaro had set the example, reforming his habits at thirty-five. Had he waited any longer, he undoubtedly would not have survived to so advanced an age. Hope lay with those whose lives and energy could still be conserved. Thus, most writers on longevity addressed the young and instructed them on ways of retaining their youth. The alleviation of the ills of old age, however, received little attention in their tracts. This was hardly surprising. The confident longevity writer promised the reader who adhered to his regimen an extended life span, and one attended with little or no experience of old age.

The only hope for the old, many longevity advocates asserted, lay in retaining the appearance and vitality of youth or, by some miracle, in having these important qualities returned to them in senescence. This, they concluded, was not entirely impossible. In 1807, for example, the English physician Sir John Sinclair listed "the color of the hair, the possession of teeth, and the clearness of vision" as the most remarkable features that separated youth from age. With awe and admiration, he then related tales in which these characteristics of the young had reappeared in the elderly. By regaining their youthful countenance, these persons had managed to live well beyond a century.[28] Old age – with all its negative qualities – was hardly the goal of writers of longevity books; instead, they looked forward to eternal middle age.[29]

Throughout the nineteenth century, the vision of the writers on longevity continued to attract wide audiences. In part, this was a response to perceived inadequacies in medical therapeutics. As the public grew increasingly skeptical of heroic cures, they began to question the theoretical constructs on which they were based; in the mid-nineteenth century, therapeutic nihilism was a fashionable – if never universal – stance. Proper hygiene and temperate habits certainly did seem to lead to a longer life. Could mercury or bloodletting deliver, or even promise, as much? Yet, although the methods of the longevity advocates gained wide recognition – and eventually become part of the physician's regular practice – their ultimate goal was subject to harsh scrutiny. Spokesmen for longevity hygiene had promised a life span that stretched over endless decades, with none of the infirmities seemingly inevitable in the last stage of life. As the century progressed, however, the final segment of the life cycle neither changed its traditional characteristics nor gave any indication of vanishing. As we have seen, numerous nineteenth-century statisticians had worked to dispel the idea of unlimited longevity. Their life tables, they asserted, had definitely proven that most persons did not survive even to seventy. Although the nineteenth century did witness a dramatic rise in life expectancy, this was due to a decrease in infant and child mortality, rather than to any sudden extension of senescence.[30] Threescore and ten remained – as it had since biblical times – a limit only a few could even hope to surpass. The old continued to grow weak with age and, with each additional year, faced increasingly numerous and debilitating illnesses.

Moreover, as we shall see, as clinicians began to subject the elderly to close examination, they discovered traits that seemed to make senescence a distinct and inescapable part of the life cycle. Using the latest medical theories and scientific techniques developed in the hospitals and laboratories of the mid-nineteenth century, interested clinicians categorized the old not merely in terms of age or lack of energy but according to their unique physiological, anatomical, and psychological conditions. These were realities that would hardly be erased by a proper diet or regimen. Instead, this new perspective caused physicians to view the elderly as a separate class of patients requiring specific age-related treatment for their characteristic ailments.

*   *   *   *

It would be difficult, if not impossible, to date this transformation precisely. Physicians did not ignore aged invalids one day and thoroughly prescribe for their ailments the next; nor did they develop a complete course of senile therapeutics overnight. The creation of a specialization in geriatric medicine was (and is) a continuing process that depended not only on the introduction of new theories and techniques by the elite but on the acceptance and implementation of these ideas by practicing physicians. But if a particular date cannot be affixed to the birth of this new concern for the elderly, the development of geriatrics did occur within a specific historical and medical context. Prior to the nineteenth century, as we have seen, few doctors devoted themselves to the study of the aged. Although most physicians believed that growing old caused weakness and made the patient more susceptible to disease, they did not conclude that this process radically altered his or her constitution. One theory of medicine, one course of therapeutics, could be applied to all adult patients. In the early nineteenth century, however, several European clinicians challenged these basic assumptions. Growing old, they asserted, involved far more than a mere loss of vitality. By the mid-nineteenth century, at least fifteen French physicians had published monographs on the unique character of the elderly.[31] In their texts, they formulated a definition of old age that separated it medically from all other age groups and required the physician's complete attention. They had, they believed, defined a clinical basis for senescence.

Initially, these physicians had not set out to explain the aging process as such. Their conception of old age as a pathological process was only one of the many novel ideas produced by the Paris school of medicine. Under the leadership of physicians such as M.-F.-X. Bichat, F.-J.-V. Broussais, and P.-C.-A. Louis, elite French doctors began to question classic assumptions about the nature of disease. Redefining the direction of medical inquiry, they first became clinicians and pathologists; the hospitals of France evolved into centers for empirical study. As a result of this new approach, these physicians discarded traditional systems of nosology. Fits, fevers, and inflammations, they declared, were only symptoms of disease, not actual illness. Instead, they attempted to correlate these external ailments with subsequent pathological findings. Disease, they believed, left unmistakable traces in the tissues of the body. Postmortem findings, such as sclerosis, fibrosis, and degeneration, were keys to the classification of disease. Viewed in these terms, illness could no longer be thought of as a general systemic condition. Instead, these clinicians and pathologists began to devise nosologies based on specific localized disease entities.[32]

In the course of this work, clinicians came to draw medical implications about the effects of aging. At the outset, much of the research had been conducted on elderly individuals. Two of the large Paris hospitals in which they worked, the Bicêtre and Salpetrière, housed not only the sick and dying but a sizable population of aged paupers as well. Initially, these elderly persons had been of particular interest to physicians because of their accessibility. Because they had been institutionalized as a consequence of destitution and illness, their homelessness made them captive subjects for long-term scientific inquiry. Research into the pathological effects of disease, however, convinced clinicians of the distinctive nature of the ailments that vexed these elderly patients. Aging, like many disease entities, appeared to cause numerous pathological transformations. In the autopsies performed on elderly persons, physicians repeatedly discovered evidence of general degeneration, ossification, and calcification. Similarly, in both the noticeably ailing and the seemingly well, they discovered unmistakable signs of arteriosclerosis. Bichat stated that this was the case in seven out of ten elderly persons, regardless of the apparent state of their health;[33] other physicians placed the percentage close to 100. Hardening of the arteries, they declared, was the universal condition of the senescent.[34] If this were true, those who survived to extreme old age had little hope of escaping debilitating illness. According to the laws of nature, the productive years of life were sharply and irreversibly limited.

The pathological findings cited by the French clinicians were not entirely novel. Even before the nineteenth century, a limited number of autopsies on extremely aged individuals had revealed anatomical alterations. In 1706, for example, an English physician, Dr. James Keill, performed an autopsy on John Boyles, a button maker who died allegedly at 130. Keill noted the same hardening of the arteries, the deterioration of various organs, and the addition of fibrous material cited by French clinicians more than a century later. The English physician, however, believed that his findings were inconclusive; too few dissections had been (or, at the time, could be) performed to justify any definitive statement about the nature of aging.[35] Most eighteenth-century physicians, however, strongly believed that the arteries played an essential role in the aging process. This theory, along with an emphasis on the importance of the bloodstream, neatly coincided with their systemic view of the body. The statement, "a man is as old as his arteries," had allegedly been coined by Sydenham in the late seventeenth century. Two hundred years later, it had achieved the status of maxim. Physicians repeated it with the frequency and authority of a classic verity.[36] In addition, doctors were hardly surprised to discover fatty deposits or fibrous material in the

59

organism. In the writings of both solidists and humoralists, the increasing substance and dryness of the elderly body had long been cited as proof of the validity of their conceptual systems.

French clinicians, however, placed these findings into a new framework. When doctors defined and classified disease by changes in the tissues, the visible transformation of the organism acquired new meaning. The pathological aspects of the anatomy were not secondary to life processes generally but constituted a primary deterioration of the fundamental elements of existence. Merely by growing old, the individual had developed the exterior symptoms and internal lesions that were the signs of specific debilitating illnesses. This degeneration of the body had not occurred merely because the patient lacked the vitality to resist. Even in the seemingly healthy and active, fibrosis, ossifications, and other lesions were found to exist. In old age, disease seemed to be a discrete condition. As revealed by the deterioration of tissues, it was an inherent, progressive part of senescence.

On the basis of these findings, Paris clinicians viewed old age as a distinctive and irreversible segment of the life cycle.[37] The changes that came with advanced age were almost always degenerative. There was little hope that the body would ever return to its original condition. To these physicians, senescence had its own distinctive physiological nature. It differed from youth in ways that the untrained observer could not begin to comprehend. A new professional tone characterized their descriptions of the elderly organism. The body was no longer portrayed as a united system, slowly disintegrating in every part. Instead, citing the findings of postmortem studies, clinicians attempted to reduce the operations and malfunctions of the old to specific pathological mechanisms and lesions. The sight of the aged, for example, could hardly regain its power of perception. The internal structure of the eye was radically different from that found in most young persons. The physiologist Francois Magendie traced its internal changes through three distinct phases:

> 1st, the diminution of the quantity of the humours of the eye, which diminishing the refractive power of the organ, prevents the old man from distinguishing with precision surrounding objects; and in order to see them distinctly he is obliged to remove them to a distance, because the light which proceeds from them is less divergent, or he is obliged to employ convex glasses, which diminish the divergence of the rays.
>
> 2nd, the opacity beginning in the crystalline, which dims the sight, and tends by its increase to bring on blindness, in producing that malady known by the name of cataract.

3rd, the diminution of the sensibility of the retina, or otherwise of the brain, which prevents the preceptions of the impression produced on the eye, and which leads to total and incurable blindness.[38]

Similar anatomical malfunctions were cited for all parts of the body. These changes had important implications for the practicing physician. He could no longer assume that a single disease would have the same symptoms in all his patients, nor could he rely upon a unified therapeutic regimen. Disease categorization, based on the pathological transformation of tissues, necessitated a clear understanding of the normal and abnormal conditions for each stage of existence. The doctor who attempted to return senile tissue to its adolescent state would be truly foolhardy, if not indeed destructive.[39] The elderly needed to be treated by standards that confirmed to their own stage of life.

Here lay the basis for a specialization in the diseases of old age. The physician was required to know what ailments plagued the elderly, their physiological and anatomical basis, and the best – if any – method of treatment. By the mid-nineteenth century, these points were being raised by German and English, as well as French, clinicians. They urged their fellow physicians to understand the importance of gerontological studies and to further work in the field. The declaration of one of the most important forerunners of geriatric medicine, Jean Charcot, way typical of the sentiment that would be repeated for decades. "The importance of a special study of the diseases of old age," he wrote in 1861, "cannot be contested at this day. We have come to recognize in reality that, if the pathology presents its difficulties, which cannot be surmounted except by long experience and a profound acquaintance with its peculiar characteristics."[40]

Despite such pleas, the concerns of the gerontologist remained rather ambiguous. Physicians lacked a well-defined set of standards by which to evaluate the condition of the old. These criteria were not easy to devise. The ideal of the field was to treat the elderly patient by recognizing the problems of old age, rather than by adhering to the standards of the young adult. As in pediatrics, the individual's development or decline was to be related to the specific life stage. No one assumed that the child was feeble who had not yet developed adult teeth or muscle control. Why then, physicians were fond of asking, was the old person labeled debilitated when his or her body continued to undergo natural anatomical transformations? Concerned doctors discovered, however, that the two stages were not precisely analogous. The child began from a position of weakness, with physical development marked by a measureable increase in both strength and capabilities. The point of origin for old age, however, was maturity; physicians continually returned to this stage to chart the individual's decline. The advent of age was then marked by the same anatomical changes that were a basis for the classification of disease. Where, then, did old age end and illness begin? And, perhaps even more perplexing, could the old ever be vigorous, or was the very notion of a healthy senescence a contradiction in terms?

Most European clinicians seemed to imply that illness and old age were inseparably intertwined, if not quite synonymous. At best, the division between the two was extremely subjective. A large proportion of the diseases of old age were attributed to natural, intractable changes in the organism. "We shall have to note," wrote Charcot in his lectures on senescence, "that the textural changes which old age induces in the organism sometimes attain such a point that the physiological and pathological states seemed to mingle by an imperceptible transition, and to be no longer distinguishable."[41] In addition, there were numerous senile diseases – diseases that might also appear in the young but would have distinct, age-related symptoms due to the transformed state of the elderly anatomy. Yet Charcot's specificity in classifying disease was not equaled by an emphasis upon therapeutics. As a clinician, he endorsed only a few remedies; along with exercise and diet, Charcot relied upon such widely used drugs as mercury and opium.[42] Once anatomical changes had begun, he confessed, there was little that could be done to reverse them.

Part of the difficulty in devising age-related therapeutics lay in the physician's ability to define the cause of aging. French clinicians had rejected the vital energy model for one based on the degeneration of tissues. With the work of Schwann and Virchow, the importance of the tissue was augmented by an emphasis on the cell. This was the basic unit of life, responsible for growth and thus for aging. Several physicians theorized that throughout a person's life, old cells were constantly dying, some to be replaced by new generations, others simply to be eliminated. In old age, the process seemed to work extremely inefficiently. The cells that were replaced appeared less able to receive and assimilate food. With the use of the microscope, the scientist became aware that the composition of the cells had changed: A larger proportion of the mass was protoplasm, a far smaller part nucleus. As a result, the old suffered from numerous "gouty" diseases in which their bodies were unable to digest proper nourishment.[43] In the course of this process, the aged organism became feeble and seemed to waste away. Moreover, some types of cells were never replaced. In the brain, this depletion became tragically apparent as the once intellectually active individual gradually lost the use of his mental facilities.

Physicians had little control over this process. They could not stop the cell from evolving into its senile state, nor were they able to isolate the mechanism that controlled aging. In effect, what the elite European physician had done was to divide the cause of aging into smaller and smaller units: General vital energy had, by the mid-nineteenth century, been replaced by a degeneration of tissues, and finally by an inexorable devolution of cells. But why this occurred remained an unanswered question. Their research, though, did convince them of the seemingly futile nature of the dreams of the more radical longevity advocates. Diet and exercise appeared to do very little to reverse the degeneration of the body's cells. In the process of aging, the organism was destined to undergo a multitude of physiological and anatomical changes. Unable to explain or deter this transformation, the clinician was gradually coming to view the entire stage of senescence as a medical problem. Growing old was itself the source of inevitable organic alterations that constituted the pathological state known as old age.

CHAPTER FOUR

Treating the Postclimacteric Stage

English and American physicians adopted this conception of senescence at a relatively late date; not until the middle and late nineteenth century did they begin to write about the distinctive nature of old age. Their ideas were based on both medical theory and practical experience. In contrast to European clinicians, they created a senile therapeutics that revealed their daily interactions with the senescent. These recommendations also vividly reflected the actual condition of old age. As demographic and economic changes in society caused the increasing isolation of the elderly, doctors endorsed an age-based regimen that justified their seclusion and retirement. By the early twentieth century, as we shall see, American physicians had developed a conception of old age that legitimated the complete separation of the aged from the rest of society.

*   *   *   *

The first book-length work on aging in the English language to reflect the ideas of the Paris school was George E. Day's *A Practical Treatise on the Domestic Management and Most Important Diseases of Advanced Life*, published in London in 1849.[1] Day was well acquainted with the French and German literature on old age, as well as versed in the pathological approach to disease. He had translated Julius Vogel's *Pathological Anatomy of the Human Body* into English, and, throughout the course of his text, cited Prus, Chomel, Magendie, and Canstatt, as well as many others.[2] Like the clinicians, he viewed the diseases of the old as distinctive. The significant anatomical transformations of the elderly body radically altered the character of their ailments. This perspective became the basis for subsequent English-language works on old age as well. Over a half-century, authors such as Daniel Maclachlan, Bernard Van Oven, A. L. Loomis, and I. L. Nascher uniformly described the pathological alterations that occurred and traced their effect on the course and nature of numerous diseases.[3]

64

These studies all owed a great deal to European pathologists and clinicians. In approach, disease nomenclature, and therapeutics (or lack thereof), they cited many of the most recent and influential studies.

It would be a mistake, however, to view these English-language works as mere imitations of their European predecessors. Unlike many French or German physicians, few mid-nineteenth-century American physicians would have extensive clinical training, study degenerated tissue, or view the "senile cell" under the microscope. The primary source of information about senescence remained their experience in treating the old. Most, therefore, continued to characterize senescence in general, descriptive terms. "Old age," according to one mid-century physician, was "that stage of life in which the vital forces show unequivocal marks of languishment and decline, where the elasticity of youth and vigor of mankind are followed by a condition in which are manifest symptoms of decay in all parts, both in body and mind."[4]

Most English-language physicians would have agreed. Consensus on such a definition was possible because most practitioners still relied implicitly upon the vitality model of growing old. As we have seen, the studies of the clinicians and pathologists did not really invalidate traditional notions of how the body aged. Although these scientists questioned the plausibility of particular theories of aging, their work produced no firm conclusion; the mechanism that controlled aging remained unexplained and ill-defined. Although pathological studies could be interpreted as replacing vital energy with mechanical or chemical processes, most English and American medical writers seemed to find no conflict between the clinical-pathological views and the age-old metaphoric model of aging.[5] In their texts, the two theories were neatly combined: The tissue or cell degenerated while the organism systemically wasted away.

In accepting this synthesis, American physicians slightly recast the traditional notion of vital energy. Once French clinical studies became publicized, the concept had to be made consistent with both the visible evidence and the postmortem findings. Loss of energy not only resulted in a worn exterior appearance but accounted for physiological and anatomical alterations as well. When the patient's resources were depleted, the body underwent numerous pathological changes: The lesions, the calcareous deposits, and the fibrous tissues were all the result of rapidly dissipating strength. Once the waning of vital energy could be made to explain the discrete lesions and other degenerative changes found in the elderly, the physician could easily link the orthodox model of aging with more novel ideas. In 1859, for example, James Copland summarized the organic transformations discovered in the elderly organism. In part, he believed that these alterations were caused by peculiarities of food, constitution, employment, acquired habits, and indulgences. "But," he concluded:

> we are not altogether justified in considering the contingencies as the primary cause of the changes now described. We are rather to view them as more or less remote effects of the failure of vital endowment of the frame manifesting itself first in the less perfect performance of the different functions and subsequently in the modifications of structure, and ultimately in the very obvious lesions of both function and structure.[6]

Throughout the nineteenth century, the notion of vital energy remained an essential aspect of the American view of aging. One or two doctors did dismiss the idea summarily, calling the concept both ridiculous and unscientific.[7] Most practitioners, however, defended the idea, primarily – I would suggest – because it reflected their daily experience. If there were cause for disagreement at all, it concerned the process through which vital energy worked, rather than its existence. Why, some doctors asked, if vital power was endowed at birth, were young adults more energetic than infants? Why were athletes likely to outlive the totally inactive? These inconsistencies, however, did not cause medical authorities to abandon the notion. They merely reshaped the hypothetical mechanics of its operation. In the new interpretation, an individual's vital energy first increased to adulthood and then began its slow decline. "It cannot really be debated," argued one physician, "that the functions of life as they may be observed in any specialized organism increase for a time in strength, range and complexity, pass through a period of comparative repose, and finally break up and disappear."[8]

This reformulation was necessary because the theory had to correspond to observation. Vital energy remained a popular concept precisely because it provided visibly – and emotionally – satisfying rationales for a process over which the physician had little control. As doctors showed increased skill in fighting the diseases of women, children, and the middle-aged of both sexes, only the illnesses of the old seemed generally impervious to modern therapeutics. Death, once feared by all individuals, gradually became thought of as the sole province of the old.[9] Vital energy explained this close relationship in a way more recent scientific hypotheses could not. In addition, before the germ theory, the traditional model of vitality could be employed to justify the high morbidity among the elderly from very contagious diseases. George E. Day, for example, despite his clinical-pathological approach to the illnesses of the old, relied upon the notion of vital energy to explain senile influenza. The disease was devastating to the aged, he believed, because "it extinguishes the vital force in old age and in persons suffering from chronic diseases."[10] Even after the introduction of the germ theory, vital energy played a central role in the physician's explanation of the ailments of the elderly. According to one doctor, it was precisely the lack of energy of the aged that caused them to be susceptible to infection; they no longer had the strength to resist the onset of the illness. "It is well established at the present time," Dr. Come Ferran wrote in 1903:

> that the interior of all our organism is full of infectious germs which are inoffensive as long as the vitality of our cells keeps them in check, but as soon as there is the least relaxation in our vitality, they then quickly appear on the scene of action. And when these germs join themselves to certain ptomaines and other products of decay which are thrown into the blood dissimilation, then it can well be conceived how the propensity of the aged to decrepitude will be so much greater and rapid.[11]

Any one of a number of illnesses could then destroy the old. Throughout the nineteenth century, the physician's enumeration of such potentially fatal diseases grew steadily. This list of ailments was the result both of a new interest in the illnesses of the old and of a more general trend in defining age-related diseases. As we have seen, prior to the nineteenth century, the death of an elderly person caused little surprise. Merely by surviving to old age, the individual was already considered to have escaped the most commonly fatal diseases. No one, after all, was expected to triumph in the battle against time. A rising professionalism and interest in specific disease entities, however, caused several physicians to question the validity of such an attitude. "The diseases and infirmities [of the aged]," wrote Daniel Maclachlan in 1863, "have been too much regarded as inescapable concomitants in advancing years, the inevitable consequences of the progressive, natural decay of the organism and decline of the vital function generally, and therefore but little if at all within the reach of the physician."[12]

At last, Maclachlan believed, this attitude was beginning to change. In growing numbers, physicians were attempting to isolate and identify the primary reasons for their elderly patients' deaths. With an ever-increasing list of possible causes, they needed to rely upon the prognosis "decay" or "mere old age" far less often; any one of a number of diseases was believed capable of terminating the patient's life. Some illnesses were merely old ailments in modern dress. "Decay from old age," for example, became "senile maramus." Yet the theory behind the disease had not changed: The body, drained of its energy, simply wasted away as the years progressed. Other illnesses were of more recent origin, the result of the physician's attempt to link the patient's exterior symptoms to subsequent pathological discoveries. As we have seen, the fits and fevers of the old had once been characterized as a general disease state. With the gradual acceptance of disease specificity, such symptoms were redefined as an ailment particular to the elderly, caused, perhaps, by an age-related heart or vascular condition.[13] The pathological alterations of the body were responsible for a number of such specific ailments. Prostatic malfunctions, apoplexy, and Bright's disease were only a few of the many organic difficulties that could present problems in old age.

European and American practitioners generally agreed in their list of age-related ailments. In this area, English-language physicians were often content to repeat the findings of their predecessors. American and English doctors, however, recognized one disease that was usually ignored by the French. This was climacteric illness, a disease believed to occur in women between forty-five and fifty-five and in men between fifty and seventy-five. As defined by one physician, climacteric disease was:

> that extraordinary decline of the corporeal powers which, before the system falls prey to confirmed old age, sometimes makes its appearance in advanced age without any sufficient ostensible cause, and is occasionally succeeded by a renovation of health and vigor though it more generally precipitates the patient into the grave.[14]

Few prominent pathologists would take great note of this ailment; no organ showed sudden signs of deterioration, nor were characteristic lesions discovered through autopsies.[15] American physicians were content to link the illness directly to the waning of vital energy. The ailment marked the point at which "the body had run its course"[16] and had irreversibly begun its final decline. For these physicians, the proof of the disease could be found not through postmortem studies but in the patient's appearance. All at once, an individual looked old: The backbone stooped, the muscles sagged, and the mind grew dim. No one factor was believed to be the source of the problem. Physicians listed accidents, overwork, anxiety, and even the common cold as possible initiating causes. Once afflicted, however, the individual could expect little real relief from the practitioner. Even in those who seemed fully recovered, their energy was spent. They now looked, acted, and felt as if they had entered the final phase of existence.

The notion of the climacteric period mirrored ideas current in classic antiquity. As we have seen, one ancient view of the body had identified key points in the individual's life. Age sixty-three, the grand climacteric, was believed to designate the start of old age. In the early nineteenth century, physicians gave new meaning to the concept. Although the climacteric retained its connotation as the start of senescence, it became designated as well as an unavoidable disease. Although the symptoms were first described in a letter to John Sinclair in 1807,[17] the discovery of the disease was generally attributed by comtemporaries to Henry Halford. In 1813, Halford wrote "On the Climacteric Disease," in which he characterized and named the ailment.[18] At first, significantly, the essay received little attention. Twenty years later, it attracted wide public notice; in the mid-nineteenth century, the diseases of the old were beginning to be a subject of some medical concern.[19] Halford's contention that the symptoms marked an abrupt change in the system, rather than a slow decline, corresponded to this new interest. The changes that came with old age, he stated, marked a specific age-related ailment.[20] After the republication of the article, few English or American doctors would discuss senescence without first introducing the notion of the climacteric. Physicians such as Bartholomew Parr would ridicule the idea of cyclical crises less often. Most medical authorities concurred that something very important indeed was happening to the aging body.[21]

Practitioners usually believed that this visible transformation could affect both men and women. Some cited the cessation of the menses as part of the illness; others said that menopause proceded the broader, more obvious ailment. Most agreed, however, that climacteric disease was far more severe in men than in women;[22] the well-marked periodicity of the female cushioned her decline into senescence. Over an extended time span, her body could adjust to the new stage of life. In men, though, the alteration was instantly apparent; their weight, facial appearance, and temperament all changed. The entire organism suddenly and obviously seemed to age.

By far the most serious sign of climacteric disease was the tendency toward insanity. The sudden loss of vital energy caused a rapid transformation of the entire system. The brain, as well as the body, was likely to suffer severe and permanent damage. The confident person lost assuredness, the diligent individual self-control. Unfounded fears, delusions, and even kleptomania could be linked to this fundamental physiological alteration.[23] "The epoch of reconstruction," wrote Dr. W. Bevan Lewis in 1890:

> is one of peril to the mind . . . Reflection wants the calm essential to its orderly operation, and judgment is liable to be warped and one-sided; hence, also it is that this age of life is one prone to bigotry, to religious fanaticism, or to conduct based upon dogmatic and immature beliefs. An unusual inordinate religious zeal is, indeed, a most frequent expression of this transition period in mental life; and this is of interest viewed in connection with the insanity of this age.[24]

During the second half of the nineteenth century, American physicians referred to this transition less often as a disease and more often as a normal – though painful – stage of existence. In one sense, they believed, Halford had been right; the climacteric period was an abrupt change rather than a slow decline. Yet, "the turning point towards the downhill course," as one physician termed it, seemed to take place in almost every individual, although the age of occurrence might differ.[25] Not every person suffered from the extreme symptoms of madness, for many would feel only irritable or uncomfortable. But to some extent, all could expect to undergo a noticeable transition in character. According to the medical literature of the nineteenth century, many personality traits were determined by sex. Men were thought to be naturally just, noble, virile, and brave; women were considered nurturant, mural, domestic, and passive.[26] In old age, however, these qualities no longer seemed appropriate. With the climacteric stage of life, a woman became unable to conceive; a man could no longer be portrayed as strong or vital. The basic male and female traits, in fact, seemed to merge in the old until they became almost indistinguishable. After the climacteric, I. L. Nascher explained, "the growth force is now mainly exerted toward the approximation of the sexes and in old age they approach a neutral type."[27] Both elderly men and women were seen as dependent, passive, and weak; their greatest concerns were (or should be) moral and religious. The affairs of the world were best forgotten. The senescent were advised to prepare themselves for their heavenly home.[28]

The climacteric period of life, therefore, marked the division between maturity and senescence. Those in this phase were neither old nor young; their bodies – as well as their status in society – were in a period of transition. Like the passage between adolescence and adulthood, the stage that separated adulthood from old age could be filled with danger.[29] The volatile nature of the body produced physical and mental instability in the climacteric sufferer. This phase, however, lasted only as long as the visible, age-related disease persisted. Once the change had occurred, the old irreversibly separated from their younger selves. It was understandable, then, that physicians considered the illness to be more severe in men than in women. The female could slowly adjust to her new stage of life, while her domestic duties remained the same.[30] For the male, though, the advent of the climacteric implied a radical break with his own past. After describing man at the peak of his strength, Dr. Charles Caldwell lamented: "And I regret to say, I have passed through the last stage of life in which it is not painful to accompany him – because it is the last in which he is comfortable to himself, useful to others or an ornament to his race."[31] In earlier segments of the life cycle, the individual had grown and developed; now he began his "downhill decline."[32]

Thus, physicians cautioned all aging persons to take note of the important divide they had crossed. To the nineteenth-century practitioner, the climacteric was more than an inevitable disease; it marked a point at which most individuals had to accept an entirely new manner of living. "It is the duty then," wrote Dr. Bernard Van Oven:

> of all persons who have attained the climacteric age, carefully to avoid excesses and undue exertions, to watch at all times for the insidious approach of disorders; never to reject any slight ailment, but regard them as forerunners of more serious derangements, seek to repair the most trifling irregularities of function and give rest at once to any organ of the body which shows debility or fatigue.[33]

Above all, physicians warned the elderly that their normal physiological condition had now become one of disease.[34] Although the individual might appear to be in perfect health, old age alone signified disability. With each passing year, the internal organs progressively decayed. Activities that had once been effortlessly accomplished could cause serious infirmities: Overwork might bring on mental exhaustion; physical labor could lead to cardiac arrest or apoplexy. From this perspective, every elderly individual, regardless of the present state of his or her health, became a potential patient. All post climacteric individuals were advised to accept unquestioningly the role of invalid and to place themselves "under the immediate and constant care of the physician."[35] Once in authority, the concerned family doctor could then determine the steps necessary to maintain the fragile existence of the elderly. "Every person," advised Dr. H. C. Wood, "when he advances in years, should go over his whole method of life and personal habits with some wise counsellor and should adopt his mode of living to the peculiarities of his particular case."[36]

In a sense, the nineteenth-century studies of pathology had legitimated this role for the physician. By defining physiological old age as a pathological process, they had placed every aspect of senescence in a medical perspective. Choices of diet, clothes, activity, and even occupation became valid professional questions. The earliest gerontological specialists, therefore, devoted much of their writings to the prescription of proper regimens. In general, these programs did not differ practically from the admonitions proffered by the advocates of longevity. In both popular health manuals and scholarly journals, medical authorities instructed the elderly to avoid red meat, be temperate in food and drink, and participate only in those activities that exercised the mind and body without causing exhaustion or worry.[37] Unlike the longevity spokesmen, however, most early gerontologists did not promise that their prescriptions would lead to an extended life. As the body decayed, there was little hope – or desire – for a century-long existence. Additional years would only bring greater organic disability.[38] A correct regimen, therefore, was simply seen as a means of making the body less susceptible to the numerous senile illnesses. Progressive decay could not ultimately be diverted.

Once a senile disease appeared, though, the physician had little beyond palliation to recommend. As the nineteenth-century medical findings broadened the legitimate sphere of the physician, they also deterred him from experimenting with therapeutics.[39] According to prominent pathologists, almost all of the peculiarly senile illnesses were potentially fatal. The organic difficulties that increased with age made the hope of curative treatment illusory. Rather than minister to specific senile diseases, a few individuals attempted to eliminate old age altogether. Through scientific experiments, they searched for the magic elixir that would bring eternal youth. But professional responses to their suggestions only emphasized how patently implausible they seemed. In the 1870s, for example, C. E. Brown-Sequard believed that he could restore the sexual power of the old through a solution derived from ground-up animal testicles. The scientific community generally greeted his experiments with ridicule.[40] In 1903, when Elie Metchnikoff presented his prescription for continuing middle age, he met a similar response. According to Metchnikoff's formula, the scientist was to inject a horse with finely minced particles of human organs such as brains, liver, heart, or kidneys; after a few weeks, he was to drain off the serum.[41] Other physicians suggested the simpler idea of injecting young blood into the old. In terms of curing diseases, however, there were far fewer recommendations. Most America physicians resorted to an assortment of traditional remedies: Opium was prescribed and withdrawn; purgatives, emetics, and diuretics were all endorsed by some and refuted by many.[42] Most senile ailments seemed to remain impervious to treatment.

Any disease, therefore, once it appeared in its senile state, was almost certain to cause the physician innumerable and often insolvable problems. It was futile, he knew, to attempt to return the anatomy of the elderly to its preclimacteric state. Instead, most medical authorities merely reclassified the symptoms of the old in terms of age-related disease entities. Even illnesses that seemed common to all age groups, such as pneumonia, bronchitis, or jaundice, were given special designations to reflect the debilitated condition of the patient. Bronchitis, for example, became "senile bronchitis," its nature and course altered by the pathological vascular tissue and mucous membrane characteristic of the elderly. Physicians believed that such "normally" diseased aspects of the aged organism sharply limited the potential efficacy of therapeutics. In the case of senile pneumonia, for example, George E. Day concluded that three-fifths of all patients would die. Their constantly congested lungs and habitual bronchorrhea gave the physician little hope of ever curing the illness.[43] Well into the twentieth century, practitioners readily agreed with this assessment. In 1907, for example, Dr. Clarence Bartlett declared that "the results from the treatment of old people with pneumonia are so poor that it is difficult to speak with any positiveness as to the efficient measures for their cure."[44]

Senile diseases, therefore, were fundamentally different from illnesses common to other age groups. After midcentury, medical authorities advised practitioners that many diseases cured themselves; the best treatment was often to allow nature to heal the patient. In the old, however, this was hardly the case. The natural course for most senile diseases was either increasing disability or the death of the patient.[45]

This fantastic medical connotation of the word *senile* quickly overshadowed all previous meanings. Before the nineteenth century – and the classification of age-specific illnesses – the term had little to do with disease; anything "suited for or incident to old age" could be considered senile. It was value neutral and, insofar as old age could

73

be considered a valuable period of life, enjoyed a positive connotation. In 1794, for example, Thomas Jefferson could look forward eagerly to the day he exchanged "the roar and tumult of the bulls and bears for the prattle of my grandchildren and senile rest."[46] By the late nineteenth century, such an expression made little sense; *senile* was strictly and monolithically applied to age-related ailments. In terms of usage, at least, the entire stage of life had acquired a medical connotation. Senility, once merely "the state of being old," had been transformed into a pathological condition that robbed the individual of both intellect and understanding.[47] The normal state of being old, it seemed, was that of debilitating illness.[48]

Few late-nineteenth-century physicians would disagree with this assessment. Senility, more than any single ailment, came to represent the extreme and inevitable incapacity of senescence. Unlike climacteric disease, however, senile dementia was not the creation of modern physicians. Even in biblical days, the loss of reason in the old had been a well-noted affliction. Medical authorities, however, had generally assumed that this was an abnormal state for the elderly rather than their usual condition. Benjamin Rush, for example, was convinced that most aged individuals would retain full use of their mental powers until they reached the grave. In 1797, in a study of a group of octogenarians, he found that although some elderly individuals had faulty memories of the recent past, their intellectual, moral, and religious powers were completely unimpaired. He did not consider the mere loss of memory a harbinger of more serious problems. For Rush, even a decayed body did not dictate the inevitable loss of one's mental faculties. The spirit and intellect were sure to outlive the material side of one's nature.[49]

With the nineteenth-century medical findings about old age, however, the ability of the senescent to retain their reason came under serious question. As proven by postmortem studies, the anatomical transformations of the organism affected both mind and body. In old age, the brain underwent numerous pathological alterations. Whether physicians believed that dementia was caused by brain lesions, starvation of tissue, dying brain cells, arteriosclerosis, softening of the brain, or even a loss of molecular vitality, most authorities agreed upon the inevitability of the process.[50] In the early nineteenth century, a few physicians, such as Isaac Ray and James Cowles Prichard, attempted to distinguish between normal senile decay and abnormal dementia.[51] The first, they believed, was unavoidable and progressive; the latter, an incurable ailment. "Were it no so," declared

Ray in 1838, "every old man would labor under a certain degree of dementia."[52] This was a conclusion he was not prepared to entertain. But Ray, as well as other early expert psychologists, struggled to differentiate between the two diseases. "It may be difficult," he conceded, "to satisfy ourselves whether or not [decay] is accompanied by [derangement], but for any practical purpose it may seldom be necessary."[53] Regardless of whether the disease was called decay or dementia, afflicted individuals slowly lost their reason. First, the memory failed, followed in turn by the powers of perception, recognition, and intellect. There was little the physician could do to deter this process. His only role was to make the patient comfortable as the old man or woman sank into a state of complete mental incompetence.

By the late nineteenth century, few physicians would attempt to distinguish between decay and dementia. "No sharp line can be drawn between ordinary senile dotage and senile dementia," wrote Dr. W. H. B. Stoddard in 1909. "The normal mental deterioration incident upon old age is itself early senile dementia."[54] Senile insanity, like other age-related diseases, had a normal physiological basis. The natural result of gradual decay, it was considered the eventual, inescapable state for all elderly individuals. The early loss of memory, therefore, could only be interpreted as an ominous sign. The pathological transformation of the brain had begun, and total loss of reason was only a matter of time. "From the beginning to the end," explained Dr. Charles Mercier in 1890:

> the process is a continuous, gradually progressive loss. Conduct, intelligence, feeling, and self-consciousness gradually diminish, and at last cease to exist . . . The decadence of old age is, in fact, a *dementia*, a deprivation of mind. It is a normal and physiological dementia, the natural and inevitable result of the gradual subsidence of the molecular movements of the nervous elements into stillness; the natural outcome of the exhaustion of the initial impetus which started the organism upon its course of life and kept it going; the natural expression of this dissipation of energy which accompanies the integration of matter in the process.[55]

Aging was a general, progressive decline; as the body decayed, so did the mind. The concept of mental immortality – endorsed by physicians as late as the early nineteenth century – found few adherents by the end of the century.[56] Vital and intellectual principles were hardly divisible. The brain, like any other organ composed of living cells, underwent physiological decay as it aged. Postmortem studies confirmed this belief. Compared to the brain of the young, clinicians

75

found that the senile organ weighed less, had a thinner cortex, and was subject to lesions and softening.[57] Given such pathological alterations, there seemed little question that as the individual entered the "senile" state, he would suffer from a constantly decreasing mental capability.

On the basis of these data, more than a few physicians began to challenge the traditional image of the old as repositories of great wisdom. The anatomy and physiology of the age appeared to limit their intellectual achievement. With each passing year, the brain of the old became less sensitive to stimulation and less able to process complicated information. By the time the individual reached senescence, the intellect was all but shattered. Thus, the apparent wisdom of the old was nothing more than the lingering traces of past talents. "When an old man utters great thoughts," the American neurologist George Beard declared, "it is not age but youth that speaks through the lips of age." In 1876, Beard believed that he had definitely proven this assertion. Compiling a list of the greatest geniuses of past and present, he claimed that their composite biography "scientifically" demonstrated their uselessness once they reached old age. "On the average," he wrote, "the last twenty years of the lives of original geniuses are unproductive." By sixty, a person could hope to retain little youthful creativity.[58]

In addition, physicians believed that the aging of the mind prevented the elderly from adapting to new circumstances. The molecules of the senile brain had become fixed into well-established arrangements. The organ no longer possessed the plasticity necessary to formulate new patterns. The aged mind, therefore, was incapable of assimilating concepts that were unorthodox or unknown. The physiology of the old, wrote Charles Mercier, confirms that "old and accurate observation that 'you cannot teach an old dog new tricks.'"[59] Business, social affairs, and even family life made little impression upon the aged brain. The old lived in the past; each day, they became less conscious of the world around them.

Intellectual achievement, however, was not the only aspect of mind affected by senility. Nineteenth-century physicians repeatedly asserted that the progressive decay of the brain noticeably altered the personality. The antisocial characteristics that first appeared during the climacteric period now assumed permanent form. The old became perverse instead of reasonable. No longer interested in other events or people, they grew increasingly involved in their own petty concerns. "A change in temper is likewise noticed," continued one late-nineteenth-century physician. "Self-control is lost and depression is apt to alternate with irritability. The aged become petulant, selfish, and indifferent to the usual interests of life and to their family."[60] Most practitioners assumed that the old had little real control over these traits. In senescence, their personalities no longer seemed the result of individual backgrounds, tastes, or ideas. Instead, they became the direct reflection of the organisms' pathological conditions. Unchecked by any higher faculty, emotions alone came to dictate the senescent personality.

These uncontrolled passions could easily lead to the old into unfortunate, if not dangerous, circumstances. Once senility overtook the aged, they tended to act on any whim. Children were suddenly denied their rightful inheritance, foolish marriages were made, and unwise business deals were transacted.[61] In such a state of mine, the aged individual could become a serious threat to his or her own safety. The suicide rate, according to Dr. Colin A. Scott, revealed "that this crime becomes more frequent at and after the grand climacteric."[62] The case of Margaret Wall, a patient at the Philadelphia Orthopaedic Hospital, was typical. At sixty-five, after her husband died, she became extremely melancholy. As her depression increased and her sense of present-day realities diminished, she made repeated attempts to throw herself down the stairs. Only the constant vigilance of her family prevented her from committing suicide.[63]

The problems posed by the senile, however, did not stop with the afflicted persons. Physicians warned that such individuals could become a serious threat to those around them. Dr. Beard, in fact, linked the Credit Mobilier affair to the advanced age of the participants in a direct causal relationship. Because the individuals were all old, he asserted, they had lost their judgment. Unable to tell right from wrong, they became involved in a scandal that finally affected the entire nation.[64]

The most widely discussed problem created by senility, though, was not intellectual corruption but moral perversion. Most late-nineteenth-century physicians believed that by the time of senescence, the individual had lost both the ability and the inclination for sexual relations. This was nature's way of preserving the body's essential seminal fluids. Through its inability to engage in sexual activity, the organism was saved from "the most exhausting expenditure of nervous and vital energy."[65] With senility, however, the desire for sexual activity often returned, although without the corresponding capability. As a result, the elderly turned into "opulent satyres" or "grotesque monsters" whose abnormal and uncontrollable cravings led them to commit numerous sexual perversions.[66] The senile old man, explained Dr. Allan McLane Hamilton, becomes "amatory, obscene, and fond of telling of the adventures of his youth and living again its gallant frivolities. His leer is lascivious and he goes about with unbuttoned clothes and is lost to all shame."[67] Slovenliness, exhibitionism, and even child molesting could arise out of this pathological mental condition.

Not all the old, of course, would suffer from these extreme symptoms of senility. Yet physicians warned practitioners to be alert to all signs of early dementia. Even in instances where the aged person seemed healthy and active, the brain could be undergoing progressive and irreversible decay. This was especially important when legal matters were involved. Called upon when a will was contested, the physician assumed the role of expert; he had to affirm or deny the mental competence of the elderly testator. In such cases, the practitioner found that he often lacked a clear set of practical guidelines. As we have seen, late-nineteenth-century physicians classified senile dementia as an inevitable part of physiological decay; no distinct line separated the forgetful old person from the insane. The final will of the aged, absentminded individual, therefore, could easily be contested – especially if the money was donated to a church or charity rather than kin. Religious zeal could be interpreted as senile fanaticism; refusal to acknowledge an heir might be explained as pathological willfullness. The degree of decay then became an issue of legal importance. Did extreme age cause the loss of reason and intellect as well as memory? Did the deterioration of brain cells prevent the individual from knowing the extent and condition of the property?[68]

These were questions, physicians asserted, that could be answered only by the cautious family doctor. Specially trained and familiar with the patient, he alone possessed the knowledge necessary to analyze the subject properly.[69] Even the most concerned judge lacked the wealth of information available to the practitioner. Although he might be able to ascertain if the individual understood the state of his or her business affairs, he was not capable of comprehending the patient's total mental state. "We should bear in mind," Dr. J. Nichols advised, "that in this advanced period though there may be apparent soundness in the operations of the mind, when movement is only in one direction, yet the harmonious play of all its faculties may be greatly disturbed or entirely destroyed."[70] Only the physician could be aware of the individual's usual habits, actions, and beliefs. The slightest change in these areas could be a sign that decay was progressing. In determining the extent of impairment, I. L. Nascher advised, "it is necessary to compare all the faculties with the faculties as they were, and not with the faculties of another at the same age."[71] This could be done only by a person who had watched the elderly individual grow old and could question his daily behavior. Did he act his age? Did he attempt youthful activity unbecoming to his years? Did he have sexual desires inappropriate to the elderly?

For the aged to qualify as mentally competent, doctors implied, they had to act old. Any degression from the standards of senescence was surely a sign of mental regression. "In the young man," T. S. Clouston wrote in 1884, "there is an organic craving for action, which not being gratified there results organic discomfort; in the old man there is an organic craving for rest and not to gratify that causes organic uneasiness."[72]

By the nature of his age and his pathological internal state, the old man was expected to want to retire from active life, to leave his work to junior associates, his family matters to heirs. "The more important parts of his business," Charles Mercier noted:

> have been for some time in younger hands. He still lingers as long as possible round the scenes of his labor, but his actual part is limited to routine work; which at length, incapable even of this, he retires altogether. The whole sphere of activities comprised in his business relations is altogether relinquished; the activities necessary for the rearing and maintenance of offspring have long been uncalled for, his daughters being married, and his sons providing for themselves. There remains to him only the simple activities requisite for the immediate conservation of life, and after a time even these are imperfectly performed . . . No longer capable of conserving himself from the ordinary risks of everyday life, he must be carefully watched and tended to prevent some accidental circumstance from exterminating the feeble germ of life that still remains to him.[73]

The old man and woman became, first and foremost, patients in need of constant medical attention. This was, doctors asserted, their physiological destiny. The organic alterations that constituted old age subverted all other possible roles. In terms of caring for the elderly, the physician then assumed the part of expert; every aspect of the senescent's routine was subject to his approval. Yet the same physiological and anatomical changes that had determined that the elderly act the part of needy invalids also stereotyped them as the most unpleasant and incurable patients. The personality characteristics of old age meant that these individuals would be difficult to control and rarely grateful for treatment. In hospitals, they merely filled necessary beds; in mental institutions, they disrupted routines without improving their own condition. "The difficulty of managing such cases satisfactorily in an asylum or out of it." wrote T. S. Clouston:

> is extreme. They are very restless, always meddling with something or somebody, very obstinate, entirely forgetful and purposeless. They are constantly making their water on the floor, in a corner of the room or in another patient's hat. They need bathing often. Their bowels are either too costive or too loose. They are liable to retention of urine from enlarged prostates and bladder paralysis. They either eat too much or will not eat at all. A slight fall breaks their bones. To lie near other maniacal or irritable patients is out of the question, for they are sure to get hurt. For them one requires to use the best attendants, the best single rooms at night, and the best parts of a fully-equipped hospital ward; and all this needs to be done by nurse and doctor under the depressing feeling that it is of no use in the long run towards the cure of the patient.[74]

This attitude, voiced by many physicians, certainly limited the growth of geriatrics.[75] In the late nineteenth century, while ambitious young physicians specialized in such fields as surgery, pediatrics, or gynecology, the diseases of the old continued to receive little attention. Therapeutically, there was little hope of implementing curative measures; clinical studies had definitely proven that old age itself was a disease. Even a medically endorsed total regimen seemed to produce few results. "For a person in the seventies," Dr. James Faugeres Bishop wrote in 1904:

> it is not worth while to make any great sacrifice in the way of money and associations to go in search of health, because the probabilities are that the disturbance of the routine to which he has been accustomed through many years will do more harm than any climate will do him good.[76]

This attitude, however, did not deter the physician from prescribing for the elderly. Autopsies on the old had proven that the senescent could not be treated like all others. They required age-related treatment for their peculiar discomforts. The exterior appearance of the elderly only further supported the need for special regimens. After the climacteric had passed, the individual lacked the necessary vital energy to participate physically or mentally in daily activities. The body had become particularly susceptible to varied and often fatal diseases. The person's only hope was to withdraw from society and submit to the physician's custodial care. Thus, concerned doctors began to categorize the last segment of the life cycle as a period of disability and disease. The classification of the superannuated no longer rested on visible infirmities alone. According to the anatomical view of disease, the internal degeneration found in the elderly body meant that the entire stage was pathological. Those who had become senile had indeed begun to suffer from a progressive and incurable illness.

The work of the late-nineteenth-century physician, therefore, broadly paralleled that of the professional social worker. Like the sociological model of senescence that linked dependence to old age, the medical conception emphasized the numerous weaknesses and diseases that were present in the last stage of life. Simply put, all persons who had grown old were likely to exhibit signs of decay. Thus, in medical and sociological terms, at least, old age was a time when separation from society was both necessary and desirable. Only under the care of experts could the elderly continue to live a peaceful – if no longer productive – existence. In large part, of course, this expanding notion of dependent superannuation was a response to broad economic and demographic changes. In the late nineteenth century, an increasing proportion of the old were indeed being separated from society, not only by the prescriptions of professionals but by their inability to retain control over family, wealth, and possessions. This loss of status was apparent not only in the writings of experts on aging but also in the establishment of institutions devised to meet the needs of the old. As we shall see, in the late nineteenth century, the almshouse, hospital, mental institution, and old-age home all reflected contemporary ideas and realities about growing old.

CHAPTER FIVE

Institutionalizing the Elderly

In 1903, Homer Folks, commissioner of New York City's charities, announced a new policy for the City Almshouse. The institution would now be called the Home for the Aged and Infirm. Writing in the pages of *Charities*, Folks explained the reason. The change of name, he asserted, was based on the improved character of the inmates. In contrast to poorhouses of the past, New York's asylum was not filled with the lazy, corrupt, or able-bodied. Most of the residents were simply old and ailing. They had entered the poorhouse in order to receive badly needed food, shelter, and medical attention. "Observation and experience lead me to the conclusion," Folks declared, "that we should regard the people with more consideration than we have been accustomed to give the inmates of the almshouse."[1] The adoption of a new name for the institution was thus intended to bring dignity to such aged sufferers. The institutionalized elderly would no longer be treated as disgraced paupers.[2]

Folks's new policy was based on far more than the kindly sentiments of one charitable commissioner. It was not only the New York City Almshouse that appeared to be dominated by the old; almost every large city reported similar inmate populations. Nor was Folks unique in suggesting that "homes" might be created to shelter the aged and infirm. Throughout the nineteenth century, such private asylums had been established across the country, attracting the once middle-class elderly who had become incapable of providing for themselves. The New York City Almshouse proposal, then, was part of a larger movement affecting the care of the senescent. As a particular institution, its policies mirrored widespread beliefs about the needs and abilities of its aged inmates. The history and policies of other asylums, such as old-age homes, mental institutions, and general hospitals, revealed similar conceptions about the superannuated. In the late nineteenth century, as we shall see, the evolution of institutional care for the elderly both reflected and significantly influenced the growing differentiation of the old from the rest of society.

* * * *

Throughout America's history, the almshouse had always served as a shelter for those who were destitute in old age. The most ancient and broken of the nation's large cities were likely to spend their final days confined to the poorhouse. In Philadelphia, for example, until the mid-nineteenth century, individuals of advanced age constituted about one-fourth to one-third of the inmate population.[3] Other cities and large towns reported similar proportions of institutionalized old persons. In 1851, a survey of the public asylums of Rhode Island revealed that 31 percent of all almshouse paupers were over the age of sixty.[4] Such persons were generally institutionalized as an act of charity rather than as a punishment. They were viewed as too sick and weak to survive outside the asylum. In Providence, for example, most elderly inmates were listed as being "partially insane and sickly," "old age and lame," or "deserted" and "friendless."[5] There was little hope that these individuals might ever improve or become self-sufficient. They were placed in the almshouse as a final resting place before death.

During the second half of the nineteenth century, the proportion of old persons in the almshouse began to rise significantly. By 1904, the national almshouse population was 160,006. Of these 69,106, or 43 percent, were over sixty.[6] In industrialized states, the increase was even more pronounced. In 1864, for example, the old constituted 26 percent of Massachusetts's almshouse population; by 1904, the proportion had risen to 48 percent.[7] This, it should be noted, was at a time when only 8 percent of Massachusetts's population was over sixty. It was little wonder, then, that welfare officials began to engage in lengthy discussions about the declining status of old age. Their new statistical approach to poverty underlined the debilitated state of Massachusetts's elderly. The authors of the 1910 *Report of the Commission on Old Age Pensions, Annuities, and Insurance*, for example, presented their findings as conclusive proof that old age had become a serious social problem. "The strikingly high proportion of persons entering the pauper institution late in life," the *Report* asserted, "points to the close connection between old age and pauperism. It is clear that such pauperism is in most cases the result of the infirmity of advancing years rather than the misfortunes of earlier years."[8]

The scores of surveys and censuses that were commissioned in the late nineteenth and early twentieth centuries all presented similar evidence of the seemingly insurmountable problems of the aged. The focus was usually the almshouse; the conclusion, based on "hard facts" and "objective figures," was always the same: Destitution among the aged was rapidly growing. The institution appeared to offer indisputable proof of the elderly's diminished power and authority. In San Francisco, for example, one sociologist, Mary Roberts Smith, was horrified to find that the average age of the city's poorhouse residents rose from $36\frac{1}{8}$ in 1870 to $59\frac{1}{8}$ in 1894. The municipal reports of the city, Smith believed, left little doubt of the growing number of dependent elderly.[9] It mattered little that 98 percent of the old remained outside the asylum.[10] To social analysts such as Smith, almshouse realities seemed to reinforce the conception that poverty and senescence were inherently connected. The advanced age of the inmates was cited as concrete evidence that the old could not succeed in modern society.

Such statistics, of course, actually revealed far more than simply the growth of poverty-stricken old age. The figures also reflected widespread and changing attitudes about the best care for the elderly. The policies of welfare administrators, as well as the debilitated state of the elderly, explained the aged's high rate of institutionalization. Numerous factors contributed to their growing numbers in the cities' pauper asylums.

In large part, this condition resulted from changes in the treatment of destitute middle-aged adults and children. By the mid-nineteenth century, scores of reform societies had begun to free redeemable young paupers from the confines of the poorhouse. Some of these organizations, as we have seen, sent adolescents to the countryside to find work and a healthy environment. Other groups placed the needy in homogeneous institutions far removed from the corrupt influence of the pauper asylum. They sent the young to homes for orphans, the insane to mental institutions, the deaf, dumb, and blind to schools for the handicapped, the able-bodied to houses of industry, and even the petty criminal to the reformatory and prison.[11] Such persons, of course, had traditionally filled the poorhouse. With their departure, the old and sick – never an insignificant element in the almshouse – became increasingly visible as the asylum's most numerous inmates.

In addition, the high percentage of institutionalized elderly had a economic basis. In most states and counties, welfare administrators assumed that the cheapest means of supporting needy old age was also the best. This philosophy translated rapidly into placing the old in the nearest and least expensive almshouse. In contrast, outdoor relief was usually judged to be both more costly and far too pleasant. Almost everyone, it was asserted, would apply for a pension if he or she did not have to suffer the consequences. The almshouse, on the other hand, was deemed disagreeable enough to attract only the most needy and destitute.

Throughout the nineteenth century, then, and as the problems of supporting a sizable class of urban poor became increasingly apparent, welfare authorities generally came to reject past claims of large outdoor pensions for the aged.[12] In Philadelphia, for example, during the first third of the century, the guardians of the poor had allotted both outdoor relief and almshouse shelter for the needy elderly. As they gave seventy-five cents a week to every pauper who could not work, the great majority – 69 percent – of their 569 pensioners in 1830 were over sixty.[13] In 1835, however, upon the completion of a large public almshouse, the city ended all such pensions. The old, if they wished support, were forced to enter the asylum. Even four years later, when outdoor aid was reinstated, the guardians of the poor made it clear that those of advanced age and great decrepitude were still expected to seek institutional shelter. Outdoor pensions, they declared, were to consist of only meager support, and that in kind. Those requiring more than an occasional cord of wood or bundle of clothing would not be able to subsist outside the almshouse.[14] Thus, in contrast to the 798 persons who had received outdoor aid in 1833, only 123 obtained such assistance when pensions again began in 1840.[15]

In many states during the mid- and late nineteenth century, this budget-minded attitude continued to determine the care and placement of the destitute elderly. In California in 1883, for instance, the state legislature appropriated $100 a year to each locality for every pauper over sixty. As a consequence, many local welfare officials sent the old to established county almshouses in which the annual cost fell below the allotted sum. In this manner, they saved on the expense of caring for the elderly.[16] They also, in turn, ensured that the state's almshouses would be quickly filled by the aged.

It was hardly surprising, then, that a large number of elderly individuals found themselves institutionalized. By the early twentieth century, the old – in contrast to all other age groups – were disproportionally more likely to receive relief in the almshouse than outside it. Their condition, it was asserted, dictated this treatment. The debilitated state of the aged meant that they would never again return to self-sufficiency. "The old men and women who are given relief," the *Report* of the Massachusetts Commission explained, "are usually of necessity sent to the almshouse."[17] Their segregation into the wards of the poorhouse marked their ultimate differentiation from their communities. They had little to ensure them an autonomous status or to reintegrate them into society.

Contemporary studies of aged almshouse inmates seemed consistent with this conception. Such surveys showed that the elderly pauper was likely to have few means of outside support or care. In Massachusetts at the beginning of the twentieth century, the great majority of inmates reported that they were no longer married; only 15.4 percent had a spouse, whereas 25.4 percent were single and 57.8 percent were widowed.[18] Moreover, more than half declared that they were without living children.[19] Even those with offspring usually asserted that it was impossible for their children to assist them. They had neither room in their small apartments nor the financial means to support their parents.[20]

This lack of assistance seemed to affect men far more than women. In almshouses across the country, males outnumbered females by almost two to one.[21] The elderly grandmother, it appeared, was seen as being able to assist the family. She might take care of the children or help around the house.[22] For men, however, old age seemed to leave few possibilities for playing a necessary role. "Children or relatives," the *Report of the Pennsylvania Commission on Old Age Pensions* declared:

> will make greater sacrifices in order to keep an aged mother at home and prevent her going to a poorhouse, than they would for an aged father or other male relative. Aside from the sentimental reasons involved, the presence of an old woman around the house – unless she is absolutely invalided – entails little burden, as she can be made useful in numerous ways. This, however, is not the case with an aged man.[23]

Just as the elderly male seemed incapable of participating in the daily activities of the family, he also appeared unable to contribute economically to its operation. The great majority of almshouse residents reported themselves to be too debilitated to remain employed. In Massachusetts in 1910, 79.5 percent of the inmates declared that they were completely disabled, and 8.4 percent were recorded as partially incapacitated.[24] Most of these individuals had been employed in manufacturing and mechanical fields (33.7 percent), as domestic workers (22.6 percent), or as common laborers (14.5 percent).[25] Now, either handicapped as the result of sickness and accidents or weakened by old age, they spent their final days as the inmates of the poorhouse.[26]

The public institution, in turn, reflected the debilitated state of its predominantly aged inmates. As we have seen, in America's history, the almshouse had always played two major functions: It had served as an asylum for the punishment of the vagrant and able-bodied and as a residence for the poverty-stricken and ailing. In the late nineteenth century, however, upon the removal of the "lazy and corrupt," the hospitallike atmosphere of the institution became dominant.[27] Most paupers entering the asylum were too weak or ill to provide for their own necessities. In admitting these individuals, therefore, the superintendents of the poorhouses assumed that, along with food and shelter, they would also have to supply medical attention. "It has become increasingly evident," the visiting medical staff of the Long Island Almshouse and Hospital of Massachusetts wrote in 1903:

> that no real line of distinction is to be drawn between the so-called Almshouse and Hospital Departments. The institution as a whole, because of the infirm character of its inmates, is gradually and inevitably assuming the general character of a hospital, rather than of an almshouse and hospital combined . . . It is an erroneous idea to suppose that the old and decrepit, and those suffering from chronic disease in its various forms do not require medical attendance.[28]

In New York, Homer Folks agreed, questioning whether "the time has not come when the inmates of our almshouses should be considered as more related to hospital patients than paupers."[29] About one-third of the elderly were placed in hospital beds. The rest resided in wards in which "only those suffering from the general breakdown accompanying old age are received."[30] There was, however, no clear line between elderly persons admitted because of sickness and debility and those institutionalized simply for shelter. Individuals seemed to move between medical and almshouse wards with some regularity. The amount of space, supplies, and personnel, as well as the old man's or woman's physical and mental state, contributed to his or her placement. "It is not possible," explained a trustee of the Long Island Almshouse:

> to discriminate between "old and infirm" and "old and sick." These terms at Long Island are interchangeable; the people are sometimes known as inmates of the institution and sometimes as patients in the hospital, but whether they are in one department or the other, they are all feeble and infirm, else they would not be at Long Island, and

no matter where they may be found to-day, they are pretty sure to become hospital patients sooner or later.[31]

Certainly, the late-nineteenth-century physicians' conception of aging as a discrete pathological process coincided with this view. According to the medical model of senescence, all old persons would eventually become patients in need of constant medical attention. This attitude helped to justify the transformation of the almshouse. By the late nineteenth century, the managers of these public asylums had begun to portray their institutions as peaceful homes perfectly suited to the needs and ailments of their aged charges. The traditional punitive institution had vanished; the poorhouse had supposedly evolved into a well-run modern facility. By the early twentieth century, for example, the chaplain of the New York City Almshouse (renamed, as noted earlier, the City Home for the Aged and Infirm in 1903), defended his asylum as a proper haven for the old. "What can a man or woman aged and infirm look for in life," he asked in the pages of *Charities and the Commons*, "more than a warm room and clean comfortable beds to sleep in – good wholesome and varied food to eat, a church to go to, plenty of papers, magazines and books to read? All of these the inmates of our home have."[32]

The chaplain concluded that his 2,700 inmates were happy and well treated.[33] The asylum, after all, coincided with the long-standing model of old-age dependency. It provided the elderly with the "family" and necessities that for so long had defined their poverty-stricken status. In addition, most welfare advocates agreed that institutionalization was advisable for needy old age. Excluded from private charity programs, the unemployed elderly were sure to suffer. In order to survive, they would have to submit to strenuous work tests or depend on the kindness of others. In the overcrowded labor market, they had little hope of competing for available jobs. An asylum for the elderly, on the other hand, removed them from this predicament. In these homes, at least, they would be saved from the disgrace of begging for their subsistence.[34]

Thus, in the second half of the nineteenth century, organizations such as the New York Association for Improving the Condition of the Poor (NYAICP) and their successors advocated institutionalization for all aged paupers. Their volunteers energetically attempted to place every needy old person – even those who resisted their charitable assistance. The NYAICP's annual report of 1893, for example, told the story of one rather stubborn old man "whose tenacious attachment to his given apartments [sic] exceeded comprehension." But the association persisted, and finally the man was put in an institution. "When the hour arrived for our aged friend to say good-bye to his poor old home," the report continued, "the scene was touching beyond words. He wept in his second childhood; but, being admonished to go, he turned a moistened eye on the lowly abode of years, bide adieu with a sign to his rickity household goods and gratefully accepted his proffered home."[35]

The almshouse was now a "home"; it had achieved a new status in the philosophy of scientific charity. Many welfare administrators agreed that it offered proper shelter for the superannuated of the lower class. The institution provided cheap, efficient care, and its hospital wards attended to inmates who were not only destitute but likely to be ailing as well.

This widely shared belief was to have a radical effect upon the acceptance of the aged into other institutions. In time, the wards of the poorhouse came to replace other medical facilities as an acceptable setting for the incapacitated aged. As we have seen, doctors generally believed that chronic senile patients were beyond real assistance. Their illness, whether mental or physical, was largely incurable. Regardless of treatment, their condition could only become worse. It followed logically, therefore, that the almshouse, rather than the mental asylum or private hospital, offered sufficient, if hardly remedial, care.

Thus, in the late nineteenth century, superintendents of private medical facilities rarely welcomed the old into their wards. Senility placed the insane elderly patient in a distinct category. In contrast to the young, the aged individual could expect little therapeutically oriented treatment. The physician's belief in the best care for the patient, in fact, dramatically changed once the ailing man or woman advanced in age. "We never intentionally send an insane patient to [the Long Island Almshouse]," Dr. Charles T. Gaynor explained, "except in the case of an old person who is pretty senile and can be treated as well at Long Island as at any other hospital. They do not like to send a person seventy-five years of age to an insane hospital."[36] Other doctors, such as George Choate, superintendent of the Massachusetts State Hospital at Taunton, recommended that the insane elderly receive no professional attention at all. "As there is no reasonable hope for cure," he wrote, "I have generally advised friends to retain them at home."[37]

The attitudes of these physicians were then vividly reflected in the rates of institutionalization of the insane elderly. In New York in 1871, for example, whereas nearly 80 percent of all insane persons aged thirty to forty were placed in state, city, or private institutions, the corresponding figure for those over sixty was only 38 percent. Most insane old persons were either left in the care of friends (30 percent) or placed in county poorhouses (28 percent). (Of those aged thirty to forty, 20 percent were with friends and only 15 percent were in county asylums.)[38] In Massachusetts in 1880, the old were four times more likely to remain outside an institution than to receive medical attention.[39] This, it must be remembered, was during a period in which institutional care was still seen as the most hopeful means of cure. Only when asylums came to be viewed as offering few therapeutic possibilities would the elderly begin to fill their wards in overwhelming numbers.[40]

To a large degree, the exclusion of the old rested on the physician's understanding of senility. The progressive physiological basis of the illness precluded extensive treatment. This assumption, in fact, often obscured actual recovery rates. Many of the elderly who were institutionalized left the asylum "cured" or at least "improved." In the late nineteenth century, for example, in the Wisconsin State Hospital for the Insane, about 26 percent of those over sixty were designated as recovered. (The highest rate – 37.7 percent – was for those aged fifteen to twenty. Yet patients forty to fifty had a recovery rate – 26.7 percent – similar to that of the aged.)[41] Most physicians, however, seemed convinced of the chronicity of mental disease in the aged. This negative diagnosis was not due to one particularly incurable ailment or symptom. *Senility*, in fact, was an all-inclusive and rather arbitrary term. Physicians applied the characterization with little regard to the patient's actual mental state. The same individual might have entered the asylum many times before he turned seventy. Suddenly, though, he would be diagnosed as senile. His symptoms had not changed, only his age. Yet his chances of being accepted by the administrators were sharply reduced.[42]

This exclusion, I believe, revealed a great deal about the physicians' and superintendents' understanding of old age. In light of their own statistics, they could not fail to see that many of the aged patients left their asylums seemingly cured. Their rejection of the elderly after the mid-nineteenth century, I would suggest, was based instead on their overshadowing belief in the future incapacity of those over seventy. Even if cured, these aged persons were likely to suffer from other debilitating and increasingly serious diseases. The old, after all, could never escape being both physically and mentally senile.[43] It was hardly surprising, then, that regardless of the recovery rates, mid- and late-nineteenth-century superintendents denied the elderly access to their mental institutions. Because of their symptoms *and* their age, the senescent were considered to be laboring under a hopeless condition.

Similarly, by the late nineteenth century, the elderly who were diagnosed as suffering from chronic physical ailments were often excluded from private general hospitals. In the past, this had not always been the case; evangelically oriented hospitals often served as homes for needy old men and women. Those who were weak, though not really ill, spent their final years confined to a ward in the hospital. In 1869, for example, when Roman Catholic Carney Hospital of Boston opened its doors, it welcomed aged patients. One of its five floors was reserved for "old people who may not be sick but come here for a home."[44] St. Luke's Hospital of Chicago reported that it had a similar philosophy of patient care. In 1866, in its eighth annual report, it proudly noted that "in our wards are a few very aged men, who are there simply because no where else could they have the decencies and comforts of life to which none who know them would deny they are entitled."[45]

By the end of the century, however, the administrators of even these religiously based hospitals had begun to reject the destitute, homeless old as patients. In the 1890s, for example, Carney Hospital declared that it did not want "chronic, lingering inmates."[46] It no longer saw its proper function to be the housing of the weak and poverty-stricken. Changes in the theory and practice of medicine had transformed the institution. It presented itself as a modern medical facility devoted to rapid and efficient cures. The hospital preferred to admit only the acutely ill, who might remain a short time and then reenter the active world, or those patients who were about to die. The chronic senile patient, however, was advised to seek shelter in institutions that welcomed incurables. The almshouse seemed a more appropriate home than the new scientific hospital.[47]

Many hospital administrators, though, did endorse one other alternative to the poorhouse. They advised the elderly to apply for admission to an old-age home. In contrast to their own hospitals, the old-age home was viewed as an ideal place for the chronically ill and incompetent. It catered not only to the ailments of the elderly but to their moral and physical necessities as well. In the second half of the nineteenth century, in fact, numerous hospitals annexed institutions for the senescent to their own facilities. In so doing, they believed, they could remove the old from their wards without forcing them to face the disgrace of the almshouse. Hartford Hospital in Connecticut, for example, followed such a course. In the 1860s, it had admitted incurable patients into the hospital because they were "suffering"; these persons, the managers explained, had few other places to go.[48] In 1873, however, the administrators applied to the state's General Assembly for a charter to build "The Old People's Home." "At present," the administrators wrote, "there are about twelve persons occupying beds in the hospital wards who would be proper subjects for this home . . . Our wards will soon be so crowded that this class must be refused admission."[49] Six years later, although the charter had been granted, the hospital found that it lacked the funds to begin the undertaking. In appealing for money, it again emphasized the great and growing need for the new institution. The home, the authors of the hospital's nineteenth annual report wrote, would relieve the institution of the care of "twenty old and destitute persons, not hospital subjects, and provide for many decrepit and infirm, whose only crime is old age."[50] For this, the report asserted, the elderly did not deserve to be punished by almshouse incarceration. Rather, the goal of the hospital was that they be placed in a benevolent asylum.

The old-age home also won the support of many late-nineteenth-century social workers. Although these professionals generally endorsed the notion of sending the old of the lower class to the almshouse, many questioned the propriety of this action in the case of the elderly who had once been middle class. To the editor of *Charities*, for instance, such a step seemed an abhorrent cruelty. These individuals, he asserted, "in their previous lives had been upright and respectable." It was their age and disabilities, rather than poor habits, that had led them into unemployment and poverty. As such, they were simply victims of the demands and pace of modern society. For this apparently growing group of needy persons, the editor wrote, the old-age home offered a sensible alternative to the almshouse. Like the asylum for the poor, it removed the superannuated from active competitive society, yet did not characterize its inmates as paupers. Instead, at least in the ideal, it gave its residents comfort and dignity in their final days.[51]

By the end of the century, in fact, a sizable number of aged men and women had become the inmates of benevolent asylums. In Massachusetts, for example, whereas 3,480 persons sixty-five and over were in the state's almshouses, 2,589 were in old-age homes;[52] in New York in 1894, 4,713 aged individuals were listed as residing in

58 private asylums.[53] These persons, like those in the poorhouse, had few ties to their communities; most reported already being severed from their families and their occupations. In Massachusetts, the great majority of inmates – 94.7 percent – were listed as wholly or partially incapacitated,[54] and 88.3 percent declared that they were no longer married.[55] But the residents did differ from almshouse inmates in two important ways. First, most – 69.4 percent – were women; second, they had paid to enter the asylum.[56] In Pennsylvania in 1911, only four of thirty-two institutions reported that they were free to all applicants; all others charged fees ranging from $10 to $500.[57] This money, in part, contributed to the higher operating costs of the homes. Whereas the Massachusetts poorhouses spent an average of $3.83 a week on each resident, the state's benevolent homes allocated $5.80 for every tenant.[58] In the late nineteenth century, elderly persons in private old-age homes were assumed to enjoy comfort and care far superior to those of the almshouse.

This ideal of the proper environment for the dependent elderly was embodied in hundreds of benevolent homes. In the century to come, of course, the institution was to become an established part of American life. In the late nineteenth century, the old-age home, although it was never the dominant form of senescent care, gave tangible expression to widely shared attitudes about the needs and abilities of the elderly. The founders of these institutions consciously attempted to build asylums that would conform to the personality and necessities of senescence. In contrast to almshouses, old-age homes were selective about their inmates; they did not simply house the destitute and ailing. Rather, they devised – and, in their annual reports, articulated – standards for the correct care, characteristics, and behavior of their aged tenants. In admitting some groups of old persons and denying entrance to others, they defined the category of deserving superannuation precisely. In Philadelphia, for example, the first old-age home, the Indigent Widows' and Single Women's Society, opened its doors in 1817 for the benefit of white, once middle-class females.[59] This group, the managers asserted, were the most worthy and defenseless. They did not deserve to die in the almshouse or to be left to beg on the street but merited the unique care offered by a private asylum. By the end of the century, at least twenty-four old-age homes had been established in the city, offering shelter not only to the once wealthy widow but to men, couples, blacks, the financially secure, and even the very poor.[60] All of these persons, the founders of the homes implied, could now be considered superannuated; they required the specialized care of a benevolent asylum. These nineteenth-century homes, therefore, were intended for lonely, tired, and sick individuals whose age alone qualified them for institutionalization.

The establishment of such homes was not limited to Philadelphia. By the beginning of the twentieth century, there were scores of old-age homes in every large American city. The development of this institution was, of course, directly tied to the nation's urban and industrial growth. As economic changes caused increasing numbers of elderly persons to be perceived as powerless and needy, private asylums were created to offer shelter and care. Not surprisingly, then, the first old-age homes were established in the large eastern cities of America during the first half of the nineteenth century. It was here, as we have seen, that the problems of aging in modern society first became apparent. And as the rate of urbanization accelerated, so did the number of homes. In the South, the cities of Charleston, South Carolina, and Jackson, Mississippi, both opened old-age homes in the late nineteenth century; in the Northwest, a private asylum was established in Minneapolis in 1868.[61]

Although these institutions differed in geographic location and date of establishment, they varied little in their history or goals. Across the nation, they attempted to offer helpless old persons a more attractive residence than the almshouse. In their foundation, the benefactors of these asylums shared the belief that there were few other real alternatives for a growing proportion of the old. As in Philadelphia, most cities first established asylums strictly for white, formerly middle-class women. In time, though, they, like Philadelphia, came to have homes for the old of all races, sexes, and backgrounds. Regardless of their former lives, most old persons were judged in need of institutional shelter.

The asylums of Philadelphia, therefore, were unique only by virtue of their date of foundation. In their practices and ideals, they were mirrored by homes throughout the nation. Yet because of their early establishment, the city's institutions may serve as a valuable case study through which to view changing conceptions of old age. Their founders were often the first to verbalize their beliefs about the elderly; their managers played innovative roles in determining the inmates' routines and duties. And as these institutions evolved, they reflected the effect changing attitudes had on the care of the senescent. By the end of the century, as we shall see, these old-age homes, along with almshouses, insane asylums, and general hospitals, had become well-defined symptoms of the new realities confronting America's elderly population.

*   *   *   *

The first old-age home in Philadelphia, the Indigent Widows' and Single Women's Society, specifically defined the proper objects of their benevolence. When the home was opened in 1817 to women only, the society declined to accept any applicant who had been born and raised in poverty. These individuals, they stated, were sufficiently cared for by the almshouse. Instead, their organization was designed for women "whose earlier lives had been passed in more refined walks of life and whom experience, therefore, had not inured to the struggles of penury."[62] Their seventh annual report explained the purpose of the society clearly:

> It is generally known that in a large city there are always a number of persons who have been in easy circumstances and enjoyed the comforts attendant on this state; but have been reduced by misfortune to poverty; who are too respectable to be classed with the poor that come under the notice of most charitable societies, are unwilling to be inmates of an Alms House, and yet are unable to procure for themselves the comforts or even the necessities of life; for such it is desirable that a place should be provided where their declining years might be rendered comfortable, without the feeling of misery and degradation incident to a state of dependency on public charity.[63]

This feeling of degradation was to be prevented by making the women see the institution as their home and the other inmates as members of their family. Thus, separate rooms were provided so that each inmate would have privacy, whereas meals taken at a general table were meant to ensure a feeling of family unity.[64]

Although concerned with the material aspects of the home, the Indigent Widows' and Single Women's Society saw a more pressing reason to rescue their charges from the almshouse. Although their home had certainly provided for the women's comfort, they explained, "What is more important, many exemplary Christians devote their best efforts to instruct [the inmates] and to induce them to prepare for the awful change from their sojourn in this life to a weary rest from their labours, and where sorrow can never intrude."[65] The society, although nonsectarian in character, emphasized its Christian orientation continuously throughout the first half of the century. Annual reports proudly enumerated tales of women whose religious devotion, strained by the conditions of poverty, had been restored

95

through the spirit of the home. Left in the almshouse, they would have died in misery. Institutionalized, they could leave the world in hopes of eternal peace.[66]

To maintain the religious mood within the home at all times, the society desired that only moral, pious women be admitted. To ensure this, they required each applicant to give proof of a "character and habits beyond reproach," along with recommendations from "respectable persons."[67] In 1823, in an attempt to further guarantee the quality of their applicants, they exacted a $150 entrance fee. This had been done, they explained, so that "unworthy objects would be excluded." Anyone who had once been middle class would, they assumed, be able to raise this amount of money.[68] Nowhere in their records did they give any indication that the fee had been assessed for financial reasons, although the home was often in need of funds. By 1887, in fact, this measure of a woman's past worth had reached $400.

The institution also attempted to "preserve perfect harmony in the family" through an elaborate set of rules and regulations enforced by a resident matron.[69] Those disagreeing more than twice with her policies were expelled. In the first seventeen years, 20 out of 140 inmates were found to be unsuitable residents.[70] The annual reports, however, never gave explicit reasons for the expulsions. In 1887, a one-year probation period was established for each incoming resident before she became a true family member.

Despite the familylike relationships emphasized by the management, the home, at the time of its founding, did resemble the contemporary image of an institutional poorhouse in one respect: All inmates were required to donate their labor to raise money for the house. This rule, the founders stressed, not only added to the financial stability of the home but also "promoted a disposition of harmony and understanding by maintaining a degree of social intercourse and . . . prevented the depressing idea of entire dependency which might otherwise produce a feeling of despondency."[71] The work instead, the society explained, made the women feel useful and filled the home with the "spirit of industry."[72] Although they did not consider the inmates able to support themselves in full, they recorded with pride the amounts of money raised by the women's sewing, knitting, and quilting.[73]

Beginning in the late 1830s, however, this attitude changed sharply. By midcentury, the thirty-third annual report solemnly explained the lack of activity in the institution. "It will be remembered," the management wrote:

> that all the beneficiaries here are very aged, the youngest considerably more than sixty years old, the rest beyond seventy, eighty and ninety, and that as a matter of course they are rarely free from infirmity and disease and few are able to contribute by their industry to their support.[74]

The women, instead, were pictured as the docile recipients of charity, desiring only to be fed, clothed, and sheltered. The managers of the home no longer recorded the belief that this treatment might lead their charges to feel worthless or depressed. Instead, they praised the "quiet, monotonous lives" of their tenants, totally apart from the productive, busy world outside the establishment's walls.[75]

This division was further emphasized by the increasing importance that the annual reports gave to the number of years each inmate had lived. When the home was first established, the society did not mention their beneficiaries' ages or the minimum number of years required for entrance. The earliest reference to life span, in 1836, divided the women into three categories: Eighteen were over eighty, forty-four beyond seventy, and four past sixty.[76] In 1844, the institutional boundary to senior status became definite. "No one," stated the new rule, "is admitted as an inmate who has not passed the limit of three score years."[77] In 1888, the threshold was raised to sixty-five.

This line clearly marked the separation of the active world from that of the unproductive elderly. As we saw above, the management's explanation of the women's inability to work included a reference to their ages. This division, once drawn, became the focus of the great contrast between the happy life of the young and the sad, tiresome hours endured by the old as they waited for death.[78] The mere entrance into senescence became a sure and incontestable sign of uselessness. "With the aged," the annual report of 1842 reflected, "we have few sympathies. They belong to a generation that has passed away; they can promise us neither reciprocation nor reward. Our reverence for them is rarely an active principle." The young had little to learn from those over sixty except the lesson of Christian charity.[79]

The sharp separation between the periods of life had an important effect on the development of institutional procedures and goals. When poverty had been the cause of the elderly's misery, an old woman could alleviate her suffering by entering the home. Now, however, she could not change her state by merely stepping inside the institution's walls. Instead, her age, her condition of uselessness, and her separation from the rest of the world all entered along with her. The society's assurance of its ability to bring joy into the lives of the aged woman had vanished; in its place, the managers expressed the hope that they could soften her rapid decline.

This task required a restructuring of the possible goals of the home. To rescue a woman from poverty was not sufficient if the society then allowed her to suffer "the burden of age." Instead, they had to prove that they could provide a healthy, happier atmosphere for their charges. By midcentury, therefore, their annual reports rarely mentioned the ominous almshouse. Instead, they began to stress the particular provisions allocated to their institutionalized inmates. "To all whom it receives," the twenty-eighth annual report explained, "it supplies a home during life, abundant food, comfortable clothing and kind attendance, watching over them in sickness and administering their last necessities in a filial spirit."[80]

In part, this change was due to the overcrowded conditions of the home. Two years after its founding, the institution had moved from Walnut to Cherry Street in order to enlarge its quarters. In 1852, the society began to erect a new wing to the Cherry Street building.

Despite these actions, the overcrowding continued. In 1857, when the new annex opened, the seventy-eight inmates immediately filled every available space. The rule that gave each tenant private quarters was amended; two or three women now filled some of the rooms. Even the establishment in 1852 of a new home for elderly women, the Pennsylvania Asylum of Philadelphia for Indigent Widows and Single Women, did not lessen the demand. The society, forced to turn away many applicants, began to select only the most worthy and needy for placement upon the waiting list. By 1864, this list covered all possible admissions for the next four years. Although the Civil War was multiplying the ranks of needy women, the home declined to accept any applications for an unspecified length of time. Instead, it continually pleaded with other charitable groups to undertake the cause of the aged.[81]

In the period between 1859 and 1890, twenty-two institutions were established in Philadelphia to fulfill this need. Similar in structure to the Indigent Widows' and Single Women's Society, they were organized to meet the special demands of the aged. These homes, however, reflected the belief that a large proportion of the old – not only the bereaved widow – needed special institutional care. In the second half of the nineteenth century, as we have seen, both the charity worker and the social scientist became convinced of the growing number of destitute, though worthy, elderly almshouse residents. The age of these inmates, it was asserted, rather than their habits, had led them to their poverty-stricken condition. For these persons, like the single once middle-class women, the poorhouse now seemed an unjust end. Instead, private welfare groups worked to develop new types of old-age homes for their care. In so doing, they created more inclusive units that reflected the public's greatly expanded conception of who among the elderly should be privately institutionalized.

Most active in this movement were the city's churches. Homes were founded by the Lutherans in 1859, the Methodists and Jews in 1865, the Baptists in 1869, the Presbyterians in 1872 and 1885, and the Evangelical Association in 1888. In their institutions, religious commitment played a leading role. The managers of the homes required the applicant to be a church member in good standing. In addition, the religious leader of the community, along with other respectable persons, had to approve of her character. In some instances, this was further verified by a visiting committee that investigated the candidate.

The Presbyterian Home for Widows and Single Women, for example, established in 1872, enumerated such rules clearly. Along with certificates attesting to her character, the applicant had to be unable to support herself, pay $150 to $250 for admission (depending on her age), sign all property over to the institution, agree to obey all rules set by the matron, and be free from any incurable physical or mental disease. In an amendment to the rules thirteen years later, the home emphasized that anyone "seriously deranged in the mind would not be retained."[82] The institution, despite the wishes of some hospital administrators, was not to be a medical facility but a place where each old woman could live out her life in "personal dignity."[83]

The Presbyterian Home, like all the newly founded institutions of this type, stressed the importance of creating a religious atmosphere. Daily Bible readings, weekly services, and consultations with the minister were provided. Moreover, most of the organizations saw a need for this spiritual environment to conform to the theology of their specific demoninations. A history of the Evangelical Association explained that, before its institution's establishment, the organization was "compelled to seek admittance [for the aged and needy members of our churches] in the Homes of other denominations, or, in some cases, the Almshouse."[84] Its new asylum could not only rescue the aged from poverty but would provide an appropriate sectarian environment as well.

As the homes separated according to religious preference, they also encompassed groups that had previously not been considered in need. As we have seen, prior to the Civil War, the old-age home was designed solely for women. Focusing their efforts upon females without male support, the organizations implicitly assumed that men were sufficient providers regardless of age. The notion of male indigence never arose in the reports of the Indigent Widow's and Single Women's Society. The growing trend toward categorization of the elderly according to age, as well as the increasing number of male almshouse inmates, however, had a clear effect upon the charities' perception of the old man. He too was now seen as superannuated, becoming as irrelevant as the aged woman to the active young world. "Men may become," the managers of one late-nineteenth-century asylum observed, "by age and misfortune, as helpless as women, and if they are equally deserving of pity and aid, difference of sex should make no difference in their claim on human sympathy."[85] Thus, in 1865, the first home for men opened its doors "as a refuge from want and suffering for decent old age."[86]

In its organization and rules, the Old Man's Home of Philadelphia closely resembled its sister institutions. Although nonsectarian in character, it required its inmates to have lived moral and religious lives, "declining to receive those who are scoffers at Christianity and known condemners of its precepts and observations."[87] The institution wanted it clearly understood that these men had not reached their state through "crime or the sin of idleness or intemperance," but merely through ill fortune or the infirmities of old age.[88]

The one major difference from the women's homes was, of course, its concern with the elderly indigent male inmate. In the early years of its establishment, the managers of the asylum emphasized the difficulties they had in convincing the public of a real need for its existence. The second annual report, therefore, explained the plight of the debilitated old man:

> The very name of manhood gives the idea of strength and ability to labor. Hence our first duty was to convince others of that which our own experience had taught us, namely that there is absolutely no class of humanity so sadly powerless to aid themselves, so useless in any of the ordinary duties of the household and so unwelcomed among strangers as destitute old men.[89]

As we have seen, late-nineteenth and early-twentieth-century studies of aged almshouse inmates revealed a similar conception of the superannuated man. The picture these institutions drew was in sharp contrast to man's stereotyped image throughout this period.[90] No longer protective, strong, or productive, he became desexed, growing even weaker, and more useless than his female counterpart. "While a woman," the management explained, "who has reached advanced age is, even with her impaired faculties, usually able to contribute in many ways to the comforts of a family, a man thus debilitated has no resource by which he can even evince his gratitude for those who befriend him."[91] By the end of the century, the managers were attacking the popular notion of masculinity less strenuously; their "family" of 128 members, as well as the almshouse population, seemed sufficient proof of their argument. They expressed only wonder that the institution had not been established earlier.[92]

The cause of the needy old man was also adopted by the Presbyterian Home for Aged Couples and Aged Single Men. Founded in 1885, this institution reflected a further broadening in the category of the institutionalized aged. As indicated by its name, the establishment had designed its facilities for married couples as well as single men. Previously, most institutional literature asked the public to commiserate with the condition of the old, lonely individual who had neither friend nor relative. One of the main aims of the earlier homes was to supply the warmth and companionship of the missing family. Any married couple wanting aid was therefore required to separate and be housed in different institutions.[93] The Presbyterian Home for Aged Couples, and Single Men, as well as the Home for Aged Couples, established in 1876, rejected this stipulation, accepting couples who could present a $500 admission fee and two new suits of clothing, and give proof that they could not support themselves or be cared for sufficiently by their children.

Like the Presbyterian Home, the Home for Aged and Infirm Colored People testified to an expansion of private institutional care. Founded by Quakers and blacks in 1865, it opened its doors to "worthy and exemplary colored people" who otherwise would be sent to the almshouse.[94] The institution at first limited its enrollment to women, but, following a move to larger quarters in 1876, began to admit both men and couples.

Established immediately after the Civil War, the home linked its purpose closely to the "uplifting" of the newly liberated black. Its very reason for existence, the managers explained, grew directly from the crimes of racism.

> If their children had been enabled to go into business as do our own, doubtless they would have been comfortable; as they were not, we

actually necessitated their dependent conditions and made ourselves liable for their maintenance.

To prevent this, then, a constant recurrence of this state of things, let us open to them, the colored people, all the avenues of trade and business, leaving them to select for themselves such occupations as shall best suit them and thus give them the opportunity at least of proving whether or not they will provide for their aged.[95]

The asylum's early reports related tales of the inmates' past lives under slavery and their subsequent escape from the conditions of poverty.[96] Within a decade, however, these issues received less emphasis; the freedom gained by blacks did not relieve the plight of their elderly. Instead, the institution increasingly turned its attention from the problems of the black in white society to those of the elderly inmates within its home. Centering discussions upon the particular concerns of the aged, it emphasized its ability to meet these needs through special food, clothing, and medicine. Due to the home, the managers stated, "the declining years of these impotent folks, which might else have been passed in unhealthy habitations and in much bodily distress, have been so much alleviated."[97] By 1880, in fact, its annual reports bore a striking resemblance to those of the other institutions.

In part, this similarity reflected the home's alteration of some of its initial rules. Although the minimum age for admittance was originally set at fifty, the institution in 1874 raised it to sixty. Like the Indigent Widows' and Single Women's Society, it modified its attitude toward the women's ability to work. A rule, reiterated during the first few years of its establishment, requiring the women to "sew, knit, or do any other service for the benefit of the Home."[98] disappeared from the annual report in 1878. Explaining their action in 1881, the managers wrote that the women could not be expected to fulfill these jobs, "but they do what they can and who shall ask for more."[99] This similarity to the other homes was apparent in another amendment as well. In 1876, the regulations officially recorded the passage of a mandatory probation period of six months for all residents. As with the other institutions, this was done "so that [the inmates'] dispositions and characters may become better known to us, and thus guard to some extent against the admission of improper inmates."[100]

Throughout this period, other groups also established old-age institutions. Trade union and fraternal organizations, concerned with the fact that the cessation of a worker's salary often left him unprepared for old age, opened asylums for the care of their members. In

Philadelphia, two such institutions existed: the Forrest Home for Aged and Infirm Actors and the Hayes Mechanics' Home.[101]

The Home for Infirm People of the Little Sisters of the Poor, opened in 1869, was still another type of private home for the elderly. In the past, all asylums had automatically charged their inmates a fee. Even the least expensive, the Home for Aged and Infirm Colored People, had raised its admission fee from $40 to $150 by the end of the century. The Little Sisters, however, accepted all aged paupers free of charge. Now, old-age homes were not only for respectable citizens previously of middle-class status; they were becoming the preferred way of caring for all the elderly. Even the managers of the Indigent Widows' and Single Women's Society, who had once stressed the importance of private homes only for those "too respectable to be classed with the poor," endorsed the idea of separate old-age homes for the lower classes. In 1875, they circulated a plea to the city's charities, an appeal that they repeated throughout the last quarter of the century. "The Managers," they wrote, "venture to suggest to those who have treasures to bestow upon objects of mercy that another institution is required for a class who after spending their lives as domestic servants become, as age advances, dependent and friendless."[102]

With these developments, the concept of private homes for Philadelphia's elderly had grown beyond its pre–Civil War definition of care for the white, formerly middle-class single woman. By 1890, it covered the single man, the married couple, the black, and the poor. Furthermore, this expansion not only affected the types of persons involved but broadened the justification for institutionalization as well.

As we have seen, beginning in the late 1830s, inmates were increasingly categorized in terms of age, which separated them clearly from the rest of society. This barrier signified another division as well; the inmates passed from the healthy world into that of the sick and dying.[103]

In their official policy statements, many of the homes emphasized that they were not created as substitutes for the hospital. In most cases, a doctor's examination was required before admittance to ensure that the applicant had no contagious disease. If an inmate showed signs of senile dementia while residing at the institution, he or she was often removed to the almshouse or hospital so as not to disturb the tranquility of the family. The Indigent Widows' and Single Women's Society, in fact, sponsored a bed at the Pennsylvania Hospital for this specific purpose. The society wanted its institution to be a home, not a shelter for the insane and dying.[104]

Throughout the last quarter of the century, however, the annual reports increasingly used terms of physical and mental illness to describe the attributes of the inmates. It seemed clear, in fact, that the asylums' managers shared the physician's conception of senescence. Aging was a disease that would eventually cause the demise of their residents. Home after home explained that the aged had minds like infants, "without the joys of that period," and bodies suffering such pain that most welcomed death.[105] Their personalities, too, reflected their condition. Absorbed in their physical ailments, "both real and imagined,"[106] the aged became the most difficult and trying of persons. The Home for Aged and Infirm Colored People, for example, thanked its matron and her assistants for their gentleness, patience, and forbearance in handling the residents, reminding the employees that the old were "but children of mature growth with strong desires natural to their years."[107] The annual reports evoked this description not merely for those patients rapidly approaching death but for all the inmates in their establishments. As in the medical model of senescence, disease was no longer an entity separate from old age; it had become the central and determining factor in that period of life.

Thus, although the homes were designed for the living, death dominated the pages of their yearly reports. If few residents had died during the course of the year, the homes often credited their sanitary conditions, good food, kind attention, or medical care. If large numbers had passed away, however, the home expressed no great concern; this, after all, seemed a reasonable expectation. "That we should have to record the deaths of eleven of the home's members," explained the managers of the Indigent Widows' and Single Women's Society, "excites but little surprise when we consider how far beyond the ordinary term of human life were the ages of those who passed away."[108] In some cases, in fact, the good health of the inmates evoked the greatest wonder.

This attitude had a notable effect upon the management of the homes. Previously, responsibility for the daily regimen of the inmates had fallen upon a wide variety of individuals. The managers, the matrons, the visiting committees, and the churches all helped structure their charges' routine. By viewing old age as a disease, however, the institutions implicitly gave ultimate responsibility for this task to the physician. During the last quarter of the century, in fact, statements from the attending physician or summaries of his reports began to appear with regularity in the annual records, replacing those of the minister. Commenting on such things as the sanitation, diet, and exercise of the inmates, he expressed the official view of conditions within the home to the public. These reports never described specific diseases or their cures. Instead, the entire normal regimen of the old had fallen within the physician's domain.[109]

The doctor was responsible for evaluating, endorsing, or revising all rules under which the patients lived. Dr. Johathan Eckhardt, who attended the women of the Presbyterian Home for Widows and Single Women, emphasized the importance of these regulations. Summarizing his statement, the managers of the home explained that the physician "reported that the health of the inmates is good, considering their ages and the climatic change coincident with changes in temperature [and] . . . attributed it to the wise precautions – the diet and the strict rules laid down by the House Committee in charge."[110]

These measures often regulated the daily schedule of the inmates' lives; they were told when to rise, wash, eat, and sleep. Furthermore, the managers made it clear that certain activities were strictly forbidden. One home, for example, banned all "discussion on exciting subjects,"[111] and another legislated against the unsupervised movement of the residents. Only under the watchful eye of the managers were they permitted to leave the building.[112]

Missing from the annual reports, however, is the description of what filled the hours between the meals and sleep. For the most part, it seems, the management emphasized the ability of the aged to sit and watch the world go by "in peace and quiet."[113] "To see the happy old men sitting around," the thirty-fourth annual report of the Old Man's Home exclaimed, "either in the cheerful pleasant hall or each in his own little room, was a sight that none of our managers at least will ever forget."[114] The administration of the Home for Aged and Infirm Colored People echoed this sentiment, commenting upon the enjoyment the inmates received through the "pleasant outlook from the windows and porch of the Home . . . [as] the birds and flowers cheer them up."[115]

Twice yearly as well, most of the homes scheduled excursions to the park for a picnic or concert. These trips, along with visits from outsiders, marked the high point of the year. "The old folks," reported the Home for the Aged and Infirm Colored People, "have received much enjoyment from the thoughtfulness of young people who have several times come out to the Home to sing to them. Such attractions aid in passing away the weary hours of old age."[116]

Generally, however, the annual reports of the institutions cited their homes' isolation and self-sufficiency as important therapeutic qualities. Housing all facilities under one roof, they allowed the tenants to remain within the asylum's gates at all times. This, in the opinion of the various managers, not only made sick individuals more comfortable but actually improved their health and lengthened their lives.[117] Inside the home, inmates no longer had to face the stress of the outside world.

The locations of the homes further added to the rejuvenating process. During the last quarter of the century, several of the institutions moved to less populated sections of Philadelphia. These new areas, it was asserted, allowed the elderly to escape the noise and tensions of the city as well as to breathe the country's fresher air. "We believe," explained the Old Ladies' Home:

> that few persons of any age can turn aside from the busy scene of the city's crowded thoroughfares to enter one of these quiet retreats for old people without a sense of relief that here at least the strife and turmoil are over for the old folks . . . and [they] can now repose in an atmosphere of undisturbed serenity surrounded with the comfortable realities of warmth and food and cherished by the ready sympathy of friends.[118]

This new, healthier environment was not designed for the poverty-stricken alone. If a man, through age, became old and therefore sick, he too needed the institutionalized care that the homes provided. The Old Man's Home noted that it had requests from middle-class men "desirous to live where they might be surrounded by congenial society of their age, where they would be certain of receiving care and kind attention during sickness."[119] The Methodist Home annexed a boardinghouse of this type to its establishment in 1876. Other institutions, such as the Home for Aged and Infirm Colored People, reported cases such as that of Lucy Taylor, "who boarded at the house and paid a monthly fee. It was of her own free will and choice that she came to this Home in her old age, to enjoy the pure air of the country and the beautiful scenery which she delighted in."[120]

Thus, although private care for the wealthy elderly did not generally develop until the twentieth century, the conceptual framework had been clearly established by the end of the nineteenth. In the future, the treatment of the old would be based on a model that defined senescence as a time of both illness and dependence. As we have seen, institutional changes reflected this belief. The treatment of the old in almshouses, general hospitals, mental asylums, and the expanding old-age home all marked the growing differentiation of the last stage of life. In the view of the administrators of these asylums, senescence was unique; the aged had needs and ailments that separated them from society. They could neither be treated alongside the acutely ill nor cared for according to procedures devised for the young. However, even if the old-age home was an improvement over the almshouse – and there can be little doubt that it was – its development reinforced the separateness of senescence. According to admission policies, all applicants had to be beyond a defined age. In America's benevolent institutions of the late nineteenth century, therefore, the differentiation of old age first took widespread and official form. Generally, from that point on, the elderly who needed extensive aid would be housed as a class apart. Their age, lack of ties to the community, and debilitated state all defined the distinctiveness of the superannuated.

CHAPTER SIX

The Pension Barrier

Not every old person, of course, spent his or her final days confined to an institution. Throughout the nineteenth century, only a small percentage of the elderly ever sought refuge in an almshouse, old-age home, or insane asylum. The great majority remained beyond the institution's walls, reliant upon their own resources and abilities or the support of relatives.

By the late nineteenth century, however, even the uninstitutionalized elderly began to be affected by the growing social differentiation of senescence. Mandatory retirement, as dictated by pension programs initiated during this period, began to place a distinctive barrier between old age and the rest of society. Adopted almost simultaneously by large industries, the military, and the civil service, pensions uniformly defined their elderly beneficiaries as diseased and dependent. No physical examination or means test would be required to prove the dire condition of their existence. According to the assumption written into these plans, the man or woman over sixty-five (or, at most, seventy) was beyond the age of usefulness. Regardless of actual physical state, this person had entered a stage distinctive for its weakness and dependence. In time, it would seem both natural and correct that such elderly persons should be denied access to employment. This attitude developed, as we shall see, out of events and ideas of the late nineteenth and early twentieth centuries. The pensions that produced and enforced mandatory retirement were a vivid response both to contemporary industrial conflict and to the growing awareness of the plight of the elderly. Without such programs, it must be remembered, many aged Americans found themselves unemployed and without means of support. By accepting a pension, the worker would at least be able to avoid ending his life amid the squalor of the almshouse. Yet, in their eventual adoption, these plans also reflected the widely shared conviction that old persons could in general be characterized as "over the hill" and, for their own sake and that of society's, should be forced to retire.

*   *   *   *

Retirement, of course, both as a concept and as a reality, was not an invention of the late nineteenth century. As we have seen, even in the colonial era, aged persons too weak to work were forced to withdraw from employment. As extreme old age approached, they were expected to cede both responsibility and leadership to the next generation. Usually, this was a decision reached with some misgivings. The unemployed elder, regardless of his former role, was likely to suffer a significant decline in status. Good works, even profound wisdom no longer assured him an exalted position.[1] In the nineteenth century, especially in urban areas, the aged population seemed even more likely to be forced into unemployment. No longer endowed with valued goods or property and deprived of physical strength, they had little to guarantee their active participation in the community.[2] By 1890, in fact, 42 percent of all men over sixty-five who had worked in nonagricultural fields reported that they were either retired or considered themselves to be permanently unemployable.[3]

Many charity workers, as has been noted, implicitly condoned this situation. Increasingly aware of the cities' overfilled labor market, they assumed that work was best reserved for the young. Adolescents, after all, were capable of reform and progress; imbued with correct habits, they might mature into productive adults. In contrast, there seemed little doubt that the value of the elderly had already been spent. The poverty-stricken old were therefore advised to withdraw from the labor force into the enforced retirement of the almshouse or old-age home.[4]

Most old persons who followed this course had little alternative. They sought institutionalization simply because they had ceased to be self-sufficient; their debilitated state, and not the advice of experts, mandated their departure from the work force. Throughout most of the nineteenth century, in fact, the timing of a worker's retirement remained linked to his own health and capabilities. Usually, the laborer would resign only when he was no longer physically able. His entrance into an institution was a sign that he had no other means of subsistence.

This, however, was not the only option for the retired. Many remained outside institutions, assisted by their children or living on

109

their own savings. In addition, by the last quarter of the nineteenth century, about 9 percent of all elderly persons were dependent upon pensions for their basic necessities.[5] Throughout the century, these annuities had been awarded to the old both by the military and (far more sporadically) by private employers. Given as an act of charity or as a sign of honor, the allowances were intended to save the incapacitated old man from certain destitution. Many businesses reported giving annuities to aged workers they believed deserving. These awards, they contended, were a tangible outpouring of the companies' benevolence. They were based on the employers' "moral obligation" to the elderly worker. "When [the employee] becomes too old or infirm to perform any bit of labor," reported one typical firm, "we supply whatever may be necessary to keep him in comfortable circumstances."[6] In their trade magazines, railroad companies also boasted of the kind, individual treatment they gave their aged employees. Before it established a standardized pension plan, for example, the Boston and Albany Railroad explained on one occasion that, as it was necessary to retire four of its elderly, infirm workers, each would be presented with a check for a year's salary; another railroad line told of its thoughtfulness to "Old Pap," who, having worked for the company for forty-five years, was now able to retire comfortably on a monthly annuity.[7] In presenting these pensions, the companies stressed their generosity. They were rewarding the worker who had served their interests long and faithfully.

During the nineteenth century, the military also awarded the aged veteran a monthly pension. In establishing an annuity for Revolutionary War veterans in 1829, and later in presenting pensions to the survivors of the War of 1812, the Indian conflicts, and the Mexican War, the government stressed that the pension was intended as a sign of honor and was awarded to those who had served their country loyally in times of war. The fact that many decades had elapsed between the conflicts and the pensions (the annuity for the War of 1812, for example, came fifty-six years after the event) ensured that the recipients would be not only extremely aged but quite few in number. The military had little intention of supporting a nation of pensioners.[8] With the enactment of Civil War pensions, however, the prospect of thousands of new recipients seemed likely. Only twenty-five years separated Appomattox and the initiation of the Civil War award. The Pension Bureau stressed, however, that this money was intended only for those in dire need; severe restrictions were attached to the annuity. The applicants had to prove that they were "suffering from

110

a mental or physical disability of permanent character, not the result of their own vicious habits, which incapacitates them from the performance of manual labor in such a degree as to render them unable to earn support."[9]

By the early twentieth century, however, the notion of who should receive a pension had considerably broadened. In the military, as well as in large industries, the pension began to assume a standardized form. Well-defined regulations, rather than charitable intentions or individual need, dictated the size and condition of the awards. Attempts to rationalize the program, as well as to assist the old in retiring, led to the creation of highly structured plans that made little distinction among elderly recipients. All persons of a particularly advanced (and, by implication, feeble) age were to be included in the pension system.

* * * *

In the military, as has been noted, Civil War annuities were initially planned only for the diseased and disabled. The government made it clear that it did not want every aged veteran clamoring for a pension. To receive the award, the applicant had to submit to a medical examination. Doctors were advised to be cautious in this certification and were required to specify the exact nature and extent of every ailment. They were also warned to omit any infirmity that might have arisen from natural old age. According to Pension Bureau regulations, such disabilities did not merit monthly support.[10] The aged veteran, it was assumed, would still be able to do manual labor.

In actual practice, though, physicians often seemed unable to distinguish between the dissipations of age and more distinct, acceptable ailments. As we have seen, contemporary medical theory defined the last stage of life as a pathological process; no clear line separated the diseased from the senescent. Doctors for the Pension Bureau, therefore, had few guidelines by which to determine the correct size of the award, or, in fact, to decide whether one should be given at all. This confusion was vividly reflected in contested pension decisions. The ruling made by one physician was likely to be overturned by another. In 1901, in evaluating one case, for example, the Pension Bureau ruled:

> that the fact that claimant has attained the age of 65 does not entitle him to a pension per se, under section 2 of the act of June 26, 1890, regardless as to what his mental or physical condition may be . . . but the evidence in this case disclosing the fact that claimant is by trade a

111

pattern maker and that by reason of his age, disease of heart, enlarged veins of legs and stiffness and limitation and atrophy of hand, he is unable to follow said occupation, the action rejecting his claim was in error and is reversed.[11]

By the turn of the century, in fact, the commissioner of pensions had attempted to construct clear, if unofficial, guidelines that would standardize awards and alleviate this problem. Although the act of 1890 had failed to include age as a pensionable disease, H. Clay Evans advised physicians to give awards based solely on old age. A claimant, he stated, "who had reached the age of 75 is allowed the maximum rate for senility alone, even when there is no special pensionable disability. A claimant who has attained the age of 65 is allowed at least the minimum rate, unless he appears to have unusual vigor and ability for the performance of manual labor."[12]

In 1904, the natural incapacity connected with old age became a standard part of pension law. In a special and somewhat controversial decree, President Theodore Roosevelt officially included every aged veteran in the pension program. According to Order 78, the applicant, upon attaining the age of sixty-two, would be considered "disabled one-half in ability"; at sixty-five he became two-thirds incapacitated; and after seventy he reached total disability.[13] Accepted by Congress in 1907 and written into law, this ruling gave precise boundaries to age-related dependence. Unless proven otherwise, those beyond seventy would be considered overaged.

This act, then, served to rationalize and simplify military pensions. Physicians, it was asserted, would be spared needless examinations; the proper award could be allotted simply by noting the applicant's age.[14] Moreover, the law seemed a tangible expression of the widespread and growing categorization of senescence. According to the new provision, all elderly persons – not only the poor and ill – would be classified as too ancient and broken to remain self-sufficient.

In 1907, at the time the law was passed, the commander-in-chief of the Grand Army of the Republic (GAR) proudly took credit for establishing the close relationship between advanced age and total disability. At the twenty-seventh national encampment of the GAR, Commander-in-Chief Brown asserted that it was the veteran of the Civil War who had convinced society that old age was an incurable – and pensionable – disease.[15] Brown's claim, of course, was somewhat exaggerated. By the early twentieth century, the public seemed to need little convincing that old age was a distinctive and less than pleasant stage of existence. The realities of growing old in modern society had been repeatedly brought to national awareness. Social science journals related the elderly's ever-increasing dependence; physicians graphically depicted their seemingly incurable illnesses. The military pension, then, was only another element in the growing segregation of old age. By nature of its age-based regulations, it turned the old soldier and sailor – regardless of their actual physical condition – into superannuated persons.

But Brown also overstated the importance of the GAR; the military was not alone in awarding such pensions. In the late nineteenth and early twentieth centuries, large industries also began to grant annuities in the belief that all old persons could be classified as disabled. This assumption was written into the provisions of their pension plans; the aged employee was defined as too debilitated to continue working. These pensions, in fact, actually enforced this conception. Whereas the military pension plans assumed that the veteran would be unfit for labor, the business-sponsored programs dictated precisely when the laborer could no longer work. Once such plans were enacted by a company, all employees beyond a specified age were forced into retirement. These pensions, then, became more than a simple act of charity. By the early twentieth century, they had evolved into programs that would structure the life of the elderly worker.

*   *   *   *

The first old-age pensions were proposed by the American Express Company in 1875 and put into full operation by the Baltimore and Ohio (B&O) Railroad in 1884. Other transportation firms followed the B&O's lead, along with companies that dealt with mining, manufacturing, banking, and steel.[16] By 1910, forty-nine pension plans had been devised; in the next fifteen years, the number rose to about 370.[17] During this period, the companies that adopted these programs were among the nation's largest. In 1926, although 73 percent of the businesses with pensions had more than 1,000 workers, less than 1 percent of the firms in the United States had staffs this large; only 6 percent of all American companies employed more than 100 workers.[18] The firms with pensions, therefore, were markedly more complex and bureaucratically organized than most. Pensions, as we shall see, were part of this rationalization process. Through their adoption, they brought order and stability to the work force. Moreover, these early plans served as a model for future programs. Once other companies increased in size, they too incorporated measures that structured their work force; the process of bureaucratization was repeated many times. Thus, although most pension programs were adopted in the twentieth century, they rarely diverged from the early companies' design. In both form and effect, they reflected their nineteenth-century origins.

Railroads were innovators in developing plans that mandated the retirement of their workers. The lines' primary concern, though, was not the needs or desires of the elderly employee. Rather, they created these programs as a tool through which to exert control over their laborers. In the late nineteenth century, transportation executives confronted the country's best-organized and most powerful unions. Repeatedly, these brotherhoods had paralyzed the nation's business by calling for strikes that demonstrated great strength. In response, management turned to paternalistic welfare programs in the hope that they would pacify the workers and create a stable labor force. In 1877, for example, in the midst of the massive railroad strikes, the chairman of the board of the Chicago, Burlington, and Quincy Railroad made this reasoning explicit. In a letter to the line's president, J. N. A. Griswold explained the advantages of a relief program. "I think," Griswold wrote to Robert Harris:

> that the sooner these plans are elaborated and adopted the better, in order to show the men that while we will not submit to their dictation we still have their interests at heart and are desirous of making them understand that the interests of the corporation and their own are mutual.[19]

Old-age pensions became an essential part of these paternalistic plans. According to the provisions of most programs, the employee was required to work without interruption for a specified number of years, usually more than twenty or thirty. Upon reaching an advanced age, he could retire. After he attained a somewhat higher age, his departure became mandatory. He then received (in most cases) an annual pension of 1 percent of his average salary times the number of years he had been in the company's service. In making this stipulation, large companies often included a maximum age for hiring (usually between thirty-five and forty-five, though at times as low as thirty). Frequently, this measure was presented as a charitable consideration. The management would hardly feel morally justified in forcing an aged worker to retire who could not qualify for his pension.[20]

Few workers, however, considered these programs a demonstration of their company's charitable instinct. Unlike other types of relief programs that were often jointly run by both management and labor, pension funds remained firmly in the hands of the executives.[21] Workers neither contributed to their treasuries nor exerted any influence in their administration. This made the annuity a gift from the industrialist rather than a right earned through years of labor. The rules of the pension guaranteed that the laborer clearly understood this condition. Each plan included (in some form) a provision that read:

> No employee shall be considered to have a right to be retained in the service of the company, or any right or claim to any pension allowance, and the company expressly reserves its right and privilege to discharge any officer, agent or employee, when the interests of the company in its judgment may so require without any liability or any claim for a pension of their allowance other than salary or wages due and unpaid.[22]

To merit his pension, therefore, the worker had to adhere closely to any regulation set by the management. Thus, he could neither make demands upon the firm nor quit to find more profitable employment. Most laborers, however, had been highly mobile; in the nineteenth century, the work force as a whole was extremely unstable. The majority of men employed by the railroads, for example, worked less than six months before seeking a transfer.[23] Once retirement plans were established, such mobility was, to some extent, less profitable. Basing their level of compensation on length of service, rather than establishing a flat rate or one based on merit, late-nineteenth-century pension programs tied the worker's benefits directly to job stability. Despite offers of better jobs or higher wages from other companies, the laborer then had an interest in remaining in the same position. "The pension," one bank president declared, "operates repeatedly as an incentive to hold men between the ages of forty and fifty when they have acquired the experience and skill which makes them especially valuable and prevents their being tempted away by slightly increased wages for a temporary period."[24]

Nor could the employee act in any way that might disturb the management. As each pension plan stated, the laborer who disrupted the company or provoked the executives would lose his pension – as well as his job. Managements hoped that this would protect them against strikes. A worker, if he were anxious to receive an annuity in his old age, might be less willing to take part in a walkout. In addition, pensions offered the company a means of exerting control over the worker's daily behavior. His conduct, not only while on the job but also after hours, and even well into the years of his retirement, had to meet with management's approval if he expected to receive lifelong monthly payments. The First National Bank of Chicago, for example, which organized a pension fund in 1899, explained its definition of improper behavior explicitly. Although it established a mandatory program that automatically collected 3 percent of the employee's wages, the management retained firm control over its administration. A *partial* listing of actions that might cause revocation of the pension privilege read:

> In the event a pensioned officer or employee shall engage in any other employment without the consent of the establishment's permission the pension will be forfeited. Any clerk who marries on a salary of less than $1,000 a year without the consent of the establishment forfeits all benefit rights and is subject to dismissal from employment. In the case of bankruptcy of the pensioner, or of his taking the benefit of any insolvency law, or on his conviction for felony or misdemeanor, or on any judgment entered against, and in the case of any widow, in her misconduct being proved to the satisfaction of the bank, all benefit rights are forfeited, provided, however, that the establishment may, in its discretion, renew the pension for any of the reasons named. Unwarrantable losses for which any officer or employee is responsible may, if they do not result in his dismissal, result in his being punished in the discretion of the establishment by forfeiture of the offending officer's or employee's interest in the fund, beyond what he himself has contributed to it, without the interest. The benefits under the fund are not treated as vested rights; they are granted at the discretion of the establishment and continue only during the establishment's pleasure.[25]

The Grand Trunk Railway Company discovered an additional use for its pension. Although the general manager of the line praised its system before the World's Railway Commerce Congress of 1893 for its "relief of the individual from anxieties attendant upon the contemplation of the period of inability to provide for himself and his family,"[26] the worries of its aged employees were far from over. In 1915, when its aged workers went out on strike, the management proceeded to recall these retired wage earners. The choice it gave the men was simple: Either they return to work or they lost all benefits.[27] With the pension as a privilege, the employees would have to remain perpetually loyal to the firm.

Unions, therefore, viewed management-controlled pension plans with grave misgivings.[28] Not only did they attempt to regulate the daily behavior of the worker, but they placed an additional restriction on his future. According to these programs, when an employee reached a specified age, he was automatically retired. Although prior to this period, as we have seen, many workers had left the labor force because of injury or ill health, their departure had not been based solely on age. The benefits granted by the workers' own beneficial societies recognized this fact. Although they allocated funds for death, accident, or disability, the societies did not provide for the old worker who had merely decided to stop working. In the nineteenth century, the individual received aid if he was disabled. Otherwise, he was expected to obtain some type of employment.[29]

Traditionally, both management and labor had enacted measures to make the continued participation of the elderly possible. Some companies set aside less strenuous positions for the old and crippled. An elderly engineer might become keeper of the roundhouse; an old steelworker was transferred to the position of plant watchman.[30] On the Chicago, Burlington, and Quincy Railroad, for example, one limited freight line, the Chariton branch, was reserved for the elderly and disabled.[31] Often, trade unions further adjusted their regulations to suit the needs of their elderly members. According to an early-twentieth-century report of the commissioner of labor:

> Many of the local unions of the various national unions that do not feel justified, under present conditions, in establishing old-age benefits have had in operation for many years provisions that permitted the old member to work for a wage rate lower than the rate fixed for the younger member; in some local unions the member has been permitted to fix his own wage rate, the only condition being that he observe union rules. Many of the unions relieve the old member from the payment of all contributions except assessment for death benefits.[32]

Pensions that eliminated the old from the work force directly countered these measures. Yet, there was surprisingly little organized union resistance. In part, this was because the provisions created by the workers' societies for their elderly members did not keep the old worker employed. Even without mandatory age limitations, companies often released their workers when they advanced in age. Although most of these individuals remained in the labor force (and thus were not recorded as permanently unemployed or retired), they had difficulty obtaining new positions.[33] As we have seen, discrimination against hiring the old was not a late-nineteenth-century innovation. Barred from higher-paying jobs, many aged workers searched for employment as unskilled laborers.[34] At least with a pension, these individuals might escape dependency. Eventually, unions would also provide benefits for their members based on years of service and age. Although these plans did not demand that the worker retire and collect a pension, their adoption testified to the need to provide for an age-limited work cycle.[35]

But union opposition to retirement was muted for another reason as well. By accepting pensions, workers won an additional concession from their companies. A basic aspect of most pension plans was management's recognition of the seniority system. With employment practices based on years of service, workers felt that they could eliminate the most extreme cases of managerial favoritism and nepotism.[36] (Even today, these two issues remain vitally interrelated. Although the AFL–CIO opposes unilateral compulsory retirement, this condition is accepted when it is tied to the seniority system.)[37] Executives, in turn, saw advantages in accepting the plan. Although they lost some control over hiring, firing, and promotions, they secured the further stability of the work force. As Robert Harris, president of the Chicago, Burlington, and Quincy Railroad, explained to his board chairman in 1877:

> It will not be disputed that it was the influence of the older men to which we owed the fact that the men at Aurora did not participate in the late troubles. The plan proposed [of graduated wages based on length of service] would operate to make the older men still more conservative . . . [They would earn extra money] which they would lose if they gave occasion for their discharge. I think that the difficulty that the Boston & Providence people experienced would be met by having the rule apply to those employed on stated service in several departments.[38]

One drawback of this program, however, was the creation of a labor force staffed by older, highly paid workers. According to the seniority system, any cutback would first affect the newest workers, leaving their elders employed and collecting relatively high wages. In adopting pension plans, companies responded in part to this dilemma; most programs included a mandatory retirement age. With the tacit cooperation of the unions, the elderly laborer was automatically pensioned at seventy or sixty-five. His place – as well as his seniority – was vacated to make room for the promotion of the mid-level employee and the hiring of the younger worker.

Obviously, industrialists would not have included this provision if they had anticipated a labor shortage.[39] At the end of the nineteenth century, however, European and country-to-city migration created an abundant supply of labor. To many Americans, this seemingly limitless pool of would-be industrial workers was vivid proof that the United States needed to reassess its immigration policy.[40] To industrial entrepreneurs, however, these migrants represented an unlimited source of employees who could easily and cheaply replace their

118

higher-paid predecessors; they saw no need for immigration restriction. Thus, like middle-class reformers who had assigned available work to the young, industrialists followed a somewhat parallel course, setting strict age limits for the hiring and firing of workers. Through their pensions, they clearly marked the point at which productive maturity merged into incapacitated senescence.

Publicly, there was little opposition to this policy. Pensions, in fact, were entirely consistent with a growing emphasis in late-nineteenth-century thought on a need to measure and categorize man's physical and mental capabilities. Experts from many fields incorporated the latest medical and protosociological theories into their disciplines in an attempt to define the proper role for each individual in mass society. In its extreme form, this ideological outlook led eugenics authorities to demand the sterilization of the measurably imcompetent; only the most worthy were to sire future generations of Americans. Similarly, if somewhat less drastically, some labor experts rejected traditional laissez-faire principles in order to assure that work was given to the most fit.[41] In their self-consciously rational design for the labor market, they automatically excluded the aged worker regardless of individual health or abilities. The work of the economist and statistician, after all, had given credence to this idea. Citing the growing number of old persons in the almshouse, policy-oriented social scientists demanded that something be done. Both the Massachusetts and Pennsylvania Commissions endorsed standardized pension plans as the ideal solution to the seemingly ever-increasing dependence of the senescent.[42]

Many physicians also supported this notion. American medical theory, as we have seen, continued to conceive of the body as containing a limited amount of vital energy; once the supply was gone, the old man had little hope of competing with the younger worker. "The old man's bank is already overdrawn," wrote J. M. French in 1892. "He is living from hand to mouth."[43] Retirement, then, became part of the medically endorsed prescription for conserving the elderly's rapidly dissipating strength, "After sixty," admonished Dr. A. L. Loomis in 1888. "failure [of the old] to recognize the changing condition of the vital powers and continuance in their business habits of earlier life, after this period, are no better than suicide."[44]

Thus, when economic experts recommended the mandatory elimination of the old from the job market, they relied upon the professional authority of both social and medical science. In their works, retirement was presented as an ideal solution. It would ease the labor problem while protecting the declining strength of the elderly. Economist Francis A. Walker, for example, combined the language of the physician and the statistician in his discussion of senescence. Viewing the overcrowded labor market with concern, he called for the creation of "factory acts prohibiting the labor of all classes beyond the term which physiological science accepts as consistent with soundness and vigor."[45] This measure would not only relieve the intense competition for jobs but was in full accord with the physician's prescription for health and longevity. The elderly worker was advised to forget the "hurly-burly" of the active life and turn to rest and meditation. It was in his own best interest.[46]

As America entered the twentieth century, an additional rationale was used to promote the mandatory separation of old from young. Endorsers of pensions rephrased their arguments. They now not only presented their programs as highly ethical and benevolent but, in addition, legitimated them with that byword of the new industrial era: efficiency. In a period of increasing mechanical complexity, this had become a national craze. Efficiency experts invaded all fields and occupations, certain that they could bring rational order and simplicity to every human activity.[47] Armed with the omnipresent stopwatch, they set out to find the standard time needed for each job – that is, "the reasonable time for a good worker to accomplish the task set."[48] In their computations, experience and past knowledge were discounted, if not altogether disclaimed. The efficiency expert hoped to revolutionize work, systematically reeducating the laborer as to the proper way to do each task. Eventually, publicists for this position contended, the scientific manager would train employees who, like pieces of machinery, could be easily interchanged or, if need be, totally replaced. On the line, one leading efficiency authority asserted:

> the youngest member is as capable potentially as the highest, and whether he rises to supreme command in five years or forty-five depends on opportunity. When he has reached the age of retirement he gives way to a junior as one day gives way to another. There was nothing worth preserving, and the elimination of the temporary head produces a desirable wriggle of life all the way down the line.[49]

No expert would have disputed this assessment. The industrial pace, all agreed, used up the laborer, leaving him at sixty-five little more than a shell of his youthful self. In an era filled with tests and measures, however, this assumption remained unproved and significantly unexamined. Few, if any, correlations between age and efficiency were ever produced to convince the public of its validity.[50]

Instead, experts cited the 1873 study of Dr. George M. Beard, who, as we have seen, had crudely attempted to relate age to productivity. Beard's conclusion, that "on the average, the last twenty years of the lives of original geniuses are unproductive," was often repeated.[51] It seemed sufficient proof of the notion of senescent inefficiency.

In an overcrowded labor market, this became a generally accepted – and highly useful – conception. "Most employers," the president of the National City Bank of New York wrote, "regretfully acknowledge that it takes but a few years to use up a worker, so high is a pace at which work is now done. The employer is not to blame. He must keep his output up to the mark or be forced to the wall."[52] Such an assessment seemed especially applicable in the face of labor's growing demand for a shorter work day. In the late nineteenth and early twentieth centuries, unions were instrumental in reducing the daily hours from ten to eight. In industry after industry, management responded by investing in new technology and demanding greater productivity from all employees. The young, able to work at a rapid pace, then became highly valued laborers. In contrast, the old were judged obstacles to increased industrial output.[53]

One solution seemed clear enough: Replace the aged worker with young and efficient counterparts through a system of retirement benefits. Explained in these terms, the rationale for pensions had significantly altered. Previously, relief had been given to the totally disabled and dependent worker. His pension represented his only hope of escaping permanent almshouse residency. With pensions awarded chiefly to enhance the company's own efficiency, however, the definition of who should retire had considerably broadened. It now included not only those completely incapacitated, but all workers whose long years of service now seemed indisputable proof of their weakened and thus inefficient condition. These employees, efficiency experts cautioned, were just as much a threat to high production as the totally disabled. Their slower pace and reduced output only inhibited the standard rate of the other wage earners.[54] Pensions, therefore, became a "wise business practice," ridding firms of their overpaid and underproductive members – the "dead weight," as one executive elected to term them.[55] Thus, like military pensions, industrial plans of the early twentieth century had come to define all elderly workers as superannuated.

A similar conception of senescence was written into the first state and municipal civil service pensions.[56] In the late nineteenth and early twentieth centuries, while industrialists praised the economic merits of pensions and began to retire their employees, social analysts drew attention to federal, state, and city employees who daily served the public. They repeated the complaints voiced by businessmen. The retention of the old, they asserted, was simply a bad business practice. The Chicago police force, for example, was labeled by one official as an "asylum for old and decrepit men"; the New York City force was characterized as filled with "dead wood."[57] Such men were judged unfit to fill the dangerous roles they had assumed. The special dangers inherent in their positions called for great strength and ability.

Thus, adopting the language of the efficiency expert, policymakers set out to catalogue the waste evident in municipal jobs. Here, after all, were workers paid by taxes and expected to serve the public. Without a watchful industrialist to retire them when aged, and without a pension if they chose to retire voluntarily, municipal employees remained in their jobs far beyond their period of greatest usefulness. This, welfare experts cautioned, had important effects on everyone: Children were not getting the best education, fires and crimes received less than full attention, and clerks and laborers paid by the government were backward and inefficient.[58] Nowhere was this point made more clearly than in the influential *Report of the Massachusetts' Commission on Old Age Pensions, Annuities, and Insurance.* A model for other states, the Massachusetts report went to great lengths to document the inefficiency evident in just one sector of Boston's municipal services:

> The returns show the following facts regarding the number of pensionable employes, their length of service, compensation and efficiency:
>
> The total number of employes over sixty-five is 491; over seventy years, 168. The amount of compensation paid to employes over sixty-five is $419,888.43; over seventy, $273,000. The number over sixty-five reported as inefficient is 296. The compensation paid to this group is $200,194.35.
>
> The percentage of inefficient employes among the employes over sixty-five is strikingly large in many departments. For example, in the cleaning and watering division of the street department 35 are employed, of whom all are inefficient; in the cemetery department 16 persons over sixty-five are employed, of whom all are reported as inefficient; in the park department, 27 are employed of whom 24 are inefficient.
>
> The period of service is over 30 years in the case of 119 employes over sixty-five or 25 percent of the total. Only 5 per cent, or 42 persons, have been in the employ of the city less than five years.
>
> The leading departments, in respect to number of pensionable employes, rank as follows: 1) paving division of the street department, 109 over sixty-five years; 2) water department, 65; 3) sanitary division,

street department, 58; 4) sewer division, street department, 47; 5) cleaning and water division, street department, 34; 6) park division, 27; 7) ferry division, street department, 26; 8) cemetery department, 16.

Although the report indicated neither the measures used to determine inefficiency nor the number of substandard nonelderly laborers, its conclusion was clearly stated: The most economical solution was to pension off the inefficient and replace them with young, unemployed workers.[59]

Other surveys reported similar problems with superannuated employees. Even the Pension Bureau declared that it was overstaffed with the elderly. Before the enactment of age-based Civil War pensions, it had been bureau policy to hire the aged veteran. In 1903, however, its annual report declared that this program was detrimental to the office's efficiency. Of its 1,714 employees, nearly 500 were over sixty; the average age of all workers was fifty-three.[60] "Some law of retirement and provision must be devised," the annual report stated, "as the present system is too unsatisfactory and too expensive."[61]

Municipal workers generally supported the establishment of old-age annuities. Many had little hope of remaining financially independent on the basis of their savings. One teachers' group, for example, explained that their unique position left them with little extra money for their senescence. According to Elizabeth A. Allen, vice-principal of a grammar school, secretary of the New Jersey State Committee on Teachers' Pensions, and a member of the Board of Trustees of the New Jersey Public School Teachers' Retirement Fund, most teachers were single women who had few friends or relatives to support them. Moreover, she asserted, because they were women, they had received very small salaries. They therefore had little choice: Teachers either remained employed until they died or spent their final years as almshouse residents. It was only reasonable, she concluded, that such individuals should turn to the state for old-age assistance.[62]

Policemen and firemen also encouraged the creation of a pension system. The analogy with the military was repeatedly made; they too were soldiers fighting in the defense of the nation. Thus, if Civil War veterans received an annuity, those who battled in the "war against fire" or the "war on crime" deserved equal consideration.[63]

Often, however, municipal pension programs included a regulation that the employees had not approved: These plans dictated the age at which the individual had to retire. Now, not only the clearly disabled but all elderly workers would be forced into unemployment.

Almost every expert on retirement believed this age-restricting provision to be essential. In 1911, for example, when the Massachusetts commission presented a bill to the Commonwealth, it included the mandatory retirement of all workers past seventy. Voluntary retirement was permitted for those beyond sixty with fifteen years of service, or for those who had been employed for thirty-five consecutive years.[64] The commission had little worry that the man of fifty-five would retire still endowed with health and ability. "The number of employees," they wrote, "who would be eligible for retirement under the thirty-five years of service clause is so extremely small as to be a negligible factor."[65] Far more pressing to the Commonwealth, they asserted, was the fear that the superannuated worker would remain on its payrolls. Once pension plans were enacted and maximum age limits set, the inefficient senescent employee had no choice but to pass into retirement. Efficiency and welfare experts, therefore, joined economists and industrialists in endorsing age-based pensions as a humane response to widespread industrial problems. They agreed, after all, on the principle behind them: The young would find work and the elderly would attain security away from the almshouse. Thus, the pension system became a multifaceted solution: It offered financial aid to the unemployable old, work to the young, seniority to the unions, efficiency to the engineer, and stability and discipline to the employer. Moreover, this seemed a profitable solution for all; once production was no longer repressed by inefficient wage earners, the output of the country would multiply. "The effect of such a policy on the struggling millions of working people," prophesied Lee Welling Squier in his often-quoted study on old-age dependency, "would be little short of electric."[66] Retirement programs, he hoped, would rectify a host of social evils.

With this enthusiasm for the pension system came a recognition of a new, age-limited work cycle. The laborer was no longer expected to continue to work until permanently disabled but merely until he attained a particular age. Mandatory retirement and the age-based pensions that justified it both reflected and furthered this transformation. They not only arose out of changing ideas about the elderly's need and ability to work but legitimated the demand that the aged should no longer be employed.[67] These programs had become a tangible expression of society's less formal classification of its aged population. Advanced age clearly separated the senescent from the rest of the community. Regardless of health or abilities, all persons beyond sixty-five could be characterized as superannuated.

CONCLUSION

Old Age in a Bureaucratic Society

By the beginning of the twentieth century, the segregation of the aged had begun to assume institutional form. In the policies and asylums designed for the old, the last years of life were secluded from the turmoil of the industrial world. Beyond sixty-five, an individual was naturally thought to be antiquated; his age alone became clear proof of his superannuated state.

This conception has had a distinctive history, evolving with the nation's urban and industrial development. Even in colonial times, of course, certain people had been characterized as useless and over-aged. Their many years brought ridicule and shame; they received little of the biblically prescribed respect. But such judgments were individual and functional, not categorical. They were based on the clear inability of these persons to retain any valued resource.

Throughout the nineteenth century, this class of aged persons continued to exist, and, it seemed, in ever-increasing numbers. As the economic organization of society changed, a significant proportion of the old could not depend on the land to assure their status. As the life cycle was transformed, they were no longer guaranteed an important position within the nuclear family. Loss of parental authority, of occupation, and of wealth all defined the existence of the overaged.

The plight of these individuals then became the subject of wide professional concern. Beginning in the mid-nineteenth century, scores of charity workers, social theorists, doctors, and businessmen focused upon the unique problems of the senescent. The writings of these experts reflected the popular belief that in industrial society most aged persons could be considered to have little purpose. In their books, articles, and surveys, these authorities centered almost entirely upon the elderly who had lost the traditional sources of prestige. They uniformly depicted old age as a time when most men and women struggled vainly against dependence and disease. At the same time, the policies of these professionals further tended to segregate

125

the elderly from their communities. In the shared perspective of these experts, not only the poverty-stricken and ill but the majority of old persons had little of significance left to contribute. Their best course was to withdraw from the hurly-burly world. If they wished to retain their precious vital energy, they were admonished to seek medical assistance and retirement.

By the late nineteenth century, American physicians had formulated a model of aging that justified such advice. Noting the changed anatomy, physiology, and psychology of the old, doctors asserted that aging itself was a disease. The elderly had little hope of ever returning to the physical or mental state of the middle-aged. To treat these patients as they would the young, therefore, would be both futile and dangerous. Instead, once past the climacteric, the elderly required a distinctive regimen and specific senile therapeutics. Regardless of apparent health or capabilities, they were defined as the proper subjects of geriatric medicine.

Similarly, late-nineteenth-century charity workers and social theorists tended to divide their clients according to age. In their recommendations for assistance, the old were viewed as existing in a completely separate stage of the life cycle. Although professional social workers offered programs of reform through work and salvation to the adolescent and the middle-aged, they endorsed only retirement and institutionalization for the elderly. As their statistical surveys appeared to demonstrate, individuals over sixty-five had little in common with other needy groups. Their personalities were too well shaped for any promise of reform; their debilitated physical and mental states precluded future achievement. Unable to return to self-sufficiency, the elderly were advised to withdraw from active competition with the young.

These attitudes were then institutionalized in measures created to assist the old. Benevolent asylums, pension plans, and geriatric medicine all worked to remove the aged from industrialized society; they sought to shelter them in a world consciously devoid of the young. In their formulation, these programs reflected the experts' belief that the old had completed their years of productivity and usefulness. Retired from society or residing in an old-age home, they could only reflect on their many decades of toil and contemplate their uncertain destinies.

Yet, despite the seemingly pessimistic view of aging on which these measures were based, they had clearly been created to assist their beneficiaries. For the unemployed elderly, pensions were a means of escaping poverty; old-age homes were preferable to the squalor of the almshouse. In a very real sense, these programs reflected a genuine awareness of and concern for the plight of the aged. Once they were enacted, the ancient and broken among the old could escape the struggle for subsistence.

But these programs did more than simply rescue some of the aged poor from the confines of the poorhouse. In contrast to measures enacted during the colonial era, these policies rarely classified their aged recipients on the basis of their abilities, nor did they minister to the old together with the young and middle-aged. After the mid-nineteenth century, few elderly persons received piecework assignments or funds from charity organizations. Instead, destitute old men and women were likely to find themselves institutionalized with other members of the aged poor. And even those who might have remained employed and self-sufficient were affected by these newly developed measures. Throughout the late nineteenth and early twentieth centuries, growing numbers became subject to pension plans that removed them from the labor market. According to these programs, age, rather than actual condition, mandated their status and treatment. Once beyond sixty-five, the elderly were expected to enter a new stage of life; they had become recognizably superannuated.

The reliance upon chronological age, though, was not directed solely at the old, nor did it indicate a sudden decline in their prestige. Rather, the age restrictions written into these plans were simply part of a rational attempt by professionals to solve myriad national problems. In an era when urban and industrial growth seemed to magnify the complexity of society, age as a determining factor eliminated many uncertainties. It became an acceptable barometer of one's position in the world. With each passing year, the person moved through planned stages; age, rather than individual needs or differences, prescribed ideal progress. For the young, such a philosophy translated into the precisely structured schoolroom classes. By the mid-nineteenth century, children in large urban areas were placed in grades according to their chronological ages. For the old, a similar categorization took place, if at a slightly later date.[1] By the early twentieth century, America's aged population had begun to feel the effects of sweeping age-based regulations.

These programs and policies, then, must be understood as part of the growing bureaucratization of America. In an era of seemingly unlimited expansion, they were adopted to structure the life course of the mass of individuals. Once pension plans and seniority systems were enacted, for example, the average laborer knew precisely when he would be promoted and fired. It was hardly coincidental that the first companies to enact these policies were also the nation's largest. The size of these firms had outdated the traditional personal solutions to the elimination of the debilitated worker. The board of trustees of the Baltimore and Ohio Railroad or even the First National Bank of Chicago had little hope of knowing each man on their staff. No benevolent manager could oversee every individual's work and decide when his debilitated state detracted from the quality of the labor force. Rather, such firms tended to categorize their employees. On the railroad line, as in the manufacturing plant, a worker's seniority dictated his salary and his position until he reached the age of retirement. He was then automatically removed from employment. His many years had become the most obvious – and least personal – indication that his ability to work had ended.

A similar system of classification was adopted by organizations and institutions deluged by applications. By the early twentieth century, many groups found it far more efficient to set precise criteria for their target populations than to deal with persons on an individual basis. Among charity organization societies, for instance, age became a convenient guide; it was used to assess a person's worth and capabilities. As a result, groups such as the New York Association for Improving the Condition of the Poor could easily and quickly reject any candidate over sixty. The philanthropists saw the individual's advanced age as a sure indication of future uselessness. Adopting the same philosophy – if to an opposite end – managers of many old-age homes required their charges to be at least sixty-five, and military boards tied the size of their pensions to the soldiers' precise age. Once this was done, social workers would no longer have to spend countless hours investigating every case; doctors would not have to determine the cause of each person's debilitated state. Instead, the individual's advanced years marked the precise point at which he should retire from society.

Throughout the nineteenth century, though, this bureaucratic system of classifying the elderly still directly affected only a limited number of persons. By 1910, just forty-nine companies had established pension plans; only 2 percent of the elderly were sheltered in old-age homes.[2] Most old persons continued to live in rural areas, reliant upon their own labor, their possessions, and the support of their families. But as the twentieth century progressed, these measures would have increasing impact. After 1910, as the majority of Americans became urban dwellers and industrial workers, they would find themselves subject to the age restrictions written into these regulations. By 1930, 434 companies had established pension plans; 69,000 persons were housed in 1,268 private asylums for the elderly.[3] And during the Great Depression, the policy of assuming that all old persons were overaged and outdated gained national recognition. In 1935, Congress enacted a social security program based on the notion that at sixty-five every worker would retire and collect a pension. Simultaneously, and quite consciously, this act served to rationalize the labor force.[4] In a period of massive unemployment, it removed the old from competition with the young and justified their jobless condition.[5] This, after all, was hardly a new idea. Social reformers of the middle and late nineteenth century had stressed similar remedies for an overcrowded job market. The programs of both the fledgling professionals and the New Dealers promised the young employment and the old "social security" away from the ominous almshouse.

In recent years, there has been little question of the great impact of these age-based measures and the beliefs on which they are based. By 1970, three-quarters of all men over sixty-five were retired; approximately 1 million old persons were housed in nursing institutions.[6] It has become a widely shared expectation that the old will require specialized care and attention. The irony of these policies and ideas, though, is that in attempting to assist the poverty-stricken and ailing, they have ensured the dependence of a large proportion of the elderly. The measures mandate the separation of the old from the very factors that once guaranteed their continued prestige. Housed in an "old folks" home or retired on a small pension, the elderly have little hope of controlling their work, family, or possessions. As a result, the entire age group (and not just the 15.7 percent that live below the poverty line) has acquired the characteristics of the colonial era's ancient and broken.[7] And not surprisingly, like that eighteenth-century group of aged persons, they too receive little respect. But this is not simply because we live in a youth-oriented society or one that at some point had suddenly come to detest the aged. Rather, over the course of a century, demographic and economic realities have combined with professional policies to enforce the powerlessness of old age. Once beyond sixty-five, most persons are bureaucratically characterized as diseased and dependent. This age-based conception of senescence has a distinctive history. In the evolving scale and nature of society and its modes of organization lie our modern notion of what it means to be overaged.

Notes

Introduction. Classifying Society's Superannuated

1 Leo W. Simmons, "Aging in Preindustrial Societies," in *Handbook of Social Gerontology*, ed., Clark Tibbitts (Chicago: University of Chicago Press, 1960), p. 87.

2 Leo W. Simmons, *The Role of the Aged in Primitive Societies* (New Haven, Conn.: Yale University Press, 1945), p. 54.

3 Ibid., pp. 235–6.

4 Ibid., pp. 226, 236.

5 For a differing view, see David Hackett Fischer, *Growing Old in America* (New York: Oxford University Press, 1977), chap. 1, "The Exaltation of Age in Early America." As the title of the chapter suggests, Fischer believes that the old were venerated in colonial America as symbols of authority and godliness. The hierarchical nature of society, as well as the comparative rareness of the elderly, contributed to their high status. There are, however, a number of problems with this interpretation. First, Fischer concedes that not every old person in colonial America was idolized. "To be old and poor and outcast in America," he writes, "was not to be venerated but rather despised" (p. 60). According to Fischer, in fact, a number of exceptions to the rule of veneration of age existed. Yet, as we shall see in Chapter 1 of this study, these paradoxical contradictions may be both more extensive and more important than his study suggests. Second, the fact that the elderly were "comparatively rare" (p. 29) does not explain their prestige. According to Leo W. Simmons, in few preindustrial societies was more than 3 percent of the population over sixty. Yet within these cultures, the range of sentiments was broad; the scarcity of the old, in fact, did not assure them respect or veneration. Simmons, "Aging in Preindustrial Societies," p. 67.

6 Cotton Mather, *The Diary of Cotton Mather*, vol. 2 (Boston: Massachusetts Historical Society, 1912), pp. 194, 219, 222, 225, 235, 653.

7 Joseph Lathrop, *The Infirmities and Comforts of Old Age: A Sermon to Aged People* (Springfield, Mass: Henry Brewer, 1805).

8 William Harlan, "Isolation and Conduct in Later Life," (unpublished Ph.D. diss., University of Chicago, 1950), pp. 225, 234; cited in Zena Smith Blau, *Old Age in a Changing Society* (New York: Franklin Watts, Inc., 1973), p. 155.

9   The transition from old to overaged based on a loss of power and authority is certainly not unique to America. It has, of course, been captured in English literature in Shakespeare's play *King Lear*. For an analysis of this drama's portrayal of Lear's transition to an overaged man and the effect it had upon his relationships with his children, see Blau, *Old Age in a Changing Society*, chap. 3.

10   Recent studies have illustrated the difficulties inherent in attempting to date precisely such a radical transformation in attitudes. Compare, for example, the conclusion of David Hackett Fischer, who finds that between 1770 and 1820 there was a "revolutionary change" in age relations (Fischer, *Growing Old in America*, p. 101), with the belief of W. Andrew Achenbaum that the period between 1865 and 1914 "constitutes an important transition in the history of ideas about growing old" (Achenbaum, *Old Age in the New Land* [Baltimore and London: Johns Hopkins University Press, 1978], p. 39). Both historians, I believe, overlook the negative attitudes toward age that existed before their selected "crucial" periods. This omission allows them to discern a radical and sudden change in American social perceptions: Once, the aged were all adored; later, whether in revolutionary or post–Civil War America, they became ostracized and hated. Even in Achenbaum's own publications, this difficulty in dating becomes obvious. In an earlier study, he places the transformation in the 1880s (Achenbaum, "The Obsolescence of Old Age in America, 1865–1914," *The Journal of Social History*, 8 [Fall, 1974], pp. 48–62). As this study will show, however, there have always been old persons whose age brought them ridicule and contempt. For a further debate over the difficulties in placing a precise date on this change, see Lawrence Stone, "Walking over Grandma," *New York Review of Books*, 24, no. 8 (May, 1977), pp. 10ff; David Hackett Fischer, "Growing Old: An Exchange," *New York Review of Books*, 24, no. 14 (September, 1977), p. 48.

11   As late as 1890, only 26.2 percent of all elderly workers considered themselves permanently nonemployed. I. M. Rubinow, *Social Insurance* (New York: Henry Holt & Co., 1913), p. 305.

12   Abraham Epstein, *The Problem of Old Age Pensions in Industry* (Harrisburg, Pa: Pennsylvania Old Age Commission, 1926), pp. 115–16.

13   Frederick L. Hoffman, "State Pensions and Annuities in Old Age," *Journal of the American Statistical Association*, 11 new series, no. 85 (March, 1909), p. 396. Almost as soon as old-age homes were established, they were deluged by applicants. Certainly, such residences were preferable to the shelter of the almshouse. For a further discussion of the development of this institution, see Chapter 5.

14   In 1970, only about one in four of all American men over the age of sixty-five held full-time employment. United States Department of Commerce, Bureau of the Census, *Detailed Characteristics*, United States Summary (Washington, D.C.: Government Printing Office, 1970), Table 215. In 1970, there were about 24,000 nursing homes housing about 1 million elderly persons. It has been estimated that about 20 percent of the old will seek residence in a nursing home sometime during their

lives. This figure does not include the millions who will be hospitalized prior to death. Robert N. Butler, *Why Survive?* (New York: Harper & Row, 1975), p. 273.

15 For two recent studies that look at images of old age in nineteenth-century philosophy and literature, see Thomas R. Cole, "Past Meridian: Aging and the Northern Middle Class, 1830–1930," (unpublished Ph.D. diss., University of Rochester, 1980); Jane Range and Maris A. Vinovskis, "Images of Elderly in Popular Magazines: A Content Analysis of *Littell's Living Age*, 1845–1882," *Social Science History*, 5, no.2 (Spring, 1981), pp. 123–70.

1. Aging in Colonial America

1 Increase Mather, *Two Discourses* (Boston: B. Green, 1716), p. 120.

2 David Hackett Fischer, *Growing Old in America* (New York: Oxford University Press, 1977), Appendix, Tables I, p. 222, II, p. 223; United States Bureau of the Census, *Historical Statistics of the United States* (Washington, D.C., Government Printing Office, 1960), p. 11, A86–94; Robert V. Wells, *The Population of the British Colonies in North America before 1776* (Princeton, N.J.: Princeton University Press, 1975), pp. 116–18.

3 Samuel Willard, *A Compleat Body of Divinity in Two Hundred and Fifty Expository Lectures on the Assembly's Shorter Catechism* (Boston: B. Eliot and D. Henchman, 1726), Sermon 180, p. 617.

4 Increase Mather, *Dignity and Duty of Aged Servants of the Lord* (Boston: B. Green, 1716), p. 52.

5 Fischer, *Growing Old in America*, pp. 48–52; Robert Gross, *The Minutemen and Their World* (New York: Hill & Wang, Inc., 1976), p. 62.

6 Cotton Mather, *Addresses to Old Men and Young Men and Little Children* (Boston: R. Pierce, 1690). Increase Mather also noted that the young often ridiculed the old for their weaknesses. In *Two Discourses*, he wrote:

To deride aged persons because of those natural infirmities which age has brought upon them is a great sin. It may be they are become weak and childish; they that laugh at them on that account, perhaps if they should live to their great age will be as childish as they. And would they be willing to be made a laughing stock by those that are younger than they? (p. 99)

7 Zena Smith Blau, *Old Age in a Changing Society* (New York: Franklin Watts, Inc., 1973), pp. 209–45. As Blau notes, the loss of these crucial roles has a serious effect upon the individual: "Marital, filial, and occupational relationships become the anchoring points of adult identity, particularly if the individual lacks other role resources that can extend the range of his influence and of the social influences that form and sustain his identity" (p. 213). As we shall see, this was as true in eighteenth-century America as it is today.

8 For a different opinion, see Fischer, *Growing Old in America*, pp. 26–76.

9 Robert V. Wells, "Demographic Change and the Life Cycle of American Families," in *The Family in History*, eds., Theodore K. Rabb and Robert

I. Rotberg (New York: Harper & Row, 1971), p. 87, Table I, p. 93; see also Fischer, *Growing Old in America*, Appendix, Table VI, p. 228.

10 Wells, "Demographic Change," p. 89; Fischer, *Growing Old in America*, p. 228.

11 For the life cycle of the Willings and the Binghams, see Robert C. Alberts, *The Golden Voyage: The Life and Times of William Bingham, 1753–1804* (Boston: Houghton Mifflin Company, 1969), esp. pp. 92, 95–6, 113, 129, 363, 394; Thomas Willing, "His Autobiography," in Burton Alva Konkle, *Thomas Willing and the First American Financial System* (Philadelphia: University of Pennsylvania Press, 1937), pp. 117–18. Of Willing's thirteen children, ten survived childhood.

12 Edmund S. Morgan, *The Puritan Family* (New York: Harper & Row, 1966), chap. 3.

13 Allan Kulikoff, "Tobacco and Slaves: Population, Economy, and Society in Eighteenth-Century Prince George's County, Maryland" (unpublished Ph.D. diss., Brandeis University, 1976), pp. 57–60; Daniel Scott Smith, "Old Age and the 'Great Transformation': A New England Case Study," in *Aging and the Elderly*, eds., Stuart F. Spicker, Kathleen M. Woodward, and David D. Van Tassel (Atlantic Highlands, N.J.: Humanities Press, Inc., 1978), pp. 294–5; Daniel Scott Smith, "Parental Power and Marriage Patterns: An Analysis of Historical Trends in Hingham, Massachusetts," *Journal of Marriage and the Family*, 35 (August, 1973), pp. 419–28.

14 Smith, "Old Age and the 'Great Transformation,'" p. 291.

15 Philip J. Greven, Jr., *Four Generations: Population, Land, and Family in Colonial Andover, Massachusetts* (Ithaca, N.Y., and London: Cornell University Press, 1970); see also Fischer, *Growing Old in America*, pp. 51–4.

16 Kulikoff, "Tobacco and Slaves," p. 139.

17 John Demos, "Old Age in Early New England," in *The American Family in Social-Historical Perspective*, 2nd ed., ed., Michael Gordon (New York: St. Martin's Press, Inc., 1978), pp. 236–7; Smith, "Old Age and the 'Great Transformation,'" p. 295; John J. Waters, "Patrimony, Succession, and Social Stability: Guilford, Connecticut in the Eighteenth Century," *Perspectives in American History*, 10 (1976), pp. 157–8.

18 Greven notes that among the first generation of settlers in Andover, only two fathers divided their land completely before their death; seven gave one son part of their land in the form of a deed, whereas the rest of the children had to await their fathers' death; two gave deeds to more than one son; and fourteen held all of their land until death. "For the great majority of the second generation," Greven writes, "inheritances constituted the principal means of transferring the ownership of land from one generation to the next." *Four Generations*, pp. 82–3.

19 Fischer, *Growing Old in America*, pp. 56–7; Wells, *Population of the British Colonies*, p. 131.

20 *Probate Records of Essex County Massachusetts*, Will No. 66, cited by Greven, *Four Generations*, p. 142. J. H. Plumb notes that until the seventeenth century, "the word 'child' expressed kinship, not an age

133

state." Plumb, "The Great Change in Children," in *Rethinking Childhood*, ed., Arlene Skolnick (Boston and Toronto: Little, Brown and Company, 1976), p. 205. The dependence of a son defined the relationship and the roles of the generations. This status took precedence over the age of either the father or the son.

21 Kulikoff, "Tobacco and Slaves," pp. 57–60.

22 Greven, *Four Generations*, chaps. 7 and 8.

23 Ibid., p. 229.

24 *A Report of the Record Commissioners of the City of Boston containing Miscellaneous Papers* (Boston: Rockwell & Churchill, City Printers, 1886), City Document 150 (1707), p. 152.

25 This seemed to be an established way for the old to support themselves, both in Philadelphia and in Boston. For some other examples from Philadelphia, see *Court Papers, Philadelphia County*, manuscripts located at the Historical Society of Pennsylvania, pp. 69, 76, 85, 87, 90. It should be noted that in every case the aged individuals declared themselves to be official inhabitants of the city.

26 *Minutes of the Common Council of the City of Philadelphia* (Philadelphia: Select and Common Councils of the City of Philadelphia, 1847), p. 490, November 26, 1747.

27 Ibid., pp. 445 (1745), 487 (1747), 521 (1749), 556 (1752). In almost all cases, the standard fine of five pounds was remitted due to the age and condition of the defendant. This, however, did not always occur. In the case of Margaret Read, for example, who was fined for keeping a "Publick House" without a license, the penalty remained, despite the fact that she claimed to be "old and poor." March 21, 1751, p. 534.

28 Fischer, *Growing Old in America*, p. 47.

29 Demos, "Old Age in Early New England," p. 242; Smith, "Old Age and the 'Great Transformation,'" pp 293–4.

30 Smith, "Old Age and the 'Great Transformation,'" p. 293.

31 Fischer states that the order of seating in meetinghouses was one sign of the esteemed position of the aged. *Growing Old in America*, pp. 38–40. More recently, however, this piece of evidence has been questioned. John Demos, for example, has suggested that wealth, rather than age, was given greatest weight in creating the seating plan. In the front row of the Hampton, New Hampshire, meetinghouse, for instance, was Thomas Ward, age thirty-one; his extreme wealth was responsible for his position of high status. Similarly, at the rear of the meetinghouse was William Cole, age seventy-nine. Although one of the oldest residents in town, he was also one of the poorest. Demos, "Old Age in Early New England," pp. 245–7. See also Lawrence Stone, "Walking over Grandma," *New York Review of Books*, 24, no. 8 (May, 1977), p. 12; Smith, "Old Age and the 'Great Transformation'", pp. 291–2.

32 Maris A. Vinovskis, "'Aged Servants of the Lord': Changes in the Status and Treatment of Elderly Ministers in Colonial America," paper given at the AAAS Symposium on "Aging from Birth to Death: Socio-Temporal Perspectives," Toronto, January, 1981.

33 Cotton Mather, *Diary of Cotton Mather*, vol. 2 (Boston: Massachusetts

Historical Society, 1912), p. 617. It is, of course, dangerous to take Increase Mather as representative, for his temperament and his position made him an unusual figure in colonial history. He had a tendency to find fault with a great many aspects of his life – including his treatment in senescence. Other important old persons as well, however, suffered in their final years. Benjamin Franklin, George Washington, John Adams, and Thomas Jefferson all voiced complaints about the physical and emotional discomforts that came with growing old. Although David Hackett Fischer explains this unhappiness as the result of their relative isolation, I believe that there are other reasons for the elderly's complaints. Fischer, after all, has suggested that one reason old age was respected was that "it was comparatively rare" (p. 29). The isolation of the old, therefore, should not have occurred; the elderly should have been valued and remained an active part of society. For many old persons – even the most powerful – this did not happen. In old age, as Fischer recognizes, these individuals were quite unhappy. Their discontent, I would suggest, arose out of the difference between their expectation of how they should be treated and their actual experience. In senescence, they were increasingly segregated from society. Fischer, *Growing Old in America*, pp. 67–8; see also Thomas R. Cole, "Past Meridian: Aging and the Northern Middle Class, 1830–1930" (unpublished Ph.D. diss., University of Rochester, 1980), pp. 207–10.

34 Cotton Mather, *Diary of Cotton Mather*, vol. 2, p. 181; see also pp. 194, 195, 196, 246, 280.

35 Ibid., pp. 186, 219, 222, 236.

36 Increase Mather, *Two Discourses*, p. 134.

37 Ibid.

38 Demos, "Old Age in Early New England," 242.

39 The only widely adopted age-based restrictions applied to military service. In these cases, it was generally the rule that a man beyond the age of sixty did not have to serve. See, for example, Charles J. Hoadley, ed., *Records of the Colony on Jurisdiction of New Haven* (Hartford, Conn.: Case, Lockwood and Company, 1858), p. 602. It was not unusual, however, for the person's physical condition, rather than his age, to be the determining factor in military regulations. Many times, it seemed, those well past the age of sixty continued to serve. See, for examples, *Records of the Suffolk County Court, Part II*, vol. 30 (Boston: Publications of the Colonial Society of Massachusetts, 1933), pp. 837, 910, 915, 1019, 1025, 1066.

40 As John Demos has pointed out, "Men past sixty voluntarily reduced their activities in work and/or public service." As he notes, this was usually a gradual, rather than a sudden, process. As the infirmities of age increased, they limited the participation of the old in both family and community affairs. Demos, "Old Age in Early New England," pp. 240–4.

41 Samuel Sewall, *The Diary of Samuel Sewall, 1674–1729*, Collections of the Massachusetts Historical Society, 5, ser. 5 (Boston: Massachusetts Historical Society, 1878), pp. 168, 359–60, 382.

42 Ibid., p. 358.
43 Ibid., p. 8.
44 Cotton Mather, *A Brief Essay on the Glory of Aged Piety* (Boston: S. Kneeland and T. Freen, 1726), p. 28.
45 Cotton Mather, for example, always attempted to find worthy pastimes for the elderly in order to keep them occupied. In his *Diary* in 1713, for example, he wrote:

> I observe diverse, especially Elder, men in the Town, who have little Business to do, I would insinuate myself into their Conversation; and project with them, and suggest to them, those Methods, with which they may improve their Leisure-time in doing Abundance of Good. Especially in visiting and counselling and comforting the Afflicted, and finding out the Indigent. (Vol. 2, p. 240)

46 Ella Chelfant, *A Goodly Heritage: Earliest Wills on an American Frontier* (Pittsburgh: University of Pittsburgh Press, 1955), p. 35; Demos, "Old Age in Early New England," p. 238.
47 Demos, "Old Age in Early New England," p. 238.
48 Will of Adam Deemes, 1798, reprinted, in part, in Chelfant, *A Goodly Heritage*, p. 35.
49 Alexander Keyssar, "Widowhood in Eighteenth-Century Massachusetts: A Problem in the History of the Family," *Perspectives in American History*, 8 (1974), p. 108.
50 A story in *Shakespeare's Jest-Books*, recorded by the Brothers Grimm, vividly portrays the plight of the parent who gave all his property to his children, failing to reserve any power for himself. According to the tale of the old man of Monmonth:

> After the deed was made, awhile the old man sat at the upper end of the table; afterwards, they sat him lower, about the middle third of the table; next at the table's end; and then among the servants' and last of all, they made him a couch behind the door and covered him with the old sackcloth, where, in his grief and sorrow, the old man died. When the old man was buried, the young man's eldest child said unto him: "I pray you, father, give me this old sackcloth." "What wouldst thou do with it?" said his father. "Forsooth," said the boy, "it shall serve to cover you as it did my old grandfather."

> Pasquil's Jest (1604), in *Shakespeare's Jest-Books*, ed., W. C. Hazlitt, cited by Keith Thomas, *Age and Authority in Early Modern England* (London: British Academy, 1976), p. 36.

51 Waters, "Patrimony, Succession, and Social Stability," p. 147; Keyssar, "Widowhood in Eighteenth-Century Massachusetts," pp. 98, 109.
52 Cotton Mather, *The Widow of Nain* (Boston, 1728), pp. 10–11, cited by Keyssar, "Widowhood in Eighteenth-Century Massachusetts," p. 99.
53 Smith, "Old Age and the 'Great Transformation,'" p. 297.
54 Wells, *Population of the British Colonies in America*, p. 132. In England in the eighteenth century, Peter Laslett has found a similar proportion of elderly nonhousehold heads. That is, 17 percent of all men and 22 per-

cent of all women were living in households other than their own. Laslett, *Family Life and Illicit Love in Earlier Generations* (Cambridge: Cambridge University Press, 1977), p. 105.

55 John Wesley, cited by Philip Greven, *The Protestant Temperament* (New York: Alfred A. Knopf, Inc., 1977), p. 27. This sentiment was also voiced a century and a half earlier by John Robinson, who wrote that "children brought up with their grandfathers or grandmothers seldom do well, but are usually corrupted by too great indulgence." Robert Ashton, ed., *Works of John Robinson*, vol. 1 (Boston: Doctrinal Tract and Book Society, 1851), p. 246.

56 *A Report of the Record Commissioners of the City of Boston containing Miscellaneous Papers*, City Document 150 (May 3, 1692), p. 62.

57 *A Report of the Record Commissioners of the City of Boston containing Boston Records from 1660–1701* (Boston: Rockwell & Churchill, City Printers, 1881), City Document 68 (1682); *A Report of the Record Commissioners of the City of Boston containing Boston Records from 1700–1728* (Boston: Rockwell & Chruchill , City Printers, 1882), City Document 77 (1722).

58 Thomas Foxcroft, *The Character of Anna* (Boston: Kneeland, 1723), p. 56.

59 Willard, *A Compleat Body of Divinity*, Sermon 180, p. 617.

60 Cotton Mather, *Addresses*, p. 37.

61 *A Report of the Record Commissioners of the City of Boston containing the Records of the Boston Selectmen 1701–1715* (Boston: Rockwell & Churchill, City Printers, 1884), p. 68.

62 John Demos, *A Little Commonwealth: Family Life in Plymouth Colony* (New York: Oxford University Press, 1970), p. 152; Michael Zuckerman, *Peaceable Kingdoms: New England Towns in the Eighteenth Century* (New York: Random House, 1970), p. 116. For a somewhat less extreme view of the lack of privacy in colonial life, see David H. Flaherty, *Privacy in Colonial New England* (Charlottesville: University Press of Virginia, 1972), esp. the introduction and chap. 2.

63 In eighteenth-century England, Peter Laslett found that the elderly who could afford to live apart did so. Wealth, he believed, allowed both aged parents and young adults greater independence. Laslett, *Family Life and Illict Love*, pp. 212–13.

64 Willard, *A Compleat Body of Divinity*, Sermon 64, p. 608.

65 *The Acts of Assembly of the Province of Pennsylvania Carefully Compared with the Originals and an Appendix . . .* (Philadelphia: Assembly of the Province of Pennsylvania, 1775), p. 160.

66 *A Report of the Record Commissioners of the City of Boston containing the Records of the Boston Selectmen 1701–1715*, p. 57; *A Report of the Record Commissioners of the City of Boston containing Miscellaneous Papers*, p. 113. For a similar case involving one William Smalcon, see *A Report of the Record Commissioners of the City of Boston containing the Records of the Boston Selectmen from 1716–1736* (Boston: Rockwell & Churchill, City Printers, 1885), City Document 77 (October 28, 1720), p. 76. The influx of a large group of elderly individuals into any community would be viewed with great dismay and fear rather than with great favor. In 1714, for example, the selectmen of Boston wrote to the governor to object to the arrival

of elderly individuals who had been dismissed from the military service. "Some among them," they wrote, are "aged or otherwise Infirm So as in likely hood [sic] they may become a further charge. Praying them So to order and direct that the burden of that charge may not lie upon ye Inhabitants of Boston." *A Report of the Record Commissioners of the City of Boston containing the Records of the Boston Selectmen 1701–1715*, 1714.

67 Cotton Mather, *Diary of Cotton Mather*, vol. 2, p. 208. For numerous other examples of Mather's concern and aid to deserted, poor old persons, see pp. 42, 44–5, 145–6, 152, 160, 228, 247, 253, 257, 272, 277, 344, 348, 364, 576, 606, 676, 763, 717.

68 See, for example, the rents paid to "old Mrs. Moore" on June 26, 1707, in *A Report of the Record Commissioners of the City of Boston containing Miscellaneous Papers*, p. 177.

69 David J. Rothman, *The Discovery of the Asylum: Social Order and Disorder in the New Republic* (Boston and Toronto: Little, Brown and Company, 1971), pp. 36, 38, 39.

70 In some large cities, the overseers of the poor attempted to separate the worthy poor from those undeserving of sympathy and comfort. In 1715, in Boston:

the overseers of the Poor with the Advise and Concurrence to the Town, Relating to makeing [sic] a division of the present Almes House & work House, So as to Accomodate Sober and aged People by themselves, and yet those put in for Vice and disorder may be Separate [sic] from them.

A Report of the Record Commissioners of the City of Boston containing the Boston Records from 1700–1728, p. 112. In Philadelphia, a similar move was made by an act of the legislature. The poor laws were modified to separate children and old persons in the almshouse from vagrants. The justices of the peace were to place vagabonds in the House of Employment. The presence of these persons in the almshouse had been a "nuisance" to children:

while the more advanced in years, to whom nothing worst than poverty or disease could be imputed, and to alleviate whose distresses the first contributions to the House of Employment were made, were confounded, with the rogues, the vagabonds and the culprits. Thus this public charity, intended to be a decent and respectable abode for the poor and infirm, was converted into a place of tumult, disorder and punishment.

Memorial to the Legislature, 1797, quoted by Charles Lawrence, *History of the Philadelphia Almshouses and Hospitals* (Philadelphia: Charles Lawrence, 1905), pp. 39–40.

71 As Maris A. Vinovskis points out, it is important to realize that attitudes toward age do evolve even in the colonial era. As the correlation of old age, wealth, and social standing changes with the division of land, veneration of the old is transformed. Vinovskis, "'Aged Servants of the Lord,'" p. 7; see also Greven, *Four Generations*.

72 Demos, "Old Age in Early New England," p. 245.
73 In 1751, there were also thirty-four outdoor pensioners receiving city relief. Gary B. Nash, "Poverty and Poor Relief in Pre-Revolutionary Philadelphia," *William and Mary Quarterly*, 33, 3rd ser. (January, 1977), pp. 6, 9; Lawrence, *Philadelphia Almshouses and Hospitals*, p. 43.
74 Priscilla F. Clement, "The Response to Need: Poverty and Welfare in Philadelphia, 1800–1850," (unpublished Ph.D. diss., University of Pennsylvania, 1977), p. 179.
75 Ibid., p. 108.
76 Ibid., pp. 64–5, 87.

2. Social Realities and Perceptions of Old Age in the Nineteenth Century

1 W. Andrew Achenbaum, *Old Age in the New Land* (Baltimore: Johns Hopkins University Press, 1978), p. 60.
2 Carl Deglar, *At Odds: Women and the Family in America from the Revolution to the Present* (New York: Oxford University Press, 1980), p. 181; David Hackett Fischer, *Growing Old in America* (New York: Oxford University Press, 1977), p. 228.
3 Peter Uhlenberg, "Changing Configurations of the Life Course," in *Transitions: The Family and the Life Course in Historical Perspective*, ed., Tamara K. Hareven, (New York: Academic Press, Inc., 1978), p. 89; Tamara K. Hareven, "The Last Stage: Historical Adulthood and Old Age," *Daedalus*, 105, no. 4 (Fall, 1976), pp. 17–18.
4 Warren S. Thompson and P. K. Whelpton, *Population Trends in the United States* (New York: Gordon & Breach, Science Publishers, 1969), p. 279. In Providence, R. I., in 1880, the average number of children among native childbearing women, ages thirty-six to forty-six, had fallen to 2.62; by 1915, it was 2.33. Howard P. Chudacoff, "The Life Course of Women: Age and Age Consciousness, 1865–1915," *The Journal of Family History*, 5, no. 3 (Fall, 1980), p. 286.
5 As Daniel Scott Smith has shown, the number of living children an elderly couple had directly affected their living situation. Only 39.5 percent of the couples that had one living child still resided with the child after the wife reached sixty-five. For those with four or more children, the proportion rose to 67 percent. Smith, "Life Course, Norms, and the Family System of Older Americans in 1900," *The Journal of Family History*, 4, no. 3 (Fall, 1979), p. 293.
6 Howard P. Chudacoff and Tamara K. Hareven, "Family Dissolution: Life Course Transitions into Old Age," *The Journal of Family History*, 4, no. 1 (Spring, 1979), p. 72.
7 In rural areas in the nineteenth century, parents who were still able to use the land to promise employment and an inheritance were far more likely to reside with their children than were sharecroppers or tenants. Daniel Scott Smith, Michel Dahlin, and Mark Friedberger, "The Family Structure of the Older Black Population in the American South in 1880 and 1900," *Sociology and Social Research*, 63 (April, 1979), pp. 544–63.

8 *Eleventh Census of the United States (1890): Housing.* "Report on Farms and Homes: Proprietorship and Indebtedness," (Washington, D.C.: Government Printing Office, 1895), pp. 216–25.

9 Lee Soltow, *Patterns of Wealthholding in Wisconsin Since 1850* (Madison: University of Wisconsin Press, 1971), p. 74.

10 Ibid., p. 75.

11 Michael B. Katz, *The People of Hamilton, Canada West* (Cambridge, Mass.: Harvard University Press, 1975), p. 161.

12 I. M. Rubinow, *Social Insurance* (New York, Henry Holt and Company 1913), pp. 305–6.

13 Achenbaum, *Old Age in the New Land*, pp. 70–1. For all male workers over ten, the respective figures are: merchants, 19.17 percent; agents, 5.5 percent; engineers, 2.6 percent; carpenters, 15.07 percent; steel-workers, 3.5 percent; printers, 2.17 percent.

14 Ibid., pp. 67–8.

15 Ibid., p. 68.

16 Rubinow, *Social Insurance*, 306.

17 John Durand, *The Labor Force in the United States* (New York: Social Science Research Council, 1948), pp. 63, 68–9; 110. Harris Schrank, "The Work Force," in *Aging and Society*, vol. 3, eds., Matilda W. Riley, Marilyn Johnson, and Anne Foner, (New York: Russell Sage Foundation, 1972), p. 165; By 1900, 93 percent of men over the age of sixty-five remained employed in agriculture, fishing, or mining. In nonagricultural fields, only 59 percent were still employed. Achenbaum, *Old Age in the New Land*, p. 103.

18 Katz, *People of Hamilton*, p. 162.

19 Ibid.

20 Abraham Epstein, *Facing Old Age: A Study of Old Age Dependency in the United States and Old Age Pensions* (New York: Alfred A. Knopf, Inc., 1922), p. 10. The figure for 1910 is an estimate, as the census groups all workers over forty-five.

21 Smith, "Life Course, Norms, and the Family System," p. 288.

22 Ibid.

23 Because of their urban orientation and their interaction with the poverty-stricken elderly, the social commentators tended to overstate the extent of old-age dependence. Yet their ideas were directly linked to the social reality of aging as it was perceived. On this point, I differ with W. Andrew Achenbaum, who believes that "Ideas about the worth and function of the elderly have a life of their own." Achenbaum, *Old Age in the New Land*, p. 86.

24 David J. Rothman, *The Discovery of the Asylum: Social Order and Disorder in the New Republic* (Boston and Toronto: Little, Brown and Company, 1971), chap. 4; Carroll Smith-Rosenberg, *Religion and the Rise of the City: The New York City Mission Movement* (Ithaca, N.Y., and London: Cornell University Press, 1971), chap. 1; William Clinton Heffner, *History of Poor Relief in Pennsylvania 1682–1913* (Harrisburg, Pa: Holzapfel Publishing Company, 1913), p. 58; Charles Lawrence, *History of the Philadelphia Almshouses and Hospitals* (Philadelphia; Lawrence, 1905; reprint ed., New

York: Arno Press, 1976), pp. 39–40; *A Report of the Record Commissioners of the City of Boston containing Boston Records from 1700–1728,* (Boston: Rockwell & Churchill, City Printers, 1882), City Document 137, p. 96.

25 For the boarding-out practices of several small towns in Rhode Island during the first half of the nineteenth century, see Thomas R. Hazard, *Report on the Poor and Insane of Rhode Island* (Providence, R.I.: J. Knowles, 1851; reprint ed., New York: Arno Press, 1973), pp. 17–18, 58–9, 76–7; see also *Massachusetts Commissioners' Report on the Pauper System* (1834), p. 23; Rothman, *Discovery of the Asylum,* pp. 23, 32, 36.

26 Mathew Carey, *Letters on the Condition of the Poor* (Philadelphia: Haswell and Barrington, 1835); Hazard, *Poor and Insane,* pp. 76–7; *Massachusetts Commissioners' Report on the Pauper System,* (Boston: Mass. House, 1883), pp. 23–4, 37; *Report to the Special Joint Committee appointed to investigate the whole system of the Public Charitable Institutions of the Commonwealth of Massachusetts* (Boston: William White, 1859), pp. 17–18; Gary B. Nash, "Poverty and Poor Relief in Pre-Revolutionary Philadelphia," *William and Mary Quarterly,* 32, 3rd ser. (January, 1979), p. 5; Rothman, *Discovery of the Asylum,* p. 29.

27 Mathew Carey, *A Plea for the Poor* (Philadelphia: L. R. Bailey, 1837), p. 5; Priscilla Clement, "Poverty and Welfare in Philadelphia 1800–1850," (unpublished Ph.D. diss., University of Pennsylvania, 1977); *Hazard's Register of Pennsylvania* 2, no. 17 (October 23, 1830), pp. 266–7.

28 Hazard, *Poor and Insane,* pp. 13, 15–16, 19, 21, 22, 32.

29 The spokesman for one reform organization estimated that in New York City during the 1830s and 1840s, about forty new associations had begun. New York Association for Improving the Condition of the Poor (NYAICP), *First Annual Report* (New York, 1845), p. 15.

30 Mathew Carey, "Essays on the Public Charities of Philadelphia," in *Miscellaneous Essays* (Philadelphia: Carey, 1830), pp. 153–203, esp. pp. 177–8; Smith-Rosenberg, *Religion and the Rise of the City,* chaps. 4 and 5 and appendix, pp. 280–1.

31 In the midst of the national depression of the 1850s, for example, authorities in Philadelphia estimated that between 20,000 and 30,000 workers were unemployed; in New York City, the number rose to between 30,000 and 40,000. Leah Hannah Feder, *Unemployment in Periods of Depression* (New York: Russell Sage Foundation, 1936), p. 19.

32 In 1870, after working with the poor for more than a quarter of a century, the NYAICP wrote, "As a result of sickness, accident, old age, or other unavoidable causes, pauperism will never be done away." NYAICP, *Twenty-Seventh Annual Report* (1870), p. 61.

33 NYAICP, *First Annual Report* (1845), p. 15.

34 NYAICP, *Twelfth Annual Report* (1855), p. 36.

35 NYAICP, *Eleventh Annual Report* (1854), p. 30.

36 NYAICP, *Tenth Annual Report* (1853), p. 66–7, and repeated consistently thereafter.

37 *Association of Charities Report II* (Boston, 1881), appendix; Nathan Irvin Huggins, *Protestants Against Poverty: Boston Charities, 1870–1900* (Westport, Conn.: Greenwood Press, 1971), p. 76; Smith-Rosenberg, *Religion*

and the Rise of the City, pp. 234–5. This policy applied especially to any effort in which education was the primary purpose. The axiom that "you can't teach an old dog a new trick" seemed reason enough to assume that all elderly persons had little chance of learning anything. *The Ninth Annual Report of the Board of State Charities of Massachusetts* (Boston, 1872), p. 26, noted that it did not list the age of mentally defective persons over the age of thirty because "few above that age [are] considered as subjects for profitable instruction."

38 NYAICP, *Seventeenth Annual Report* (1860), p. 30.
39 *Third Annual Report of the Children's Aid Society* (New York, 1856), p. 5.
40 This was the philosophy of such midcentury reform groups as the Female Moral Reform Society, the Children's Aid Society, the Five Points Mission, the Five Points House of Industry, and the Juvenile Society. Smith-Rosenberg, *Religion and the Rise of the City*, p. 251. In the second half of the nineteenth century, the NYAICP became increasingly disillusioned with the migration plan. Not only did city-oriented children and adolescents fail to assimilate into the countryside, but their loss, it was feared, would leave the city with only the most hopeless welfare cases – a category in which the old, of course, were included. In 1861, the NYAICP wrote that if the able-bodied migrated, "the city would be impoverished. It would retain thousands of poor widows, and deserted wives with dependent children – indigent females of such sickly or delicate habits as to be mostly unfitted for labor – the aged, the impotent and infirm of both sexes." NYAICP, *Eighteenth Annual Report* (1861), p. 39; also, pp. 34–6; see also *The Fifth Annual Report of the Board of State Charities of Massachusetts* (1869), p. 195.
41 The Women's Protective Emigrant Society, established in 1858, was founded, its spokesman explained, "to aid and encourage the emigration of families from the city to the country and especially to the Western States, for the improvement of their moral and physical condition." NYAICP, *Eighteenth Annual Report* (1861), p. 34; New York Citizens Association and Committee on Public Charities, "Labor Bureau," quoted by NYAICP, *Twenty-Seventh Annual Report* (1870), p. 73.
42 Edward T. Devine, *The Principles of Relief* (New York: Macmillan Company, 1904), p. 128. One rationale behind this policy was that young adults could contribute to the welfare of an entire family, whereas the old had few responsibilities other than themselves. In the late nineteenth century, for example, the Citizen's Relief Committee declared that charity work would be given only to those who had others dependent upon their labor. Huggins, *Protestants Against Poverty*, p. 146. For an example of piecework employment being given to the old in the early nineteenth century, see Carey, *A Plea for the Poor*, p. 5. In this essay, Carey described the activities of the Provident Society, which was supplying women – both old and young – with material for shirts. Carey made it clear that the elderly were receiving employment, although he assumed that their output, as well as their earnings, would be less than those of the young.
43 Amos Warner, *American Charities* (New York: Thomas Y. Crowell Com-

pany, 1894), p. 203; see also Hace Sorel Tishler, *Self-Reliance and Social Security, 1870–1917* (New York and London: Kennikat Press, 1971), p. 60.

44   NYAICP, *Eleventh Annual Report* (1854), p. 59.
45   L. A. Quetelet, *A Treatise on Man and the Development of His Faculties* (Edinburgh: William and Robert Chambers, 1842).
46   Ibid.
47   Ibid., p. v.
48   On the influence of Quetelet and the importance of the concept of the "average man," see Erwin H. Ackerknecht, "Villerme and Quetelet," *Bulletin of the History of Medicine*, 26 (Fall, 1952), pp. 317–29; James E. Birren, "A Brief History of the Psychology of Aging," *The Gerontologist*, 1, no. 1 (June, 1961), pp. 69–70; F. H. Hankins, *Quetelet as Statistician* (New York: Columbia University Press, 1908); George Rosen, "Problems in the Application of Statistical Analysis to Questions of Health 1700–1800," *Bulletin of the History of Medicine*, 29 (Spring, 1953), p. 44.
49   For a similar, if somewhat more crude, collection of biographies and the effect of old age, see George M. Beard, *Legal Responsibility in Old Age Based on Researches into the Relation of Age to Work* (New York: Russells' American Steam Printing House, 1873), p. 7.
50   Quetelet, *A Treatise on Man*, p. 32.
51   For a history of ideas about longevity prior to 1800 see Gerald Gruman, *A History of Ideas about the Prolongation of Life* (Philadelphia: American Philosophical Society, 1966). On the use of life tables, see L. L. Bernard and Jessie Bernard, *Origins of American Sociology: The Social Science Movement in the United States* (New York: Russell & Russell, Publishers, 1965); I. S. Falk, *The Principles of Vital Statistics* (Philadelphia and London: W. B. Saunders Company, 1928); Robert Gutman, *Birth and Death Registration in Massachusetts* (New York: Milbank Memorial Fund, 1959); Richard Price, *Observations on Reversionary Payments on Schemes for Providing Annuities for Widows and for Persons in Old Age*, vols. I and II (London: T. Cadell, 1792); Charles F. Stillman, *The Life Insurance Examiner* (New York: Spectator Company, 1888). On the advice of longevity experts about the old in the nineteenth century, see Thomas R. Cole, "Past Meridian: Aging and the Northern Middle Class, 1830–1930," (unpublished Ph.D. diss., University of Rochester, 1980), part II.
52   William J. Thoms, *Human Longevity: Its Facts and Fiction* (London: John Murray Publishers, 1873); Edward Jarvis, *Increase of Human Life* (Boston: David Clapp & Sons, 1872).
53   Thoms, *Human Longevity*, p. 1.
54   Southwood Smith, *The Philosophy of Health or an Exposition of the Physical and Mental Constitution of Man with a View to the Promotion of Human Longevity and Happiness* (London: C. Cox, 1847), p. 118; see also John Bell, *On Regimen and Longevity* (Philadelphia: Haswell & Johnson, 1842), pp. 395–6.
55   Bell, *On Regimen and Longevity*, pp. 394–6; Charles Caldwell, *Thoughts on the Effect of Age on the Human Constitution* (Louisville: John C. Noble, 1846), pp. 8, 9; Smith, *The Philosophy of Health*, pp. 112–13.

56 Daniel Maclachlan, *A Practical Treatise on the Diseases and Infirmities of Advanced Life* (London: John Churchill & Sons, 1863), p. 37.

57 Smith, *The Philosophy of Health*, p. 115, Maclachlan explained the law of mortality as rising gradually from age fifteen to fifty-five and then doubling every ten years (p. 31).

58 Davis R. Dewey, "Irregularities of Employment," *Publications of the American Economic Association*, 9, no. 6 (December, 1894), pp. 523–39; F. J. Kinsbury, "Pensions in a Republic," *Journal of Social Science*, 12 (March, 1881), pp. 1–11; Mary Roberts Smith, "Almshouse Women," *American Statistical Association*, 4, no. 31 (September, 1894), pp. 219–62; Amos Warner, "Notes on the Statistical Determination of the Causes of Poverty," *American Statistical Association*, new ser. 1, no. 5 (March, 1889), pp. 183–205. See also F. Spencer Baldwin, "The Findings of the Massachusetts Commission on Old Age Pensions," *American Statistical Association*, 12, no. 89 (March, 1910), pp. 417–30; Baldwin, "Old Age Pension Schemes: A Criticism and a Program," *The Quarterly Journal of Economics*, 24 (August, 1910), pp. 713–42; Frederick L. Hoffman, "The Problem of Poverty and Pensions in Old Age," *American Journal of Sociology*, 14 (September, 1908), pp. 182–96; Arthur J. Todd, "Old Age and the Industrial Scrap Heap," *American Statistical Association*, 14, no. 110 (June, 1915), pp. 550–7; Amos Warner, "The Causes of Poverty Further Considered," *American Statistical Association*, 4, no. 27 (September, 1894), pp. 46–8.

59 *Tenth Annual Report of the Bureau of the Statistics of Labor of Massachusetts* (Boston, 1879), p. 116.

60 For the argument of Carroll Wright, see C. Wright, *Outline of Practical Sociology with special reference to American Conditions* (New York: Longmans, Inc., 1899); *Some Ethical Phases of the Labor Question* (Boston: American Unitarian Association, 1902); *The Value and Influence of Labor Statistics* (Washington, D.C.: U.S. Labor Department, 1901). See also Francis Amasa Walker, "The Causes of Poverty," in Walker, ed., *Discussions in Economics and Statistics* (New York: Henry Holt, 1899), vol. 2, pp. 455–71; *The Wages Question* (New York: Henry Holt & Co., 1876), esp. pp. 414–415.

61 I am arguing that by the late nineteenth century, social analysts had begun to link old-age dependency primarily to industrialization rather than simply to the indulgences of the aging individual. As a result, they foresaw a not too distant future when most aged persons would become superannuated. On this point, I differ with W. Andrew Achenbaum, who believes that in the late nineteenth century, "most analysts concluded that instances of old-age dependency resulted mainly from physical debility, mental imparity, a spouse's death, or loss of property – circumstances that had always threatened the old – rather than industrialization *per se*." Achenbaum, *Old Age in the New Land*, p. 85.

62 Charles Booth, *The Aged Poor in England and Wales* (London: Macmillan Company, 1894); *Pauperism and the Endowment of Old Age* (London: Macmillan Company, 1892). On the significance of Booth, see T. S. Simey

and M. B. Simey, *Charles Booth: Social Scientist*, (London: Oxford University Press, 1960).

63   See, for example, Hoffman, "Poverty and Pensions in Old Age," p. 364; Smith, "Almshouse Women,"p. 253; Todd, "Industrial Scrap Heap," p. 258; and Warner, "Causes of Poverty Reconsidered," p. 58.

64   Massachusetts Commission on Old Age Pensions, Annuities and Insurance, *Report of the Commission on Old Age Pensions, Annuities and Insurance* (Boston: Wright and Potter, 1910); *Report of the Pennsylvania Commission on Old Age Pensions* (Harrisburgh: J. L. L. Kuhn, 1919); see also Baldwin, "The Findings of the Massachusetts Commission on Old Age Pensions."

65   Edward T. Devine, *Economics* (New York: Macmillan Company, 1898); *The Principles of Relief* (New York: Macmillan Company, 1904); *Efficiency and Relief* (New York: Columbia University Press, 1906); *Misery and Its Causes* (New York: Macmillan Company, 1909); *Disabled Soldiers and Sailors Pensions and Training* (New York: Oxford University Press, 1919); *American Social Work in the Twentieth Century* (New York: Frontier Press, 1921); Abraham Epstein, *Facing Old Age: A Study of Old Age Dependency in the United States and the Old Age Pensions* (New York: Alfred A. Knopf, Inc., 1922); *The Problem of Old Age Pensions in Industry* (Harrisburg: Pennsylvania Old Age Commission, 1926); *The Challenge of the Aged* (New York: Vanguard Press, 1929); *Primer on Old Age Pensions in Industry* (Harrisburg: Pennsylvania Old Age Commission, n.d.); I. M. Rubinow, *Social Insurance* (New York: Henry Holt & Co., 1913); *The Quest for Security* (New York: Henry Holt & Co., 1934); Lee Welling Squier, *Old Age Dependency in the United States* (New York: Macmillan Company, 1912). See also Homer Folks, "Disease and Dependence," *Charities*, 10, no. 20 (May 1903), pp. 499–500; "Disease and Dependence," *Charities*, 2 no. 14 (October, 1903), pp. 297–300; Edward Everett Hale, "Old Age Pensions," *Charities and the Commons*, 18 (June, 1907), pp. 275–8; Maurice Law, "The English Workingmen's Compensation Act," *Journal of Social Science*, 40 (June, 1902), pp. 19–30; Henry R. Seager, "Old Age Pensions," *Charities and the Commons*, 21 (October, 1908), pp. 10–12; Seager, *Social Insurance: A Program of Social Reform* (New York: Macmillan Company, 1910); Todd, "Industrial Scrap Heap."

66   Rubinow, *Social Insurance*, p. 302

67   Squier, *Old Age Dependency*, pp. 28–9.

68   Achenbaum, *Old Age in the New Land*, pp. 50–1; Cole, "Past Meridian," Chap. six.

3. Medical Models of Growing Old

1   I. L. Nascher, "Geriatrics," *New York Medical Journal*, 90, no. 8 (August, 1909), pp. 358–9.

2   This contrasts to other stages of life, such as childhood or adolescence, which, as recent studies allege, were "discovered" in modern times.

See, for examples, Philippe Aries, *Centuries of Childhood: A Social History of Family Life* (New York: Vintage Books, 1962), and Joseph Kett, *Rites of Passage: Adolescence in America, 1790 to the Present* (New York: Basic Books, Inc., Publishers, 1977).

3   P. M. Roget, "Age," in *The Cyclopedia of Practical Medicine,* eds., John Forbes, Alexander Tweedie, John Conolly, and Robley Dunglison (Philadelphia: Blanchard and Lea, 1833), p. 57. In the early nineteenth century, the notion of the grand climacteric was discussed particularly in works of forensic medicine. See, for example, J. Chitty, *A Practical Treatise on Medical Jurisprudence* (London: Rowoth & Sons, 1834), p. 432; J. A. Paris and J. S. M. Fonblanque, *Medical Jurisprudence,* vol. 1 (London: W. Phillips, 1823), pp. 179–80.

4   Bartholomew Parr, *The London Medical Dictionary* (Philadelphia: Mitchell, Ames, and White, 1819), p. 448.

5   According to Philippe Aries, the concept of the ages of life did not originate in antiquity but rather in the sixth century. Aries, *Centuries of Childhood,* pp. 20–1. This statement, however, ignores the cycles defined by the Greeks.

6   Thomas Browne, *Religio Medici, Letter to a Friend, Christian Morals, Urn-Burial, and Other Papers,* Part III, Section 8 of *Christian Morals* (London: Andrew Cooke, 1643), cited by Herant A. Katchadourian, "Medical Perspective on Adulthood," *Daedalus,* 105, no. 2 (Spring, 1976), p. 29.

7   Owsei Temkin, "German Concepts of Ontology and History around 1800," in Temkin, *The Double Face of Janus and Other Essays in the History of Medicine* (Baltimore and London: Johns Hopkins University Press, 1977), pp. 373–4.

8   For a discussion of the theoretical system on which traditional therapeutics was based, see Charles E. Rosenberg, "The Therapeutic Revolution: Medicine, Meaning and Social Change in Nineteenth-Century America," *Perspectives on Medicine and Biology,* 20, no. 4 (Summer, 1977), pp. 485–506.

9   Richard Harrison Shryock, *The Development of Modern Medicine* (New York: Alfred A. Knopf, Inc., 1947), p. 29.

10   This is Benjamin Rush's terminology. See Esmond Ray Long, *A History of American Pathology* (Springfield, Ill.: Charles C. Thomas, Publisher, 1962), p. 17.

11   "I am convinced," Anthony Carlisle wrote, "that the feebleness of age, when produced by sanguineous oppression, can only be removed by diminishing the quantity of blood, and that, on the promptitude of such measures, the safety of the patient will depend." Carlisle, *An Essay on the Disorders of Old Age and the Means of Prolonging Human Life* (Philadelphia: Edward Earle, 1819), p. 14; see also Benjamin Rush, "An Account of the State of the Body and Mind in Old Age and Observations upon its Diseases and their Remedies," in Rush, *Medical Inquiries and Observations* (Philadelphia: Thomas Dobson, 1797), p. 320.

12   Henry Holland, *Medical Notes and Reflections* (Philadelphia: Haswell, Barrington, and Haswell, 1839), p. 154.

13 Richard Mead, *The Medical Works of Richard Mead* (London: C. Hatch, L. Hawes, et al., 1762), p. 609.
14 Ibid., p. 602.
15 Throughout the eighteenth century and the first half of the nineteenth, physicians expressed the opinion that the old did not fear death. Holland, for example, wrote: "The earnestness to live abates as the possession of life, from whatever cause, is gradually withdrawn. Every physician is witness to these things, as he watches occasionally over existence slowly ebbing away, without toil, suffering, or alarm." *Medical Notes and Reflections*, p. 154. See also George E. Day, *A Practical Treatise on the Domestic Management and Most Important Diseases of Advance Life* (London: T. and W. Boone, 1849), p. 5; Rush, "An Account," p. 313; Sir John Sinclair, *The Code of Health and Longevity* (Edinburgh: Arch. Constable & Co., 1807), p. 8. By the end of the nineteenth century and the beginning of the twentieth, however, several doctors expressed the opinion that all persons, including the old, feared death and clung to life. See, for examples, J. Bandaline, "The Struggle of Science with Old Age," *Medical Record*, 64, no. 3 (July, 1903), p. 86, and I. L. Nascher, "Treatment of Disease in Senility," *The Medical Council*, 15, no. 8 (August, 1910), p. 357.
16 Joseph Lathrop, *The Infirmities and Comforts of Old Age: A Sermon to Aged People* (Springfield, Ill., Henry Brewer, 1805), pp. 1–13; John Reid, *The Philosophy of Death: General Medical and Statistical Treatise on the Nature and Cause of Human Mortality* (London: S. Highley, 1841), p. 357.
17 Richard Harrison Shryock, *Medicine and Society in America 1660–1860* (Ithaca, N.Y. and London: Cornell University Press, 1975), p. 93.
18 In the American colonies in the period 1650–1700, 33.8 percent of the population survived to sixty, 23.1 percent to sixty-five, and 12.3 percent to seventy. David Hackett Fischer, *Growing Old in America* (New York: Oxford University Press, 1977), Appendix, Table V, p. 227.
19 Cotton Mather, *The Angel of Bethesda*, ed. Gordon W. Jones (Boston: American Antiquarian Society, 1972), p. 315.
20 Rush, "An Account," pp. 293–322.
21 Gerald Gruman, *A History of Ideas About the Prolongation of Life* (Philadelphia: American Philosophical Society, 1966), pp. 6–8.
22 For examples of this belief, see "Review of 'On the Diseases of Old Age and their Care,' by Dr. C. Canstatt," *British and Foreign Medical Review*, 17 (January–April, 1844), p. 104; James H. Cassedy, *Demography in Early America: Beginnings of the Statistical Mind, 1600–1800* (Cambridge, Mass.: Harvard University Press, 1969), p. 262; Joel Pinney, *An Exposure of the Causes of the Present Deteriorated Condition of Human LIfe* (London: Longman, Rees, Orme, Brown, & Green, 1830), p. 6; Sinclair, *Code of Health and Longevity*, Appendix V, pp. 7–9.
23 John M. O'Donnell, "Moral Physiology: Prolongevity Hygiene in Nineteenth-Century America" (unpublished paper, University of Pennsylvania, 1977), pp. 9–10.
24 Gruman, *A History of Ideas about the Prolongation of Life*, and Gruman,

"The Rise and Fall of Prolongevity Hygiene," *Bulletin of the History of Medicine*, 35 (1961), pp. 221–7.

25 Christopher William Hufeland, *The Art of Prolonging Life* (1797), ed., Erasmus Wilson (Boston: Ticknor, Reed, and Fields, 1854), p. 202.

26 J. R. Hayes, *How to Live Longer and Why We do not Live Longer* (Philadelphia: J. B. Lippincott Company, 1897), p. 8.

27 The French *philosophes*, in particular, looked forward to an era when old age and death could be indefinitely postponed. This was the hope, for example, of both Condorcet and the American Benjamin Franklin. Shryock, *Modern Medicine*, p. 78.

28 Sinclair, *Code of Health and Longevity*, p. 51, Appendix VI, pp. 9–28, and Appendix 24, pp. 120–4.

29 Because many longevity publicists advocated endless middle age, it is necessary to understand their ambiguous attitude toward the old. We cannot assume, as some scholars have, that the elderly were unquestionably venerated for their long lives. Although their many years were to be envied, their weakened condition and numerous diseases were often feared and despised. The qualities described in the longevity tracts were hardly the physical traits or mental characteristics traditionally associated with senescence. For a different view of the importance of longevity, see W. Andrew Achenbaum, "Growing Old in the New Land" (unpublished Ph.D. diss., University of Michigan, 1976), chap. 1, and Fischer, *Growing Old in America*, chap. 1.

30 In the United States in 1850, a man at birth had an average life expectancy of 38.3 years; a woman, 40.5. By 1920, comparative figures had risen to 54.0 and 56.56 years, respectively. In 1850, a man at age sixty could expect to live an average of 15.6 more years; a woman, 17.0. By 1920, these figures had not risen but, in fact, had shown a slight drop to 14.4 and 15.4 years, respectively. U.S. Department of Commerce, *Historical Statistics of the United States* (Washington, D.C.: Government Printing Office, 1960), Table B. 76–91, p. 24.

31 In the first half of the nineteenth century, the French physicians who wrote on old age were Delseries (1802), Auchner (1804), Mauvid-Montergon (1804), Delphin-Lamothe (1806), Millot (1807), Junin (1813), Brossar-Ysabeau (1815), Vinache (1816), Bellior (1817), Secretain (1827), and Venus (1837). Erwin H. Ackerknecht, "Hygiene in France, 1815–1848," *Bulletin of the History of Medicine*, 22, no. 2 (March–April, 1948), pp. 122ff.

32 Erwin H. Ackerknecht, *Medicine at the Paris Hospital, 1794–1848* (Baltimore: Johns Hopkins University Press, 1967), chap. 7, in which he discusses the philosophy of Corvisart, Bayle, and Laennec. See also Oswei Temkin, "Health and Disease," in *The Double Face of Janus*, pp. 429–30.

33 Ackerknecht, *Medicine at the Paris Hospital*, p. 56.

34 Demange, cited by Elie Metchnikoff, *The Nature of Man: Studies in Optimistic Philosophy* (New York and London: G. P. Putnam's Sons, 1903), p. 36; see also Julius Althaus, "Old Age and Rejuvenescence," *The Lancet*, 1 (January, 1899), p. 150; Frederick N. Brown, "Some Observations upon Old Age and its Consequences," *The Providence Medical Journal*, 10, no. 1 (January, 1909), p. 58; J. Madison Taylor, "The Conservation

of Energy in Those of Advancing Years," *The Popular Science Monthly* 64 (March, 1904), p. 406.

35 Sinclair, *Code of Health and Longevity*, Appendix VI, pp. 21–2.

36 Reynold Webb Wilcox, "The Therapeutics of Old Age," *American Medicine*, 4, no. 4 (April, 1909), p. 178.

37 The importance of the different life segments was also emphasized by the development in the nineteenth century of the study of embryology. Temkin, "German Concepts of Ontology and History," pp. 373–89.

38 Francois Magendie, *An Elementary Compendium of Physiology: For the Use of Students*, trans. W. Milligan (Philadelphia: James Webster, 1824), pp. 61–2.

39 "Review of 'On the Diseases of Old Age and their Care,'" p. 111.

40 J. M. Charcot and Alfred Loomis, *Clinical Lectures on the Diseases of Old Age* (New York: William Wood & Company, 1881), p.18. The parallel with pediatrics was continually stressed, despite the fact that, when Charcot first wrote this statement (1861), pediatrics as a specialty was still being debated. Yet the link between the two studies seemed natural: If children were not to be treated by adult therapeutics and standards, neither should the elderly. Thus, many of the physicians who defended the need for a study of children's diseases also called for the creation of geriatrics. The introduction to I. L. Nascher's *Geriatrics: The Diseases of Old Age and their Treatment* (Philadelphia: P. Blakiston's Son & Co., 1914) was written by Abraham Jacobi, often credited as the father of pediatrics. See also Clarence Bartlett, "Clinical Lectures on Diseases in Old Age," *The Hahnemannian Monthly*, 41 (February, 1906), p. 107; R. R. Hopkins, "Diseases and Conditions Peculiar to Old Age," *The Cincinnati Medical Journal*, 11, no. 7 (July, 1896), p. 393; S. Newton Leo, "A Consideration of the Senile State," *New York Medical Journal*, 74, no. 25 (December, 1906), p. 1226; J. M. Taylor, "The Hygiene and Management of Old Age," *Journal of Orificial Surgery*, 7 (1899–1900), p. 74.

41 Charcot and Loomis, *Diseases of Old Age*, p. 20.

42 Ibid., pp. 74–5.

43 Althaus, "Old Age and Rejuvenescence," p. 151; Bandaline, "Struggle of Science with Old Age," pp. 82–3; J. W. Bell, "A Plea for the Aged," *Journal of the American Medical Association*, 33, no. 19 (November, 1899), p. 1137; Charcot and Loomis, *Diseases of Old Age*, p. 21; on gouty diseases, pp. 38–92; John D. Covert, "The Pathology of Old Age: Can It Be Delayed?" *Texas State Journal of Medicine*, 4, no. 11 (March, 1909), p. 277; W. M. Gibson, "Some Considerations of Senescence," *New York State Journal of Medicine*, 9, no. 9 (September, 1909), pp. 380–2. I. N. Love, "The Needs and Rights of Old Age," *Journal of the American Medical Association*, 29, no. 21 (November, 1897), p. 1034; Joseph C. Martindale, *Human Anatomy, Physiology, and Hygiene* (Philadelphia: Eldridge & Brother, 1872, p. 213; Charles Sedgwick Minot, *The Problem of Age, Growth and Death* (New York: Popular Science Monthly, 1907), p. 487; Nascher, *Geriatrics*, pp. 1–4, 43–7; Rudolf Virchow, *Cellular Pathology* (New York: Robert M. DeWitt, 1858), pp. v, 29, 84–5, 358–9; Ernst Wagner, *A Manual of General Pathology* trans. John Van Drugen and E. C.

Sequin (New York: William Wood & Company, 1876), p. 50; Wilcox, "Therapeutics of Old Age," p. 178.

4. Treating the Postclimacteric Stage

1 George E. Day, *A Practical Treatise on the Domestic Management and Most Important Diseases of Advanced Life* (London: T. and W. Boone, 1849).
2 Ibid.; see the frontpiece for the books consulted; also, for the citation of Prus, see pp. 17, 76, 77, 78, 87, 145, 147; Chomel, 87; Magendie, 9; and Canstatt, 112, 162.
3 Bernard Van Oven, *On the Decline of Life in Health and Disease* (London: John Churchill & Sons, 1853); Daniel Maclachlan, *A Practical Treatise on the Diseases and Infirmities of Advanced Life* (London: John Churchill & Sons, 1863); A. L. Loomis, "The Climate and Environment Best Suited to Old Age in Health and Disease," *Transactions of the Fifth Climactological Association* (1888), pp. 1–10, and, with J. M. Charcot, *Clinical Lectures on the Diseases of Advanced Life* (New York: William Wood & Company, 1881), Lectures No. 22–32; I. L. Nascher, "Longevity and Rejuvenescence," *New York Medical Journal*, 74, no. 16 (April, 1909), pp. 795–800; "Geriatrics," *New York Medical Journal*, 90, no. 8 (August, 1909), pp. 428–9; "The Treatment of Diseases in Senility," *The Medical Record*, 76, no. 24 (December, 1909), pp. 987–92; "Anatomical Changes in Senility," *The Medical Council*, 15, no. 1 (January, 1910), pp. 17–22; "Physiological Change in Old Age," *The Medical Council*, 15, no. 2 (February, 1910), pp. 52–6; "Pathology of Old Age," *The Medical Council*, 15, no. 3 (March, 1910), pp. 94–9; "Pathology of Old Age," *The Medical Council*, 15, no. 4 (April, 1910), pp. 119–21; "Hygiene and Regimen in Old Age," *The Medical Council*, 15, no. 5 (May, 1910), pp. 166–9; "Hygiene and Regimen in Old Age," *The Medical Council*, 15, no. 6 (June, 1910), pp. 200–1; "The Treatment of Disease in Senility," *The Medical Council*, 15, no. 7 (July, 1910), pp. 235–8; "The Treatment of Diseases in Senility," *The Medical Council*, 15, no. 8 (August, 1910), pp. 271–5; *Geriatrics: The Diseases of Old Age and their Treatment* (Philadelphia: P. Blakiston's Son & Co., 1914).
4 J. Nichols, "Old Age," *The Rise, Minutes and Proceedings of the New Jersey Medical Society, 1766–1859* (1850), p. 519.
5 Harry Campbell, "Correspondence – The Cause of Senile Decay," *The Lancet*, 2 (August, 1905), p. 403; Henry Holland, *Medical Notes and Reflections* (Philadelphia: Haswell, Barrington and Haswell, 1839), p. 188.
6 James Copland, "Age – 'Of the Conditions of a Function Characterising the Advance of Age,'" in *A Dictionary of Practical Medicine*, vol. 1, ed., Charles A. Lee (New York: Harper & Brothers, 1859), pp. 53–4. Holland linked the deposits and alterations of the blood to a loss of vital energy (p. 169).
7 S. W. Caldwell, "The Possible Suspension of Old Age," *Mississippi Valley Monthly*, 3 (March, 1885), p. 104; W. C. Goodno, "Senility, with especial reference to the Changes Developing in the Circulatory Organs, their exciting Causes, and Symptoms," *Transactions of the Thirty-Third*

Session of the Homeopathic Medical Society of the State of Pennsylvania, 33rd issue (1897), p. 245; Nascher, *Geriatrics*, pp. 39, 41.

8   Colin A. Scott, "Old Age and Death," *The American Journal of Psychology*, 8, no. 1 (October, 1896), p. 67; Van Oven, *On the Decline of Life*, p. 53.

9   Ann Douglas, "Heaven our Home: Consolation Literature in the Northern United States, 1830–1880," *American Quarterly*, 26, no. 5 (December, 1974), pp. 496–515; David E. Stannard, *The Puritan Way of Death* (New York: Oxford University Press, 1977), pp. 53, 57, 65, 188–9.

10   Day, *A Practical Treatise*, p. 129.

11   Come Ferran, "Medicine of Senility and the Validity of Prolongation of Senility by Dosimetric Alkaloidotherapy," trans. E. M. Epstein, *The Alkaloidal Clinic*, 9, no. 1 (January, 1903), pp. 18–19.

12   Maclachlan, *A Practical Treatise*, p. iv.

13   Richard Harrison Shryock, *Medicine and Society in America 1660–1860* (Ithaca, N.Y., and London: Cornell University Press, 1975), p. 96.

14   John Mason Good, *The Study of Medicine* (New York: Harper & Brother, 1835), p. 15.

15   Professor O'Connor, for example, chastised the clinicians for their failure to recognize climacteric disease because of their reliance on postmortem findings. "It is," he wrote, "perhaps too much the custom to disregard the consideration of diseases not founded on pathological changes." O'Connor, "On Climacteric Changes," *The Dublin Journal of Medical Science*, 60, no. 42 (July, 1875), p. 78.

16   T. S. Clouston, *Clinical Lectures on Mental Disease* (Philadelphia: Henry C. Lea's Sons, 1884), p. 388.

17   Sir John Sinclair, *The Code of Health and Longevity* (Edinburgh: Arch. Constable & Co., 1807), vol. 1, pp. 23–4.

18   Henry Halford, "On the Climacteric Disease," *Medical Transactions of the Royal College of Physicians*, 4, (1813), pp. 316–28.

19   Henry Halford, "On the Climacteric Disease," in Halford, *Essays and Orations* (London: J. Murray, 1831), pp. 1–15.

20   "And I venture to question," Halford wrote, "whether it be not, in truth, a *disease* rather than a mere decline in strength and decay of the natural power." Halford, "On the Climacteric Disease," p. 317.

21   See, for examples, James Clark, *The Sanative Influence of Climate* (Philadelphia: A Waldie, 1841), p. 53; Good, *The Study of Medicine*, pp. 23–4; Henry Kennedy, "Observations on Climacteric Disease, with Cases," *The Dublin Journal of Medical Science*, 25, no. 74 (1844), p. 245; Maclachlan, *A Practical Treatise*, p. 73; Nascher, *Geriatrics*, pp. 19–21; O'Connor, "On Climacteric Changes," p. 78; W. Tyler Smith, "The Climacteric Disease in Women: A Paroxysmal Affection occurring at the Decline of the Catamania," *London Journal of Medicine*, 1, no. 7 (July, 1849), pp. 601–9; George W. Wells, "The Medical Examiner – What He Does and Why He Does it – The Age of the Applicant," *The Medical Examiner: A Medico-Insurance Journal*, 6, no. 7 (July, 1896), p. 133.

22   See, for example, Day, *A Practical Treatise*, p. 66; C. M. Durrant, "On the Commencing Climacteric Period in the Male," *The British Medical Journal*, 2 (September, 1865), pp. 233–5; Good, *The Study of Medicine*, p.

24; Sir R. Douglas Powell, "Advanced Life and Its Diseases," *The Hospital*, 4, no. 102 (February, 1909), p. 507; J. Madison Taylor, "The Conservation of Energy in Those Advancing Years," *The Popular Science Monthly*, 64 (March, 1904), p. 414; Van Oven, *On the Decline of Life*, pp. 104–13; Wells, "The Medical Examiner," p. 133. Physicians believed that, in old age, both men and women were limited by their physiology. For a discussion of medical attitudes toward women, see Carroll Smith-Rosenberg, "Puberty to Menopause: The Cycle of Femininity in Nineteenth-Century America," in *Clio's Consciousness Raised*, eds. Mary S. Hartmann and Lois Banner (New York: Harper & Row, 1974), pp. 23–7.

23 See, for example, Clouston, *Clinical Lectures*, pp. 388–92; Durrant, "Commencing Climacteric Period," p. 223; Kennedy, "Observations," p. 252; W. Bevan Lewis, "Insanity at the Puerperal, Climacteric and Lactational Periods," *Wood's Medical and Surgical Monographs*, 6 (1890), p. 331; Scott, "Old Age and Death," p. 119.

24 Lewis, "Insanity," p. 341.

25 Durrant, "Commencing Climacteric Period," p. 233.

26 Charles E. Rosenberg, "Sexuality, Class, and Role in Nineteenth-Century America," *American Quarterly*, 25, no. 2 (May, 1973), pp. 131–54; Carroll Smith-Rosenberg and Charles E. Rosenberg, "The Female Animal: Medical and Biological Views of Women and Her Role in Nineteenth-Century America," *Journal of American History*, 60, no. 2 (September, 1973), p. 334.

27 Nascher, *Geriatrics*, pp. 6, 16. Charles Mercier believed that in old age man began to "take the feminine view in matters of justice that it would be cruel to punish the offender." Mercier, *Sanity and Insanity* (New York: Scribner & Welford, 1890), p. 309. See also Clouston, *Clinical Lectures*, p. 388; Maclachlan, *A Practical Treatise*, p. 5; Van Oven, *On the Decline of Life*, p. 41.

28 Henry Belfrage, *Discourses on the Duties and Consolations of the Aged* (London: Oliver & Bay, 1827); Joseph Lathrop, *The Infirmities and Comforts of Old Age: A Sermon to Aged People* (Springfield, Ill., Henry Brewer, 1805); John Reid, *The Philosophy of Death: General Medical and Statistical Treatise on the Nature and Cause of Human Mortality* (London: S. Highley, 1841). See also Thomas R. Cole, "Past Meridian: Aging and the Northern Middle Class (unpublished Ph.D. diss., University of Rochester, 1980), pp. 100–2.

29 The concept of transitional stages was first developed by Arnold Van Gennep in 1909. He wrote:

The life of an individual in any society is a series of passages from one age to another and from one occupation to another. Whenever there are fine distinctions among age or occupation groups, progression from one group to the next is accompanied by special acts, like those which make up apprenticeship in our trades.

The Rites of Passage, trans., Monika B. Vizedom and Gabrielle L. Caffee (Chicago: University of Chicago Press, 1960), pp. 2–3; see also Mary

Douglas, *Purity and Danger* (New York: Praeger Publishers, 1970), pp. 115–18. Recently, historians have focused upon the importance of these transitional periods, especially in terms of adolescence. See Joseph Kett, *Rites of Passage: Adolescence in America 1790 to the Present* (New York: Basic Books, Inc., Publishers, 1977).

30 In addressing an audience of "ladies," Samuel Sheldon Fitch emphasized the important role women could play after menopause. "Although after the cessation of the months," he wrote:

she cannot again give existence to another, yet she can enjoy the highest charms of society and social intercourse. She can guide the young and everywhere enliven and adorn, and instruct society, by the fervor of her affections to her family, the brilliance of her wit, the polish and charm of her accomplishments, and the generous diffusion of her knowledge and experience, resulting from the stores of her reading and the extent of her observations.

Six Lectures (New York: H. Carlisle, 1847), p. 199. In the mid-nineteenth century, a woman who attained the climacteric period of life was likely to have growing children in the home. Thus, her role as a mother and her domestic duties would continue undisturbed. See Robert V. Wells, "Demographic Change and the Life Cycle," in *The Family in History*, eds., Theodore K. Rabb and Robert I. Rotberg (New York: Harper & Row, 1971), pp. 85–94.

31 Charles Caldwell, *Thoughts on the Effects of Age on the Human Constitution* (Louisville, Ky.: John C. Noble, 1846), p. 14.

32 John Foster, "Old Age," *The Medical Press and Circular*, 27 (February, 1884), p. 203; see also Durrant, "Commencing Climacteric Period," p. 233.

33 Van Oven, *On the Decline of Life*, pp. 110–11.

34 "The weight of evidence," wrote W. H. Curtis, "seems to establish the fact that old age is never physiological, but always pathological, at least its visible and appreciable evidences are pathological ones." Curtis, "Disease in the Aged," *Illinois Medical Journal*, 10, no. 4 (October, 1906), p. 401; see also, as examples, Frederick N. Brown, "Some Observations upon Old Age and Its Consequences," *The Providence Medical Journal*, 10, no. 1 (January, 1909), p. 91; W. C. Bunce, "Some of the Influences that Determine Age," *The Ohio State Medical Journal*, no. 1, (April, 1906), p. 467; Goodno, "Senility," p. 244; William Kinnear, "Postponing Old Age," *The Medical Age*, 17, no. 2 (January, 1899), p. 49; E. N. Leake, "At What Period of Life Does Old Age Begin?" *The Medical Examiner*, 6, no. 10 (October, 1896), p. 191; S. Newton Leo, "A Consideration of the Senile State and its Treatment," *New York Medical Journal*, 84, no. 25 (October, 1894), p. 757; Charles G. Stockton, "The Delay of Old Age and the Alleviation of Senility," *Buffalo Medical Journal*, 61, no. 1 (August, 1905), p. 3; Taylor, "Conservation of Energy," p. 407; William Gilman Thompson, *Practical Dietetics* (New York and London: D. Appleton & Co., 1906), p. 312.

35 Day, *A Practical Treatise*, p. 46.

36 H. C. Wood, "The Hygiene of Old Age," *The Therapeutic Gazette*, 2, no. 5 (May, 1886), p. 304.
37 See Chapter 6, which discusses the development of retirement policies for the aged.
38 Kinnear, "Postponing Old Age," p. 48.
39 Nascher wrote that "the old man is a poor subject for experimental therapy." He noted, in fact, that ten persons had died from Brown-Sequard's extract. "Treatment of Disease in Senility," *The Medical Council*, 15, no. 8 (August, 1910), p. 274.
40 Peter N. Stearns, *Old Age in European Society: The Case of France* (New York: Holmes & Meier, Publishers, Inc., 1976), p. 98.
41 Metchnikoff did admit two problems in this plan: (1) the removal of organs from dead bodies within twenty-four hours, and (2) deciding the correct dose. Elie Metchnikoff, *The Nature of Man*, (New York: G. P. Putnam's Sons, 1903), p. 246; Stearns, *Old Age in European Society*, p. 98; Cole, "Past Meridian," 275–84.
42 Physicians rarely agreed on their prescriptions; therapeutics endorsed by some were often rejected by others. Sir Anthony Carlisle, *An Essay on the Disorders of Old Age and the Means of Prolonging Human Life* (Philadelphia: Edward Earle, 1819), p. 51, Maclachlan, *A Practical Treatise*, p. 42, and Canstatt, "Review of 'On the Diseases of Old Age and their Care,'" p. 111, favor bloodletting, whereas Day, *A Practical Treatise*, pp. 54–5, and Van Oven, *On the Decline of Life*, p. 165, oppose it. In the case of alkalis, Carlisle, *An Essay*, p. 48, Charcot, *Clinical Lectures*, p. 160, and Ferran, "Medicine of Senility," p. 1192, favor them, whereas Day, *A Practical Treatise*, p. 57, opposes them. In the case of narcotics, Charcot, *Clinical Lectures*, p. 75, and Henry F. Walker, "Our Counsel to Patients, especially in the Later Part of Life," *Medical Record*, 53, no. 13 (March, 1898), p. 456, suggest them, whereas Day, *A Practical Treatise*, p. 59, disagrees. In the case of purgatives, Maclachlan, *A Practical Treatise*, p. 45, recommends them, whereas Day opposes them. In the case of diuretics, Maclachlan, p. 50, favors them, whereas Canstatt disagrees (cited by Maclachlan, p. 50). Within the same work, in fact, a physician often contradicted his own prescriptions. See, for example, Day on opiates, pp. 59, 129; on metals, pp. 57, 216–17.
43 Day, *A Practical Treatise*, p. 78; see also Charcot and Loomis, *Clinical Lectures*, pp. 194–5.
44 Clarence Bartlett, "Clinical Lectures on Diseases of Old Age," *The Hahnemannian Monthly*, 41 (February, 1906), p. 115.
45 According to I. L. Nascher, "In maturity nature cures; in senility, nature kills. In maturity, the physician tries to aid nature; in senility, he tries to thwart nature and retard the natural senile process which ends in death." "The Treatment of Diseases in Senility" p. 988; Day, *A Practical Treatise*, pp. 52–3.
46 *Oxford English Dictionary* (Oxford: Clarendon Press, 1961), p. 454.
47 In 1828, Noah Webster included "senility" in his dictionary, although the word did not appear in medical dictionaries. Webster noted that the term was "not much used." By the late nineteenth century, it had be-

come a standard term in medical – and popular – terminology. W. Andrew Achenbaum, *Old Age in The New Land* (Baltimore: Johns Hopkins University Press, 1978), p. 31.

48 *Oxford English Dictionary*, p. 454.

49 Benjamin Rush, *Medical Inquiries and Observations* (Philadelphia: Thomas Dobson, 1797), pp. 308–10.

50 On brain lesions: Clouston, *Clinical Lectures*, p. 408; B. Furneaux Jordan, "Pathological and Clinical Notes with Especial Reference to Disease in the Aged," *The Birmingham Medical Review*, 32 (July, 1892), p. 7.

On starvation of tissue, Julius Althaus, "Old Age and Rejuvenescence," *The Lancet*, 1 (January, 1899), p. 150; Maclachlan, *A Practical Treatise*, p. 21.

On dying brain cells: Althaus, "Old Age and Rejuvenescence," p. 150; W. M. Gibson, "Some Considerations of Senescence," *New York State Journal of Medicine*, 9, no. 9 (September, 1909), p. 382; I. N. Love, "The Needs and Rights of Old Age," *Journal of the American Medical Association*, 29, no. 21 (November, 1897), p. 1038; W. H. B. Stoddart, *Mind and Its Disorders* (Philadelphia: P. Blakiston's Sons & Co. 1909), p. 340.

On arteriosclerosis: Louis Faugeres Bishop, "The Relation of Old Age to Disease, with Illustrative Cases," *The American Journal of Nursing*, 9, no. 9 (June, 1904), p. 677; E. C. Spitza, *Insanity: Its Classification, Diagnosis and Treatment* (New York: Bermingham & Co., 1883), p. 174; F. H. Stephenson, "Senility, Senile Dementia and their Medico-Legal Aspects," *Buffalo Medical Journal*, 40, no. 8 (March, 1901), p. 448.

On softening of the brain: Clouston, *Clinical Lectures*, p. 406; Stoddart, *Mind and Its Disorders*, p. 341.

On loss of the molecules' vitality: Henry Maudsley, *Responsibility in Mental Disease* (New York: D. Appleton & Co., 1874), pp. 259–60; Mercier, *Sanity and Insanity*, pp. 305–6.

51 Isaac Ray, *A Treatise on the Medical Jurisprudence of Insanity* (1838), ed., Winfred Overholse (Cambridge, Mass: Belknap Press, 1962), pp. 205–10; James Cowles Prichard, *Treatise on Insanity and Other Disorders affecting the Mind* (Philadelphia: Haswell, Barrington and Haswell, 1837), pp. 29–30.

52 Ray, *A Treatise*, p. 205.

53 Ibid.

54 Stoddart, *Mind and Its Disorders*, p. 340.

55 Mercier, *Sanity and Insanity*, p. 305.

56 Canstatt termed this the "soul-life" "Review of 'On the Diseases of Old Age and their Care,'" p. 103; Caldwell, *Effects of Age*, p. 6; Henry Holland, *Medical Notes and Reflections* (Philadelphia: Haswell, Barrington and Haswell, 1839), p. 106.

57 Charles Segwick Minot, "On Certain Phenomena of Growing Old," *Proceedings of the American Association for the Advancement of Science*, 39 (August, 1890), p. 387; J. Montgomery Mosher, "Old Age," *Yale Medical Journal*, 15, no. 2 (October, 1908), pp. 49–59; Stoddart, *Mind and Its Disorders*, p. 341.

58 George M. Beard, *Legal Responsibility in Old Age based on Researches into the Relation of Age to Work* (New York: Russells' American Steam Printing House, 1873). As we have seen in Chapter 2, this study reflected the work of statistician Quetelet, who, in the first half of the nineteenth century, had attempted to correlate intellectual ability with age. According to Quetelet, after fifty-five, a man's productivity decreased, "especially if the value of work is considered." Quetelet, *A Treatise on Man and the Development of His Faculties* (Edinburgh: William and Robert Chambers, 1842), p. 75.

59 Mercier, *Sanity and Insanity*, p. 305.

60 Althaus, "Old Age and Rejuvenescence," pp. 150–1.

61 Maudsley, *Responsibility in Mental Disease*, p. 261; Mercier, *Sanity and Insanity*, pp. 307–8; Mosher, "Old Age," p. 55; Nascher, *Geriatrics*, p. 38; Spitza, *Insanity*, pp. 172–3.

62 Scott, "Old Age and Death," p. 119.

63 Case of Margaret Wall, December 24, 1908, Case Histories, 2:85, Philadelphia Orthopaedic Hospital Casebook located at the College of Physicians of Philadelphia.

64 Beard, *Legal Responsibility in Old Age*, p. 33.

65 J. H. Kellogg, *Plain Facts for Old and Young* (Burlington, Iowa: J. F. Seyner, 1877; reprint ed. New York: Arno Press, 1974), p. 385; see also Van Oven, *On the Decline of Life*, pp. 99–100.

66 Kellogg, *Plain Facts*, pp. 385, 388. Many physicians believed that the senile individual was unable to control his acts, despite the fact that he knew them to be improper. William N. Williams, who entered Philadelphia Orthopaedic Hospital in 1908, was a case in point. At age sixty-seven, he was discharged from work and, according to his case history, "was mentally disturbed as a result." His senile dementia took the form of sexual perversions. "He tampers with little girls and boys. Has been arrested for this; he was let go the next day. Says he knows this is wrong." Case of William N. Williams, June 18, 1908, Case Histories, Philadelphia Orthopaedic Hospital, vol. 2, pp. 67–8. Casebook kept at the College of Physicians of Philadelphia.

67 Allan McLane Hamilton, *A Manual of Medical Jurisprudence* (New York: Bermingham & Co., 1883), pp. 27–8.

68 Ibid., pp. 79–80; Francis Wharton, *A Monograph on Mental Unsoundness* (Philadelphia: Kay and Brother, 1855), p. 16.

69 Ray, *A Treatise*, pp. 211–13; Stephenson, "Senility, Senile Dementia," pp. 560–1.

70 Nichols, "Old Age," p. 522.

71 Nascher, *Geriatrics*, p. 489.

72 Clouston, *Clinical Lectures*, p. 395.

73 Mercier, *Sanity and Insanity*, pp. 307–8; see also, Loomis, "Old Age in Health and Disease,", pp. 8–9; Nichols, "Old Age," pp. 523–4.

74 Clouston, *Clinical Lectures*, pp. 401–2.

75 Many other physicians expressed similar opinions about the difficulties of treating the aged as patients. See, for example, Bishop, "Relation of Old Age to Disease," p. 676; Brown, "Some Observations," p. 90; Cur-

tis, "Disease in the Aged," pp. 401–6; Clement Dukes, "The Restlessness of Old Age and Its Treatment," *The British Medical Journal*, 2 (December, 1899); p. 1542; J. H. Emerson, "A Group of Aged Patients," *Medical News*, 72, no. 7 (February, 1898), p. 204.

76 Bishop, "Relation of Old Age to Disease," p. 679.

5. Institutionalizing the Elderly

1 Homer Folks, "Disease and Dependence," *Charities*, 10, no. 20 (May, 1903), p. 500.
2 Ibid., pp. 499–500, and 11, no. 14 (October, 1903), pp. 297–300.
3 Priscilla Clement, "The Response to Need: Poverty and Welfare in Philadelphia, 1800-1856," (unpublished Ph.D. diss., University of Pennsylvania, 1977), p. 87.
4 Thomas R. Hazard, *Report on the Poor and Insane of Rhode Island* (Providence, R.I.: J. Knowles, 1851; reprint ed. New York: Arno Press, 1973), pp. 11, 13, 15, 19, 21, 23, 25, 30, 32, 34, 36, 37, 38, 39, 43, 44, 46, 48, 51, 53, 54, 56, 57, 59, 63. The proportions range from 85 percent in Charlestown (five out of six) to 8 percent in Cranston (1 out of 12).
5 Ibid., pp. 25–7.
6 Frederick L. Hoffman, "State Pensions and Annuities in Old Age," *Journal of the American Statistical Association*, 11, new series 85 (March, 1909) p. 395.
7 Ibid.
8 Massachusetts Commission on Old Age Pensions, Annuities, and Insurance, *Report of the Massachusetts Commission on Old Age Pensions, Annuities and Insurance* (Boston: Wright & Potter, 1910; reprint ed. New York: Arno Press, 1976), p. 37.
9 Mary Roberts Smith, "Almshouse Women," *American Statistical Association*, 4, no. 31 (September, 1895), p. 240.
10 Hoffman, "State Pensions and Annuities," p. 396.
11 Edward T. Devine, *The Principles of Relief* (New York: Macmillan Company, 1904), pp. 129–32; David J. Rothman, *The Discovery of the Asylum: Social Order and Disorder in the New Republic* (Boston and Toronto: Little, Brown and Company, 1971), chaps. 4–9.
12 This is not to say that the old did not receive any outdoor pensions. The sums they received after the mid-nineteenth century, however, were usually so small as to force any truly needy elderly person into the almshouse. In Massachusetts, for example, by the beginning of the twentieth century, the state was spending $693,076 annually on the 3,480 persons over sixty-five who lived in the poorhouses. At the same time, it allotted less than one-quarter of that figure – $189,900 – to the 3,075 aged persons on outdoor relief. For the most incapacitated of the old, this support was not enough to allow them to live outside of the almshouse. Massachusetts Commission, *Report*, p. 29.
13 Clement, "The Response to Need," p. 161; Mathew Carey, *Letters on the Condition of the Poor* (Philadelphia: Haswell & Barrington, 1835), p.

12; *Hazard's Register of Pennsylvania*, 11, no. 17 (October, 1830), pp. 266–7.

14 Clement, "The Response to Need," p. 341.
15 Ibid., pp. 179, 299.
16 Smith, "Almshouse Women," p. 223.
17 Massachusetts Commission, *Report*, p. 33.
18 Ibid., p. 37. In Pennsylvania, in the second decade of the twentieth century, the corresponding figures for almshouse inmates were 40.0 percent single, 39.0 percent widowed, and 16.9 percent married. *Report of the Pennsylvania Commission on Old Age Pensions* (Harrisburg: J. L. L. Kuhn, 1919), p. 12.
19 Massachusetts Commission, *Report*, p. 37. In Pennsylvania, 63.51 percent had no children. *Pennsylvania Commission*, p. 22.
20 In Massachusetts, 7.7 percent of the almshouse population reported having adult children or near relatives able to aid them at present. Massachusetts Commisssion, *Report*, p. 43. In Pennsylvania, 10.07 percent reported having offspring who were able to assist them. *Pennsylvania Commission*, p. 22.
21 In the United States, the proportion of males and females in the almshouse was 64 percent males and 36 percent females; in Massachusetts, the proportion was 61.4 percent males and 38.6 percent females. Massachusetts Commission *Report*, p. 36.
22 For an interpretation of the functional economic role played by grandmothers, see Michael Anderson, *Family Structure in Nineteenth Century Lancashire* (Cambridge: Cambridge University Press, 1974), chap. 10.
23 *Pennsylvania Commission*, p. 20.
24 Massachusetts Commission, *Report*, p. 68.
25 Ibid., pp. 69–70.
26 The Massachusetts Commission found that about one-third reported disability from old age; the rest declared that serious diseases and accidents had caused their incapacitation (p. 40).
27 In 1902, the managers of the Boston almshouse at Long Island noted the change in the institution. In the past, the city had maintained an almshouse with a small hospital. Now, however, they wrote, the hospital "is the most important of the work of the Long Island institute." *Fifth Annual Report of the Pauper Institutions Department for the year ending 1902* (Boston, 1903), p. 2.
28 "Report of the Visiting Medical Staff, Long Island Hospital," *Seventh Annual Report of the Pauper Institutions Department for the year ending 1904* (Boston, 1905), p. 15.
29 Folks, "Disease and Dependence," (1903b), p. 298.
30 Ibid., (1903a), p. 499.
31 *Majority and Minority Reports of an Investigation of Boston Alms House and Hospital at Long Island* (Boston: Municipal Printing Office, 1904), p. 1730.
32 *Charities and the Commons*, "New York City Homes," vol. 17 (August 27, 1900), p. 133. The minister is Ithamar W. Beard.
33 Ibid.

34 New York Association for Improving the Condition of the Poor (NYAICP), *Forty-Fifth Annual Report* (New York, 1888), p. 28.
35 NYAICP, *Fiftieth/Fifty-First Annual Report* (1893–4), pp. 64–5.
36 Ibid., p. 114.
37 *Seventh Annual Report of the Trustees of the State Lunatic Hospital at Taunton* (Boston, 1860), p. 34; also cited by Herbert Goldhamer and Andrew Marshall, *Psychosis and Civilization* (Glencoe, Ill.: The Free Press, 1953), pp. 81–82.
38 *Sixth Annual Report of the Board of State Commissioners of Public Charities of the State of New York* (New York, 1873), pp. 97–124.
39 Goldhamer and Marshall, *Psychosis and Civilization*, p. 79.
40 *Fifth Biennial Report of the Wisconsin State Hospital for the Insane* (Madison, Wis., 1892), p. 55.
41 Barbara G. Rosenkrantz and Maris A. Vinovskis, "The Invisible Lunatics: Old Age and Insanity in Mid-Nineteenth-Century Massachusetts," in *Aging and the Elderly: Humanistic Perspective in Gerontology*, eds., Stuart F. Spicker, Kathleen M. Woodward, and David D. Van Tassel, (Atlantic Highlands, N.J.: Humanities Press, Inc., 1978), pp. 109–11. The diagnosis of "senility" or "insanity from old age" seemed to vary greatly. One hospital could diagnose all its elderly patients as senile, whereas another would list other causes for its patients' insanity. Even within the same hospital, the number of senile patients might vary sharply from one year to the next or even from one ward for the elderly to another. As the disease could include any symptom occurring in a person who had reached senescence, the diagnosis seemed to reflect more the preference of the attending physician than any distinct illness. In Pennsylvania in 1888, for example, whereas there were no cases of senile dementia diagnosed at the Harrisburg institution, there were thirty-four at Norristown. *Nineteenth Annual Report of the Board of Public Charities of the State of Pennsylvania* (Harrisburg, 1888), pp. 204–8. See also *First Annual Report of the Board of State Commissioners of the State of Pennsylvania* (Harrisburg, 1871), p. 77, in which old age as a cause of insanity is not listed. Also *Biennial Report of the Insane Asylum, State of Louisiana*, for the year 1877, p. 13; for the year 1887 (New Orleans, 1888), p. 14; *Fifth Biennial Report of the Wisconsin State Hospital for the Insane* (1892), p. 60.
42 In 1903, at an investigation of the Boston Almshouse and Hospital at Long Island, Alderman Nolan asked Dr. F. P. Lord, "What are the symptoms of senility? It seems to me to cover every case here." Dr. Lord's reply, which brought laughter from the audience, was, "It is old age itself." *Majority and Minority Reports*, p. 106.
43 Morris Vogel, "Boston's Hospitals 1870–1930, A Social History" (unpublished Ph.D. diss., University of Chicago, 1974), p. 138.
44 *Eighth Annual Report of St. Luke's Hospital for the Year 1866* (Chicago, 1867), p. 9.
45 Vogel, "Boston's Hospitals," p. 138.
46 In 1903, Dr. Gaynor, of the Long Island Alms House noted that many

of the aged inmates in his institution had been dismissed from other hospitals as chronic cases. *Majority and Minority Reports*, p. 1146.

47 *Report of the Executive Committee of Hartford Hospital* (Hartford, Conn., 1862), pp. 17–18.

48 *Thirteenth Annual Report of Hartford Hospital* (Hartford, Conn., 1873), p. 11; see also *Sixteenth Annual Report* (1876), pp. 8–9.

49 *Nineteenth Annual Report of Hartford Hospital* (1879), p. 8. See also "Julius Weiss Home for the Aged," *Twenty-Seventh Annual Report of the Tours Infirmary and Hebrew Benevolent Association* (New Orleans, 1901), p. 8; *Eighth Annual Report of St. Luke's Hospital* (Chicago, 1866), p. 9.

50 *Charities*, "Charitable Needs of New York," 1, no. 7 (June, 1898), p. 7. The appeal was repeatedly printed throughout the year.

51 *Charities and the Commons*, "A Need for Homes for the Aged," 17, no. 15 (February, 1907), p. 875.

52 Massachusetts Commission, *Report*, p. 22.

53 *Twenty-Eighth Annual Report of the State Board of Charities for the Year 1894* (New York, 1894), pp. 546–7.

54 Massachusetts Commission, *Report*, p. 69.

55 Ibid., p. 59.

56 Ibid.

57 *Pennsylvania Commission*, pp. 73–4.

58 Massachusetts Commission, *Report*, p. 30.

59 Prior to 1817, Christ Church Hospital had housed indigent old women. This institution, however, did not restrict its applicants in age. Founded in 1769 through the will of John Kearsley, it was established as "an almshouse or infirmary" for poor and distressed women of the communion of the Church of England . . . (preferring clergymen's widows before others)." Throughout the 1860s, however, it still seemed to accept women in their forties. In 1865, for example, Rosanne Rogers, age forty-eight, was admitted; in 1868; Sarah Walton, forty-six, was accepted (Case Book, Christ Church Hospital, Philadelphia). By the end of the century, although it did not limit its admissions by age, the home required that its members be "of sufficient age." Moreover, it repeatedly referred to its "elderly" inmates and often noted the advanced years of a tenant at her death, as well as the high average age of the household. See, for example, *Annual Report of Christ Church for 1893* (Philadelphia, 1893), p. 3, and *Annual Report of Christ Church for 1897*, pp. 5, 6.

60 *Medical Directory of Philadelphia* (Philadelphia: P. Blakiston's Son and Company, 1889), pp. 273–85. This is the most complete available list. To the twenty-two homes for the aged, I have added two that do not appear on this list: the Evangelical Manor and the Philadelphia Protestant Home for the Aged. Wards of hospitals devoted to the old have been excluded.

61 City Department Records, Charleston, S.C., William Enston Home for the Aged (1883–1938); Mississippi Department of Archives and History, William T. Walthall Papers, Old Ladies Home, Jackson, Miss.; Ethel McClure, *More than a Roof: The Development of Minnesota Poor Farms and Homes for the Aged* (St. Paul: Minnesota Historical Society, 1968), p. 44;

see also State Historical Society of Wisconsin, Ladies Benevolent Home, Oshkosh, Wisconsin (1890–   ); Oregon Historical Society, Patton Home, Portland, Ore. (1887–1975).

62 *Twenty-Eighth Annual Report of the Indigent Widows' and Single Women's Society for the Year 1844* (Philadelphia, 1845), p. 3 (hereafter cited as IWSWS).

63 *Seventh Annual Report of the IWSWS for the Year 1823*, p. 3.

64 *Annual Report of the IWSWS for the Year 1817*, p. 4.

65 *Twenty-Fourth Annual Report of the IWSWS for the Year 1840*, p. 3.

66 *Seventh Annual Report of the IWSWS for the Year 1823*, p. 3; *Eighth Annual Report of the IWSWS for the Year 1824*, p. 3; *Sixteenth Annual Report of the IWSWS for the Year 1832*, p. 4.

67 "Act to Incorporate," printed in the *Second Annual Report of the IWSWS, for the Year 1818*, p. 14.

68 *Seventh Annual Report of the IWSWS for the Year 1823*, p. 4.

69 "Act to Incorporate," p. 14.

70 *Seventeenth Annual Report of the IWSWS for the Year 1833*, p. 3.

71 *Second Annual Report of the IWSWS for the Year 1818*, pp. 4–5.

72 Ibid., p. 5. The statement also appears as late as the *Nineteenth Annual Report of the IWSWS for the Year 1835*, p. 3.

73 *Second Annual Report of the IWSWS*, p. 5; *Third Annual Report of the IWSWS for the Year 1819*, p. 4; *Eleventh Annual Report of the IWSWS for the Year 1827*, p. 4.

74 *Thirty-Third Annual Report of the IWSWS for the Year 1849*, p. 4.

75 Ibid.

76 *Twentieth Annual Report of the IWSWS for the Year 1836*, pp. 5–6.

77 *Twenty-Eighth Annual Report of the IWSWS for the Year 1844*, p. 3.

78 *Twentieth Annual Report of the IWSWS for the Year 1836*, p. 3.

79 *Twenty-Seventh Annual Report of the IWSWS for the Year 1843*, p. 4.

80 *Twenty-Eighth Annual Report of the IWSWS for the Year 1844*, p. 3.

81 *Forty-Eighth Annual Report of the IWSWS for the Year 1874*, p. 3; *Fifty-Third Annual Report of the IWSWS for the Year 1869*, p. 3; *Fifty-Ninth Annual Report of the IWSWS for the Year 1875*, p. 4.

82 *Charter, Constitution and By Laws of the Presbyterian Home for Widows and Single Women* (hereafter cited as PHWSW) (Philadelphia: Jasper B. Rodgers, 1885), p. 18.

83 *PHWSW Rules and Regulations* (Philadelphia: Henry B. Ashmead, 1872), p. 17.

84 *A History of the Evangelical Manor* (unauthored pamphlet published by the Evangelical Association; Philadelphia, 1960), p. 1.

85 *Fifth Annual Report of the Old Man's Home for 1870* (Philadelphia, 1871), p. 6.

86 *Tenth Annual Report of the Old Man's Home for 1875*, p. 9.

87 *First Annual Report of the Old Man's Home for 1866*, p. 8.

88 *Fourth Annual Report of the Old Man's Home for 1869*, p. 6.

89 *First Annual Report of the Old Man's Home for 1866*, p. 8.

90 Charles E. Rosenberg, "Sexuality, Class and Role in Nineteenth-Century America," *American Quarterly*, 25 (May, 1973), pp. 131–51.

91 *First Annual Report of the Old Man's Home for 1866,* p. 8.
92 *Thirty-Fourth Annual Report of the Old Man's Home for 1898,* p. 8.
93 *Eighth Annual Report of the Managers of the Presbyterian Home for the Aged Couples and Aged Single Men* (hereafter cited as PHACAM) (Philadelphia, 1892), p. 2.
94 *Constitution, By Laws and Rules of the Home for Aged and Infirm Colored People* (hereafter cited as HAICP) (Philadelphia: Merrihew & Sons, 1865), p. 11.
95 *Proceedings of the Third Annual Meeting of the HAICP for 1867,* pp. 6–7.
96 *Proceedings of the Second Annual Meeting of the HAICP for 1866,* pp. 4, 11; *Proceedings of the Third Annual Meeting of the HAICP for 1867,* p. 6; *Proceedings of the Fifth Annual Meeting of the HAICP for 1869,* p. 7; *Proceedings of the Sixth Annual Meeting of the HAICP for 1870,* p. 4.
97 *Proceedings of the Eighth Annual Meeting of the HAICP for 1872,* p. 5.
98 *Charter and By Laws of the HAICP* (Philadelphia: Merrihew & Sons, 1865), p. 10. This rule is repeated annually throughout the reports.
99 *Seventh Annual Report of the HAICP for 1881,* p. 8.
100 *Twelfth Annual Report of the HAICP for 1876,* p. 10.
101 *Medical Directory of Philadelphia,* pp. 273–85; see also Lee Welling Squier, *Old Age Dependency in the United States* (New York: Macmillan Company, 1912), pp. 55–71.
102 *Seventh Annual Report of the IWSWS for 1871,* p. 3.
103 *Fifty-Ninth Annual Report of the IWSWS for 1875,* p. 4.
104 *Sixty-First Annual Report of the IWSWS for 1877,* p. 4. This specifically refers to the issue of sponsoring the bed. The attitude of the institution as home is repeated in almost every single issue.
105 *Twenty-First Annual Report of the HAICP for 1885,* p. 12. This is the source of the quotation. Endless examples from the homes may be cited. For example, see *Eighteenth Annual Report of the HAICP for 1882,* p. 6; *Thirteenth Annual Report of the PHSCAM for 1897,* p. 5; *Sixty-Nineth Annual Report of the IWSWS for 1885,* p. 5; *Fifteenth Annual Report of the Old Ladies' Home for 1891,* p. 4.
106 *Thirteenth Annual Report of the HAICP for 1872,* p. 5.
107 *Nineteenth Annual Report of the HAICP for 1883,* p. 8.
108 *Forty-Sixth Annual Report of the IWSWS for 1862,* p. 3.
109 *Sixteenth Annual Report of the Old Ladies' Home for 1891,* p. 7. In New York, *Charities* magazine often commended physicians for the thoroughness of their reports that appeared in the homes' annual statements. Of Dr. S. Newton Leo, of the Home for Aged Infirm Hebrews, it wrote that his report "may be recommended as a model for all medical men serving in a similar capacity in institutions; it is more than a medical report; it is a social and psychological study of the inmates." The editors of *Charities* also chastised the house physician of a Yonkers institution for not meeting Dr. Leo's standard. The physician would, they wrote, "perform a more satisfactory service to the public if he would model his own report more closely after that of Dr. Leo." "The Strenuous Life and the Home for the Aged," *Charities,* 11, no. 16 (October, 1903), pp. 347, 348.

110 *Eighth Annual Report of the PHACAM for 1893*, p. 9.
111 *Thirteenth Annual Report of the Old Man's Home for 1877*, p. 6.
112 *Proceedings of the Sixth Annual Meeting of the HAICP for 1871*, p. 18.
113 *Eighteenth Annual Report of the Old Ladies' Home for 1893*, p. 9.
114 *Thirty-Fourth Annual Report of the Old Man's Home for 1896*, p. 8.
115 *Twenty-First Annual Report of the HAICP for 1885,*, p. 8.
116 *Nineteenth Annual Report of the HAICP for 1883*, p. 8.
117 References to improved health fill the final pages of the century's reports
     in all the homes. See, for example, *Eighth Annual Meeting of the HAICP
     for 1872*, p. 7; *Eighteenth Annual Report of the Old Ladies' Home for 1893*,
     p. 9; *Thirty-Third Annual Report of the Old Man's Home for 1894*, p. 8.
118 *Third Annual Report of the Old Ladies' Home for 1877*, p. 6.
119 *Sixth Annual Report of the Old Man's Home for 1870*, p. 6.
120 *Sixteenth Annual Report of the HAICP for 1880*, p. 12.

6. The Pension Barrier

1 See Chapter 1, esp. the remarks of Cotton Mather and Samuel Sewall.
2 As there were always elderly people in America who, if separated from
   work, wealth, and family, suffered discrimination, I disagree with the
   belief of William Graebner that "age discrimination was born and nur-
   tured at the hands of a capitalist economy." Rather, the industrial economy only expanded the proportion of aged persons who were perceived
   to be powerless and thus could be categorized as overaged. Retirement
   programs, therefore, must be seen as a reaction to the assumed needs
   of these people as well as a symptom of society's disregard for old age.
   Most importantly, as we shall see, they grew primarily out of an attempt
   to control the labor market. William Graebner, *A History of Retirement:
   The Meaning of an American Institution, 1885–1978* (New Haven, Conn.:
   Yale University Press, 1980), p. 18.
3 W. Andrew Achenbaum, *Old Age in the New Land* (Baltimore: Johns
   Hopkins University Press, 1978), p. 103. Of those in agriculture, fishing,
   or mining, 89 percent remained employed. In all occupations, the proportion is 77 percent. See also M. Rubinow, *Social Insurance* (New York:
   Henry Holt & Co., 1913), p. 305.
4 See Chapter 5 of this study.
5 This is, of course, a very rough estimate. Before the enactment of standardized programs, most industries kept few records of the number of
   pensioners. In all cases, however, the total was quite small. The military, however, listed their pensioners in extensive records. In 1870,
   there were 87,521 men on the pension rolls, a figure that does not include their wives and children. According to both I. M. Rubinow and
   William Glasson, authorities on pensions, these annuities could be considered old-age pensions, as almost every veteran was quite aged. Thus,
   out of the 989,516 men over sixty in 1870, about 9 percent were receiving
   pensions. By 1910, 744,188, or about 18 percent of men over sixty-five
   were listed as United States pensioners. Rubinow, *Social Insurance*, pp.

310–11, 406, 409; William Glasson, *Federal Military Pensions* (New York: Oxford University Press, 1918), pp. 117–19, 149, 264, 271.

6 Cited by the Pennsylvania Commission on Old Age Pensions, *Report of the Pennsylvania Commission on Old Age Pensions* (Harrisburg: J. L. L. Kuhn, 1919), p. 139. See also L. J. Seargeant, "Superannuation of Railway Employees" in *The World's Railway Commerce Congress – Official Report* (Chicago: The Railway Age and Northwestern Railroader, 1893), p. 174.

7 "Notes and News," *Railway Age*, 24 (May, 1898), p. 329; "Communications – He Ran an Engine 45 Years," *Railway Age*, 24 (October, 1897), p. 835. See also *Railway Age*, 24 (November, 1897), p. 955, concerning the pension given by the Chicago and Northwestern Railroad to Israel H. Blodgett, who had been a ticket agent for thirty years. For early, unregulated pensions given by the Standard Oil Company, see Ralph W. Hidy and Muriel E. Hidy, *Pioneering in Big Business* (New York: Harper & Brothers, 1955), p. 601.

8 In 1887, for example, President Cleveland signed a bill that granted pensions to Mexican War veterans but vetoed another that would have allowed for Civil War annuities. He reasoned that whereas there would be few survivors from the Mexican conflict, many ex-soldiers were still alive to demand Civil War annuities. Glasson, *Federal Military Pensions*, pp. 117–18.

9 Disability Pensions Act of 1890, cited in ibid., p. 234.

10 Bureau of Pensions, *Instructions to Examining Surgeons* (Washington, D.C.: Government Printing Office, 1887), rule 14, p. 5, which reads, in part, "The disability, per se, of old age is not pensionable."

11 Bureau of Pensions, *Digest of Decisions of the Department of Interior*, eds., Eugene B. Payne and Vespasian Warner (Washington, D.C.: Government Printing Office 1905), p. 121.

12 *Report of the Commissioners of Pensions for 1900* (Washington, D.C., 1901), statement of Commissioner H. Clay Evans, p. 26.

13 *Report of the Commissioners of Pensions for 1904*. In the first year this new order was issued, 47,080 Civil War pensioners were added to the rolls. Glasson, *Federal Military Pensions*, pp. 246–7.

14 *Bureau of Pensions, Instructions to Examining Surgeons* (Washington, D.C.: Government Printing Office, 1913), rule 124, p. 20. See also "The Pension Inquiry," *The Nation*, 78, no. 2021 (March, 1904), p. 224.

15 *Twenty-Seventh Annual Report of the National Encampment of the Grand Army of the Republic* (Washington, D.C., 1907), pp. 77–8; Glasson, *Federal Military Pensions*, p. 250.

16 Banks were one of the first totally white-collar organizations to establish pension funds; yet, their motives did not differ greatly from those of other large industries. Bankers were concerned with the large turnover of their staffs, particularly when large amounts of money were handled by numerous employees unknown to the management. (Bankers Trust, for example, had a staff of 1,500 employees.) With a pension, one bank president explained, the workers "are apt to devote their best efforts exclusively to their careers, and to be in less danger of diverting their

energies into side channels of money making – channels which may easily lead them on dangerous grounds." E. A. Vanderlip, "Insurance from the Employer's Standpoint," *Proceedings of the National Conference of Charities and Corrections* (1907), p. 462. Banks did differ from other large industries, however, in often making their funds contributory, automatically subtracting 3 percent of their employees' wages.

17 Abraham Epstein, *The Problem of Old Age Pensions in Industry* (Harrisburg, Pa.: Pennsylvania Old Age Commission, 1926), pp. 115–16.
18 Ibid., p. 455.
19 J. N. A. Griswold to Robert Harris, October 5, 1877, in Thomas Cochran, *The Railroad Leaders 1845–1890* (Cambridge, Mass.: Harvard University Press, 1953), p. 344.
20 See, for example, F. Spencer Baldwin, "Retirement Systems for Municipal Employes," *Annals of the American Academy of Political and Social Science*, 38, no. 1 (July, 1911), pp. 6–14, and Epstein, *Old Age Pensions*, pp. 76–7.
21 Generally, these relief plans allocated benefits for accidents, infirmity, and death. In 1903, there were about 350 company plans that were administered by the workers with management approval, if not direct intervention. More than 100 plans were jointly run by the executives and the workers. Another thirty programs were totally funded by the management. *Twenty-Third Annual Report of the Commissioner of Labor (1908): Workman's Insurance and Benefit Funds in the United States* (Washington, D.C.: Government Printing Office, 1909), pp. 271, 308, 607.
22 This particular restriction comes from the Western Electric Company Pension System (1906), as cited in the *Twenty-Third Annual Report of the Commissioner of Labor*, pp. 646–7. Similar disclaimers can be found in all establishment-controlled programs.
23 Walter M. Licht, "Nineteenth-Century American Railway Men: A Study in the Organization and Nature of Work" (unpublished Ph.D. diss., Princeton University, 1977), chap. 2. Similar high turnover rates were reported in a number of large industries throughout the late nineteenth and early twentieth centuries. In 1912, for example, 48 percent of the employees of the Ford Motor Company either quit or were fired; in 1907, ninety-one southern textile mills hired 57,000 new employees for 30,000 places. Daniel Nelson, *Managers and Workers: Origins of the New Factory System in the United States* (Madison: University of Wisconsin Press, 1975), p. 86. The knowledge that few men would stay long enough to receive pensions surely influenced the employer's willingness to implement these programs. See, for example, the description of the pension program set up by Alfred Dodge and Sons in 1882. In this company, only 40 percent of the workers remained for a year and only 10.8 percent for five years. Out of a total of 2,046 employees who had been hired over the course of twenty years, only ten remained for fifteen years. Paul Monroe, "An American System of Labor Pensions and Insurance," *American Journal of Sociology*, 2, no. 4 (January, 1897), p. 510.
24 Vanderlip, "Insurance from the Employers' Standpoint," p. 462.

25 First National Bank of Chicago Pension Fund (1899) as reported in the *Twenty-Third Annual Report of the Commissioner of Labor*, pp. 645–6.
26 Seargeant, "Superannuation of Railway Employees," p. 175.
27 *Report of the Pennsylvania Commission on Old Age Pensions*, p. 114.
28 Frank Tracy Carlton, *The History and Problems of Organized Labor* (Boston: D.C. Heath & Company, 1920), pp. 315–16; E. E. Cummins, *The Labor Problem in the United States* (New York: D. Van Nostrand Company, 1932), p. 522; Henry Rogers Seager, *Social Insurance: A Program of Social Reform* (New York: Macmillan Company, 1910), pp. 121–2.
29 In Pennsylvania, the law regulating and incorporating fraternal organizations (passed in 1893) also failed to consider the idea of pensions based solely on age. It allowed only for provisions in "case of sickness, disability or death." *Report of the Pennsylvania Commission on Old Age Pensions*, p. 198. This was also true of the Massachusetts law that incorporated fraternal organizations in that state. Massachusetts Commission on Old Age Pensions, Annuities and Insurance, *Report of the Massachusetts Commission on Old Age Pensions, Annuities and Insurance* (Boston: Wright & Potter, 1910; reprint ed. New York, Arno Press, 1976). In the first decade of the twentieth century, when unions did begin to adopt pension plans, they continued to make it clear that payment was for complete disability rather than for old age as such. The Order of Railroad Conductors (1908) demanded that the worker be "totally disabled and without means of support"; the Bricklayers, Masons, and Plasterers International (1905) described their retirees as men "unable to secure sustaining employment at any occupation." *Twenty-Third Annual Report of the Commissioner of Labor*, pp. 204, 205.
30 See, for example, Massachusetts Board of Railroad Commissioners, *Twelfth Annual Report* (Boston, 1880), p. 59 and Emory R. Johnson, "Railway Department for Relief and Insurance of Employes," *Annals of the American Academy of Political and Social Science*, 6 (November, 1895), p. 68.
31 Paul V. Black, "The Development of Management Personnel Policies on the Burlington Railroad, 1860–1900" (unpublished Ph.D. diss., University of Wisconsin, 1972), pp. 379–80.
32 *Twenty-Third Annual Report of the Commissioner of Labor*, p. 33.
33 Harris Schrank, "The Work Force," in *Aging and Society*, vol. 3, eds., Matilda W. Riley, Marilyn Johnson, and Anne Foner (New York: Russell Sage Foundation, 1972), p. 177. In the nineteenth century, however, most men continued to see themselves as part of the labor market. In hospital death records – which surely concerned the most debilitated members of society – almost every elderly man reported having some occupation. In the *Report of the Board of Administration of Charity Hospital (New Orleans) for the year 1876* (New Orleans, 1876), for example, eighty-eight men over the age of sixty died during the year. Of these, only four, or less than 5 percent, were listed without occupations. Although one may logically question whether many of these men worked immediately before their deaths, they did not see themselves as retired.
34 A study done by the Pennsylvania Commission on Old Age Pensions

that interviewed almost 4,000 aged workers in Pittsburgh, Reading, and Philadelphia concluded:

men past a certain age must quit even the skilled trades in which they have been engaged the greater part of their lives . . . While 36 per cent stated that they were skilled or semiskilled mechanics in their earlier days, only 23.8 per cent of men past 50 years of age were still engaged in the same occupation.

Report of the Pennsylvania Commission on Old Age Pensions, p. 101.

35 In 1919, Samuel Gompers explained, in part, why unions needed to recognize this new age-limited work cycle. In a letter to the Committee on Miners' Home and Pensions, he wrote:

Many of the proposals for social insurance are of a compulsory nature. Wage earners now find themselves confronted by this alternative: either labor organizations must make more comprehensive and more adequate provisions for trade union benefits or else they will have forced upon them compulsory social insurance under the control and direction of governmental agencies.

Cited in the *Report of the Pennsylvania Commission on Old Age Pensions*, p. 200.

36 Dan H. Mater, "The Development and Operation of the Railroad Seniority System," *Journal of Business of the University of Chicago*, 13, no. 4 (October, 1940), pp. 399–402.

37 Harvey D. Shapiro, "Do Not Go Gently . . ." *The New York Times Magazine* (February 7, 1977), p. 36. On the connection between mandatory retirement and seniority, see Leonard Z. Breen, "Retirement – Norms, Behavior and Functions of Aspects of Normative Behavior," in *Processes of Aging*, eds., Richard H. Williams, Clark Tibbits, and Wilma Donahue (New York: Atherton Press, 1963), p. 384.

38 Robert Harris, Letter to J. N. A. Griswold, December 10, 1877, Harris Letters, Chicago, Burlington & Quincy Papers, Newberry Library, Chicago.

39 During the wars, in contrast, companies loosened their regulations to adapt to the tightened labor situation. See Schrank, "The Work Force," p. 163. During the Civil War, in fact, the efficiency of the Confederate railroad was disrupted because young workers were pressed into the military. To rectify this situation, the board of directors of the Virginia Central resolved:

that the superintendent be instructed to employ men over forty years old in every case when a suitable person to perform the duties can be found, and that no assistant agent be retained who is between the age of eighteen and forty-five unless he is exempt from military duty.

Charles W. Turner, *Chessie's Road* (Richmond, Va.: Garrett & Massie, 1956), p. 45.

40 Labor unrest, unemployment, and the growth of the cities' slums were

all cited as visible evidence that America was no longer able to absorb all the world's hunger and poverty. John Higham, *Strangers in the Land* (New York: Atheneum Publishers, 1972), chap. 7.

41 Frank J. Furstenberg and Charles A. Thrall have noted the presence of a "job rationing ideology" in a limited job market. This "system of shared beliefs about who should have the greatest access to the limited supply of jobs" tended to eliminate the elderly from the legitimate job market. Furstenberg and Thrall cite the Social Security system and private pension plans as making the old feel "less obligated to work and less entitled to a job." Furstenberg and Thrall, "Counting the Jobless: The Impact of Job Rationing in the Measurement of Unemployment," *The Annals of the American Academy of Political Science*, 418 (March, 1975), pp. 45–9; see also Juanita Kreps, "Economics of Retirement," in *Behavior and Adaptation in Later Life*, eds., Ewald Busse and Eric Pfeiffer (Boston: Little, Brown and Company, 1969), p. 81.

42 *Report of the Massachusetts Commission on Old Age Pensions, Annuities and Insurance*, pp. 316–21; *Report of the Pennsylvania Commission on Old Age Pensions*, pp. 179–81; see also Rubinow, *Social Insurance*, pp. 389–412; Epstein, *Old Age Pensions*, pp. 111–14. Many social analysts who endorsed the idea of industrial or govenment pensions used European models as the basis for their arguments.

43 J. M. French, "Food and Hygiene of Old Age," *The Journal of the American Medical Association*, 19, no. 21 (November, 1892), p. 596.

44 A. L. Loomis, "The Climate and Environment Best Suited to Old Age in Health and Disease," *Transactions of the Fifth Annual Meeting of the American Climatological Association* (1888), pp. 8–9.

45 Francis A. Walker, *The Wages Question* (New York: Henry Holt & Co., 1876), pp. 414–15. This work, it should be noted, was written during a severe national depression.

46 J. Madison Taylor, "The Conservation of Energy in Those Advancing Years," *The Popular Science Monthly*, 64 (February, 1904), p. 345. See Chapter 4 for a more extensive study of the American physician's view of senescence.

47 Samuel Haber, *Efficiency and Uplift: Scientific Management in the Progressive Era 1890–1920* (Chicago: University of Chicago Press, 1964).

48 Harrington Emerson, *Efficiency as a Basis for Operations and Wages* (New York: The Engineering Magazine, 1909), p. 98.

49 Ibid., p. 68.

50 At least, I have not been able to find any. This has also been the conclusion of Robert Atchley, *The Sociology of Retirement* (Cambridge, Mass.: Schenkman Publishing Co., Inc., 1976), p. 15.

51 George M. Beard, *Legal Responsibility in Old Age Based on Researches into the Relation of Age to Work* (New York: Russells' American Steam Printing House, 1873), p. 8.

52 Vanderlip, "Insurance from the Employers' Standpoint," p. 458; see also *The Carnegie Foundation for the Advancement of Teaching*, "The Moral Influence of a Pension System," 6 (1911), pp. 23–31.

53 Graebner, *History of Retirement*, pp. 24–9.
54 Reinhard Bendix, *Work and Authority in Industry* (New York and Evanston, Ill.: Harper & Row, 1956), p. 279; Emerson, *Efficiency*, pp. 70, 159–60; Abraham, Epstein, *Facing Old Age Dependency in the United States and Old Age Pensions* (New York: Alfred A. Knopf, Inc., 1922), p. 162; Epstein, *Old Age Pensions*, p. 6; Rubinow, *Social Insurance*, p. 389.
55 Vanderlip, "Insurance from the Employers' Standpoint," p. 438; Baldwin, "Retirement Systems," p. 14.
56 According to the Bureau of Labor, in 1910 there were forty-eight teacher pensions. Of the twenty-five largest cities, all but one had an established fund. Six states also had pension programs. In 1910, there were 167 pension plans for policemen and firemen. Of the nation's forty largest cities, all but six had funds; of the nation's seventy-five largest cities, sixty had funds. Department of Labor, *Pension Funds for Municipal Employees and Railroad Pensions in the United States* (Washington, D.C.: Government Printing Office, 1910), cited by Rubinow, *Social Insurance*, p. 399. See also Robert M. Fogelson, *Big-City Police* (Cambridge, Mass.: Harvard University Press, 1977), p. 83.
57 Alexander R. Piper, *Report of an Investigation of the Discipline and Administration of the Police Department of the City of Chicago* (Chicago: The Lakeside Press, 1904), p. 14: William McAdoo, *Guarding a Great City* (New York: Harper and Brothers, 1906), p. 64, cited by Robert Fogelson, "The Morass," *Social History and Social Policy*, eds., David Rothman and Stanton Wheeler (New York, Academic Press, Inc. 1981), p. 151.
58 Baldwin, "Retirement Systems," pp. 6–8; *Carnegie Foundation for the Advancement of Teaching*, 4 (1909), p. 70; 6 (1911) p. 23; 7 (1912), p. 71; Epstein, *Facing Old Age*, p. 183; F. MacVeagh, "Civil Service Pensions," *The Annals of the American Academy of Political and Social Science*, 28, no. 1 (July, 1911), pp. 305–6.
59 *Report of the Massachusetts Commission on Old Age Pensions, Annuities and Insurance*, pp. 270–1.
60 *Report of the Commissioners of Pensions for 1903*, p. 42.
61 Ibid., p. 48.
62 Elizabeth A. Allen, "Teachers Pensions – The Story of a Women's Campaign," *The Review of Reviews*, 15, no. 6 (June, 1897), pp. 700–11; see also Paul Studensky, *Teachers' Pension Systems in the United States* (New York and London: D. Appleton & Co., 1920).
63 Fogelson, *Big-City Police* chap. 2.
64 Bureau of Statistics, *A Special Report on the Cost of Retirement Systems for State and County Employees in Massachusetts – January, 1911* (Boston: Wright and Potter, 1911), p. 8.
65 Ibid., p. 11.
66 Lee Welling Squier, *Old Age Dependency in the United States* (New York: Macmillan Company, 1912), p. 321.
67 Companies without pension plans tend to retain a much higher percentage of workers over sixty-five than do companies with such plans. The adoption of these policies, therefore, tends to legitimatize the re-

lease of the aging employee. Clarence D. Long, *The Labor Force under Changing Income and Employment* (Princeton, N.J.: Princeton University Press, 1958), p. 167.

Conclusion. Old Age in a Bureaucratic Society

1 Lawrence Stone, "Walking over Grandma," *New York Review of Books*, 24, no. 8 (May, 1977), p. 10; John Modell, Frank F. Furstenberg, Jr., and Theodore Hershberg, "Social Change and Transitions to Adulthood in Historical Perspective," *Journal of Family History*, 1, no. 1, (Autumn, 1976), pp. 7–32.
2 Abraham Epstein, *The Problems of Old Age Pensions in Industry* (Harrisburg: Pennsylvania Old Age Commission, 1926), pp. 115–16; Frederick L. Hoffman, "State Pensions and Annuities in Old Age," *Journal of The American Statistical Association*, 11 new series 85 (March, 1909), p. 396.
3 Abraham Epstein, *Insecurity: A Challenge to America* (New York: Harrison Smith and Robert Haas, 1933), pp. 143, 514.
4 For the development of the age-based ideas behind the Social Security system, see William Graebner, *A History of Retirement: The Meaning and Function of an American Institution, 1885–1978* (New Haven, Conn., and London: Yale University Press, 1980), chap. 7.
5 It is important to emphasize that these programs were based on the very real problems of the aged. Even without Social Security or mandatory retirement programs, many aged persons found themselves unemployed and unsupported. During the Great Depression, the elderly were often quick to be fired and were not easily rehired. In 1934, men aged sixty-five to sixty-nine had an unemployment rate of nearly 30 percent. These elderly persons must have accepted old-age benefits with great relief. Paul H. Douglas, *Social Security in the United States* (New York: McGraw-Hill Inc., 1939), p. 6.
6 United States Department of Commerce, Bureau of the Census, *Detailed Characteristics*, United States Summary, (Washington, D.C.: Government Printing Office, 1970), Table 215; Robert N. Butler, *Why Survive?* (New York: Harper & Row, 1975), p. 273.
7 Spencer Rich, "13% of Americans in Poverty Last Year," *The Charlotte Observer*, August 21, 1981, p. 1. The year 1980 was the second consecutive year in which there was a rise in the percentage of Americans age sixty-five and over living below the poverty line. This reverses the pattern of decline that occurred in the 1960s and 1970s.

A Note on Secondary Sources

Traditionally, historians, like the rest of society, have ignored old age. Only in the past few years have a number of scholars begun to investigate the roles and conditions of the elderly in America's past. So much of this work is of recent origin, in fact, that any bibliography runs the risk of being out of date even before it goes to press. Yet, although the subject is still in the process of being formulated, several important works have raised issues and concerns that have made – and will undoubtedly continue to make – the field one of lively debate.

In 1977, David Hackett Fischer proposed one framework through which to understand old age. In *Growing Old in America* [New York: Oxford University Press, 1977], he argued that prior to 1770, the aged were venerated as symbols of authority and godliness. During the period 1770–1820, however, there was a radical change in age relations. The hierarchy was destroyed; all members of the family suddenly became equal. As a result, the old were not venerated but displaced and despised. From 1820 to the present, Fischer stated, "the lines of change have been straight and stable." Once a gerontocracy, America turned into a nation of gerontophobics. Simply put, we have come to hate anyone who has grown old.

In contrast, W. Andrew Achenbaum argued that in antebellum America the old were still respected members of society. ["The Obsolescence of Old Age in America, 1865–1914," *Journal of Social History*, 8 (Fall, 1974), pp. 48–62; "Old Age in America," (unpublished Ph.D. diss., University of Michigan, 1976; *Old Age in the New Land* (Baltimore: Johns Hopkins University Press, 1978).] In the early nineteenth century, their advanced age brought them deference rather than ridicule. They continued to be honored for their wisdom, productivity, and virtue. According to Achenbaum, 1865–1914 (rather than the postrevolutionary era) marked the critical period in the history of attitudes toward the elderly. After the Civil War, old age was no longer considered an enviable time in which to be alive.

Despite the obvious difference in periodicity, Fischer and Achenbaum appeared to agree on one central issue: In some long-distant past, the elderly were respected for their knowledge, esteemed for their experience, and admired for their God-granted longevity. Then – whether in postrevolutionary or Civil War America – these attitudes were transformed. Adoration turned into hatred; veneration became disdain. To be old was to have entered a phase of clear obsolescence.

More recent work, however, has begun to challenge the notion of a radical transformation in attitudes toward old age. In a review of David Hackett Fischer's book, Lawrence Stone argued that sentiments about senescence "are not so different today from those of Shakespeare's." ["Walking over Grandma," *New York Review of Books*, 24, no. 8 (May, 1977), pp. 10–16; "Growing Old: An Exchange," *New York Review of Books*, 24, no. 14 (September, 1977), p. 48.] Even in the colonial period, Stone stated, the elderly received respect only when they possessed valued property. The loss of wealth caused veneration to vanish rapidly. Other historians have also questioned whether a gerontocracy ever existed in colonial America. In the works of John Demos, Daniel Scott Smith, and others, a far more ambiguous picture of old age emerged. According to these scholars, the old of the eighteenth century were not always awarded honor, nor did they automatically assume positions of power. Patriarchy rested more on a man's wealth and property than simply on the length of his life.

[John Demos, "Old Age in New England," *The American Family in Social-Historical Perspective*, 2nd ed., ed., Michael Gordon (New York: St. Martin's Press, Inc., 1978, pp. 220–56); Philip Greven, Jr., *Four Generations: Population, Land, and Family in Colonial Andover, Massachusetts* (Ithaca, N.Y.: Cornell University Press, 1970); Alexander Keyssar, "Widowhood in Eighteenth-Century Massachusetts: A Problem in the History of the Family," *Perspectives in American History*, 8 (1974), pp. 83–119; Daniel Scott Smith, "Old Age and the 'Great Transformation': A New England Case Study," in *Aging and the Elderly*, ed., Stuart F. Spicker, Kathleen M. Woodward, and David D. Van Tassel (Atlantic Highlands, N.J.: Humanities Press, Inc., 1978), pp. 285–302; Smith, "Parental Power and Marriage Patterns: An Analysis of Historical Trends in Hingham, Massachusetts," *Journal of Marriage and the Family*, 35 (August, 1973), pp. 419-- 28; Maris A. Vinovskis, "'Aged Servants of the Lord': Changes in the Status and Treatment of Elderly Ministers in Colonial America," paper given at the AAAS symposium on "Aging from Birth to Death: Socio-Temporal Perspectives," Toronto, 1981; John J. Waters, "Patrimony, Succession, and Social Stability: Guilford, Connecticut in the Eighteenth Century," *Perspectives in American History*, 10 (1976), pp. 131–60. For old age in early modern England, see Peter Laslett, *Family Life and Illicit Love in Earlier Generations* (Cambridge: Cambridge University Press, 1977), chap. 5; Laslett, "The Traditional English Family and the Aged of Our Society," in *Aging, Death and the Completion of Being*, ed., David D. Van Tassell (Philadelphia: University of Pennsylvania Press, 1979), pp. 97–113; Keith Thomas, *Age and Authority in Early Modern England* (London: British Academy, 1976). For an anthropological view, see Leo W. Simmons, "Aging in Preindustrial Societies," *Handbook of Social Gerontology*, ed., Clark Tibbitts (Chicago: University of Chicago Press, 1960); Simmons, *The Role of the Aged in Primitive Society* (New Haven, Conn.: Yale University Press, 1945).]

As these works made clear, the status of the aged in colonial America was tied not only to prescription but also to their actual social condition. Crucial turning points in the lives of the old – giving up the role of household head, retiring, or having all their children leave home – were likely to influence their prestige. These turning points have also become central to a growing body of literature on old age in the nineteenth century. Using census material, several scholars have focused upon the typical life course of the elderly a century ago. Generally, these historians have discovered that, unlike today, a majority of the old reached at least sixty-five before experiencing the critical turning points. Until recent times, the passage into superannuation had remained ambigious and indistinct.

[Howard P. Chudacoff, "The Life Course of Women: Age and Age Consciousness, 1865–1914," *Journal of Family History*, 5, no. 3 (Fall, 1980), pp. 274–92; Chudacoff and Tamara K. Hareven, "Family Transition into Old Age," in *Transactions: The Family and the Life Course in Historical Perspective*, ed., Tamara K. Hareven (New York: Academic Press, Inc., 1978), pp. 217–43; Chudacoff and Hareven, "From the Nest Egg to Family Dissolution: Life Course Transition into Old Age," *Journal of Family History*, 4, no. 1 (Spring, 1979), pp. 69–83; Hareven, "Family Time and Historical Time," in *The Family*, ed., Alice S. Rossi, Jerome Kagan, and Hareven (New York: W. W. Norton & Company, Inc., 1978), pp. 57–70; Hareven, "The Last Stage: Historical Adulthood and Old Age," *Daedalus*, 105, no. 4 (Fall, 1976), pp. 13–23; Daniel Scott Smith, "Life Course, Norms, and the Family System of Older Americans in 1900," *The Journal of Family History*, 4, no. 3 (Fall, 1979), pp. 285–98; Smith, Michel Dahlin, and Mark Friedberger, "The Family Structure of the Older Black Population in the American South in 1880 and 1900," *Sociology and Social Research*, 63 (April, 1979), pp. 544–63; Peter Uhlenberg, "Changing Configurations of the Life Course," in *Transitions: The Family and Life Course in historical Perspective*, Tamara K. Hareven (New York; Academic Press, Inc., 1978), pp. 65–97. For England, see Michael Anderson, *Family Structure in Nineteenth-Century Lancashire* (Cambridge: Cambridge University Press, 1971). For Canada, see Michael Katz, *The People of Hamilton, Canada West* (Cambridge, Mass.: Harvard University Press, 1975).]

Many of the same works have also investigated the effects of modernization upon the elderly. According to these scholars, the old were not consistently or rapidly affected by the major social and economic forces that transformed the nation. As W. Andrew Achenbaum and Peter Stearns have pointed out, the elderly were far too diverse and varied a group to be uniformly influenced by the process of modernization. The traditional theory, they stated, needs to be revised to be applied to the history of senescence. ["Old Age and Modernization," *The Gerontologist*, 18 (June, 1978), pp. 307–12; see also Stearns, *Old Age in European Society* (New York: Holmes and Meier Publishers, Inc., 1977); M. Clark and B. G. Anderson, *Culture and Aging* (Springfield, Ill.: Charles C. Thomas, Publisher, 1967); D. Cowgill and L. D. Holmes, *Aging and Modernization* (Englewood Cliffs, N.J.: Prentice-Hall, Inc., 1972).]

In addition, Achenbaum and Stearns argued that attitudes toward the old do not always mirror precise economic or demographic conditions. In the past, neither prescriptive ideal nor social reality completely dictated how the elderly were perceived and treated. In the nineteenth century, for example, although most aged persons remained employed and independent, their last stage of life was often portrayed as one of disease and dependence. As several studies have shown, this image of old age was especially apparent in the works of doctors, charity workers, and social planners who dealt with the

173

problems of the elderly. According to Barbara G. Rosenkrantz and Maris A. Vinovskis, in the 1840s, Massachusetts's insane asylum superintendents began to characterize the elderly as unsuitable patients despite statistics that indicated a high rate of cure. ["The Invisible Lunatics: Old Age and Insanity in Mid-Nineteenth Century Massachusetts," in *Aging and the Elderly*, ed., Stuart F. Spicker, Kathleen M. Woodward, and David D. Van Tassel (Atlantic Highlands, N.J.: Humanities Press, 1978), pp. 95–126.] Similarly, the founders of old-age homes chose to depict their clients as the most needy and helpless of people. [Carole Haber, "The Old Folks at Home: The Development of Institutional Care for the Aged in Nineteenth-Century Philadelphia," *The Pennsylvania Magazine of History and Biography*, 110, no. 2 (April, 1977), pp. 240–57; Ethel McClure, *More than Just a Roof: The Development of Minnesota Poor Farms and Homes for the Aged* (St. Paul: Minnesota Historical Society, 1968).] Clearly, the goals of these welfare authorities, as well as their expectations, helped shape the way they perceived and presented senescence. [See also James W. Birren, "A Brief History of the Psychology of Aging," *The Gerontologist*, 1, no. 1 (June, 1969), pp. 66–7.]

Such ideals and assumptions also played a major role in the formulation of the first mandatory retirement programs. The image of senescence written into these plans emphasized the poverty-stricken and decrepit nature of the elderly. Retirement programs, though, were not created simply to assist needy old age. Rather, as recent studies have shown, they were adopted in the hope that they would provide support for the aged, work for the young, efficiency for the engineer, and seniority and discipline for the employer. Thus, although the programs' conception of all elderly persons as disabled and needy did not reflect the condition of most, it obviously served a useful purpose. With its acceptance, everyone beyond sixty-five could legitimately be removed from the labor force. [William Graebner, *A History of Retirement: The Meaning and Function of an American Institution, 1885–1970* (New Haven, Conn.: Yale University Press, 1970); Carole Haber, "Mandatory Retirement in Nineteenth-Century America: The Conceptional Basis of a New Work Cycle," *Journal of Social History*, 12, no. 1 (Fall, 1978), pp. 77–97; Gail Buchwalter King and Peter N. Stearns, "The Retirement Experience as a Policy Factor: An Applied History Approach," *Journal of Social History*, 14, no. 4 (Summer, 1981), pp. 589–625.]

Thomas R. Cole has provided one explanation for the widespread acceptance of the plans' negative view of old age. In his dissertation, "Past Meridian: Aging and the Northern Middle Class, 1830–1930" [University of Rochester, 1980], Cole argued that in the early nineteenth century, attitudes toward senescence were at best ambivalent. With the Second Great Awakening, though, theology began to sentimentalize the old into irrelevance. In an era of progress and action, the elderly seemed little more than weak and passive; their best and only hope was to prepare for their heavenly reward. This perception of old age was then confirmed by experts on prolongevity. In their writings, they dreamed of the elimination of senescence. No longer would the last stage of life lead directly to death and decay. Instead, they would live in a state of perpetual – and active – middle age. [See also Gerald A. Gruman, *A History of Ideas about the Prolongation of Life* (Philadelphia: American Philosophical Society, 1966); Gruman, "The Rise and Fall of Prolongevity Hygiene," *Bulletin of the History of Medicine*, 35 (1961), pp. 221–7.]

It is not at all clear, however, that all nineteenth-century writers portrayed senescence in this manner. In a quantitative study of magazine articles, Jane Range and Maris A. Vinovskis discovered little animosity toward the old. In the stories published in *Littell's Living Age* from 1845 to 1882, the elderly continued to be depicted as useful, if somewhat less visible, members of society. ["Images of Elderly in Popular Magazines: A Content Analysis of *Littell's Living Age*, 1845–1882," *Social Science History*, 5, no. 2 (Spring, 1981), pp. 123–70.]

These contrasting findings should not be surprising; they simply underscore the complexity of the subject. In studying old age, historians are only starting to discover the wide range of responses to the last stage of life. As many of these works have shown, we need to go beyond one-dimensional frameworks if we wish to understand the past. No golden age of gerontocracy ever existed, nor have all elderly persons fallen into disrespect. Such a perspective may actually conceal more about the history of old age than it reveals. The lives of the old differed according to ethnic background, economic strata, and cohort experience; attitudes about senescence reflected a variety of beliefs and purposes. Ideas about death, work, religion, and the family all affected perceptions of aging, as did individual experiences. These are factors that still require further investigation. Clearly, the study of the history of old age in America is just beginning.

Index

Abbot, Joseph, 2
AFL-CIO, 118
age restrictions, 125–9
  in medical tracts, 7, 48, 62, 71–2, 79–
    80, 89–91, 126
  in old age homes, 7, 103, 125, 128
  in retirement plans, 7, 108, 110–12,
    117–18, 123–4
  in welfare policies, 38, 99, 125, 126
Aged Poor in England and Wales, 44
Allen, Elizabeth, A., 123
almshouse
  composition of, 27, 83, 86–7
  in colonial America, 24, 27
  in nineteenth-century America, 27, 34,
    35–6, 40, 83–7, 109, 127
  transition to hospital, 87–8, 89
American Express Company, 113
The Angel of Bethesda, 53–4
apoplexy, in the old, 52, 68, 71
arteries, importance in aging, 59
arteriosclerosis, 59, 74
autopsies, 53, 58–9, 65, 68, 74, 75
"average man," as statistical concept,
    41–3

Baltimore and Ohio Railroad, 113, 128
Barbor, John, 22–3
Bartlett, Clarence, 73
Beard, Dr. George, 76, 77, 121
Bicêtre, 58–9
Bichat, M.-F.-X., 58, 59
Bingham, Anne, 11
Bingham, William, 11
Bishop, James Faugeres, 80
blood injections, as cure for old age, 72
bloodletting, 51, 57
boarding-out practices, 23–4
Booth, Charles, 44–5
Boston and Albany Railroad, 110
Boston and Providence Railroad, 118

Boyles, John, 59
brain, transformation in old age, 62–3,
    70, 74–5
Bright's disease, 68
bronchitis, 73
Broussais, F.-J.-V., 58
Brown-Sequard, C.-E., 72
Browne, Sir Thomas, 48–9
Byrd, William, 15–16, 17

Caldwell, Charles, 71
calomel, 49
  see also mercury
Canstatt, C., 64
Carlisle, Anthony, 51
cells, degeneration in old age, 62–3, 65,
    74, 75
Charcot, Jean, 61, 62
Charities, 82, 92
Charities and the Common, 88
Charity Organization Societies, 27, 128
Chicago, Burlington, and Quincy
    Railroad, 114, 117, 118
childrearing, 10–11, 22
children
    compared to the old, 38–9, 61–2
    effect on the old, 10–14, 21, 26, 29–30
Children's Aid Society (New York), 38–9
Choate, George, 89
Chomel, A. F., 64
Cicero, 54
City Home for the Aged and Infirm, *see*
    New York City Almshouse
Civil War pensions, 110–11
    see also pensions, military
climacteric disease, 68–71, 74
climacteric insanity, 69–71
climacteric stage of life, 69, 80, 126
climacterics, 48
Clouston, T. S., 78, 79–80
Commissioner of Labor, 117

176